Oxford International Resources

Computing
Student Book

Alison Page
Karl Held
Diane Levine
Howard Lincoln

OXFORD
UNIVERSITY PRESS

OXFORD
UNIVERSITY PRESS

Great Clarendon Street, Oxford, OX2 6DP, United Kingdom

Oxford University Press is a department of the University of Oxford. It furthers the University's objective of excellence in research, scholarship, and education by publishing worldwide. Oxford is a registered trade mark of Oxford University Press in the UK and in certain other countries.

© Oxford University Press 2025

The moral rights of the authors have been asserted

First published in 2025

All rights reserved. No part of this publication may be reproduced, stored in a retrieval system, transmitted, used for text and data mining, or used for training artificial intelligence, in any form or by any means, without the prior permission in writing of Oxford University Press, or as expressly permitted by law, by licence or under terms agreed with the appropriate reprographics rights organization. Enquiries concerning reproduction outside the scope of the above should be sent to the Rights Department, Oxford University Press, at the address above.

You must not circulate this work in any other form and you must impose this same condition on any acquirer

British Library Cataloguing in Publication Data
Data available

9781382047258

10 9 8 7 6 5 4 3 2 1

The manufacturing process conforms to the environmental regulations of the country of origin.

Printed in China by Golden Cup

Acknowledgements

The publisher and authors would like to thank the following for permission to use photographs and other copyright material:

Cover: Pauline Gregory. **Photos: p7, 14, 15, 66(b):** Oksana Klymenko / Shutterstock; **p8, 42 and 43 bkg:** Ground Picture / Shutterstock; **p9, 70 and 71 bkg:** Steve Allen / Shutterstock; **p10, 98 and 99 bkg:** Oqbas / Shutterstock; **p11, 126 and 127 bkg:** Olya Maximenko / Shutterstock; **p12, 154 and 155 bkg:** mpohodzhay / Shutterstock; **p13, 36(b), 39(l), 49(d), 64(r), 65(l), 130, 158, 182 and 183 bkg, 216(a):** Gorodenkoff / Shutterstock; **p21:** izusek / Getty Images; **p27:** antoniodiaz / Shutterstock; **p28(t):** petrroudny43 / Shutterstock; **p28(b), 191:** indigo_design / Shutterstock; **p29, 81(t):** Rawpixel.com / Shutterstock; **p32:** The Studio / Shutterstock; **p36(a):** Kite_rin / Shutterstock; **p36(c):** aslysun / Shutterstock; **p36(d):** David Pereiras / Shutterstock; **p37(tl), 57(b):** McLittle Stock / Shutterstock; **p37(tm):** Peppinuzzo / Shutterstock; **p37(tr):** evgenii mitroshin / Shutterstock; **p38(t):** Aleksandr Bognat / Alamy Stock Photo; **p40:** SasinT Gallery / Getty Images; **p41:** Rich Carey / Shutterstock; **p42(inset):** Cast Of Thousands / Shutterstock; **p43(inset):** amenic181 / Shutterstock; **p44(l):** Inna Zakharchenko / Shutterstock; **p44(m):** Africa Studio / Shutterstock; **p44(r):** SmileStudio / Shutterstock; **p45(inset t):** Filip Fuxa / Shutterstock; **p45(inset b):** AYO Production / Shutterstock; **p46:** AzmanL / E+ / Getty Images; **p47:** Heijo / Shutterstock; **p48(t), 58(r), 216(d):** Andrey_Popov / Shutterstock; **p48(m):** ZinetroN / Shutterstock; **p48(b), 69:** Kaspars Grinvalds / Shutterstock; **p49(a):** Cienpies Design / Alamy Stock Vector; **p49(b):** tynyuk / Shutterstock; **p49(c):** Gagarin Iurii / Shutterstock; **p49(e):** Anatoliy Karlyuk / Shutterstock; **p51:** Watcharawut / Shutterstock; **p52(t):** rinelastefan / Shutterstock; **p52(b):** pixelfit / Getty Images; **p53(t):** Creativa Images / Shutterstock; **p53(b):** Asier Romero / Shutterstock; **p55:** umarazak / Shutterstock; **p57(a):** Meawstory15 Production / Shutterstock; **p57(c):** Nearbirds / Shutterstock; **p57(d), 90(r):** fizkes / Shutterstock; **p58(l):** Belozersky / Shutterstock; **p60(t):** Fotokostic / Shutterstock; **p61(t, b):** Johnstocker Production / Shutterstock; **p62:** Wayhome Studio / Shutterstock; **p63:** Prostock-studio / Shutterstock; **p64(l):** Krunja / Shutterstock; **p64(b):** Lightspring / Shutterstock; **p65(r):** vectorfusionart / Shutterstock; **p66(t):** DimaBerlin / Shutterstock; **p66(m):** insta_photos / Shutterstock; **p68:** Chaosamran_Studio / Shutterstock; **p70(inset a):** sergioluno / Shutterstock; **p70(inset b, c, d, e):** Shutterstock AI Generator; **p72:** IvanGrabilin / Shutterstock; **p74:** metamorworks / Shutterstock; **p76(t):** 3rdtimeluckystudio / Shutterstock; **p76(b):** Peter Baier / Shutterstock; **p78(t):** Summit Art Creations / Shutterstock; **p78(b):** Peshkova / Shutterstock; **p80(l):** MONOPOLY919 / Shutterstock; **p80(r):** Scharfsinn / Shutterstock; **p82(t):** Alan Budman / Shutterstock; **p82(b):** Master the moment / Shutterstock; **p83:** Dragana Gordic / Shutterstock; **p89:** mountainpix / Shutterstock; **p90(l):** Sharomka / Shutterstock; **p92:** CherylRamalho / Shutterstock; **p93:** Boumen Japet / Shutterstock; **p95:** GHOSTAHSAN / Shutterstock; **p98(inset t):** Pongsak14 / Shutterstock; **p98(inset b), 138(t), 140:** Pixel-Shot / Shutterstock; **p99(inset):** 963 Creation / Shutterstock; **p100(l):** SasmitaKrt / Shutterstock; **p100(r):** Edinaldo Maciel / Shutterstock; **p101:** Poh Smith / Shutterstock; **p103:** Jahangir Alam Onuchcha / Shutterstock; **p104:** At My Hat / Shutterstock; **p107:** GOLFX / Shutterstock; **p108:** Dadann / Shutterstock; **p111:** Vladimir Konstantinov / Shutterstock; **p113:** Vibrant Image Studio / Shutterstock; **p115:** YAO DEKANG / Shutterstock; **p116:** neenawat khenyothaa / Shutterstock; **p117:** reuerendo / Shutterstock; **p118:** Jane Kelly / Shutterstock; **p119:** Litvalifa / Shutterstock; **p120(t):** arrowsmith2 / Shutterstock; **p120(b):** Steve Travelguide / Shutterstock; **p122:** Gts / Shutterstock; **p124:** Jessica Kirsh / Shutterstock; **p125:** maxbelchenko / Shutterstock; **p126(inset):** Daisy Daisy / Shutterstock; **p132:** Bakhtiar Zein / Shutterstock; **p136:** alphaspirit.it / Shutterstock; **p138(b):** dizain / Shutterstock; **p142:** NicoElNino / Shutterstock; **p144:** filadendron / E+ / Getty Images; **p149:** Song_about_summer / Shutterstock; **p150:** Thapana_Studio / Shutterstock; **p152:** PanuShot / Shutterstock; **p153:** Photo Veterok / Shutterstock; **p154(inset):** L-51 / Shutterstock; **p155(inset):** vanitjan / Shutterstock; **p156:** Szasz-Fabian Jozsef / Shutterstock; **p160:** PRILL / Shutterstock; **p163:** AlenKadr / Shutterstock; **p164:** SeneGal / Shutterstock; **p165:** DedeSupriadi / Shutterstock; **p166(l):** Stone36 / Shutterstock; **p166(r):** KAWEESTUDIO / Shutterstock; **p168:** Gleb Usovich / Shutterstock; **p170(t):** valdis torms / Shutterstock; **p170(b):** Elena Voynova / Shutterstock; **p171:** Zerbor / Shutterstock; **p172:** Frame Stock Footage / Shutterstock; **p176(t):** FeelGoodLuck / Shutterstock; **p176(b):** Zapp2Photo / Shutterstock; **p177(t):** Javier LARREA / Alamy Stock Photo; **p177(b):** Imago / Alamy Stock Photo; **p178:** Guillem Lopez / Alamy Stock Photo; **p179:** Chesky / Shutterstock; **p181:** rapisan sawangphon / Alamy Stock Photo; **p183(inset):** Olana22 / Shutterstock; **p184:** YnetteT / Shutterstock; **p187:** Martial Red / Shutterstock; **p188:** DenPhotos / Shutterstock; **p196, 198, 199, 200, 202:** Dzha33 / Shutterstock; **p207:** maicasaa / Shutterstock; **p216(b):** Jacob Lund / Shutterstock; **p216(c):** ViDI Studio / Shutterstock; **p216(e):** G-Stock Studio / Shutterstock.

All Audacity screenshots © 2024 Muse Group & contributors.
All Google screenshots © 2024 Google.
All Python Screenshots © 2001-2024 Python Software Foundation.
All Microsoft screenshots © Microsoft 2024. Used with permission from Microsoft.
All SoundCloud screenshots © 2024 SoundCloud Global Limited & Co. KG.
All WordPress screenshots © Automattic Inc.
QuotesCover screenshot © 2012-2024 QuotesCover.com. All rights reserved.
Cosmote Chronos app screenshot © Cosmote.
XR Viewer (Augmented Reality) screenshot © SevenD GmbH.
Trello screenshot © 2024 Atlassian.
YouTube screenshot © 2022 Google LLC.

Every effort has been made to contact copyright holders of material reproduced in this book. Any omissions will be rectified in subsequent printings if notice is given to the publisher.

Links to third party websites are provided by Oxford in good faith and for information only. Oxford disclaims any responsibility for the materials contained in any third party website referenced in this work.

FSC MIX Paper | Supporting responsible forestry
FSC™ C110497

Contents

How to use this book 4
Your learning journey 6

1 Creative media: Multimedia content 14
1.1 Create a multimedia platform 16
1.2 Create text content 20
1.3 Create audio content 24
1.4 Create video content 28
1.5 Host and embed content 32
1.6 Extended reality: new kinds of content 36
What have you learned? 40

2 Digital literacy: Make good choices 42
2.1 Your online self 44
2.2 Types of social media 48
2.3 Ethics of care 52
2.4 Healthy balance 56
2.5 You, money and the internet 60
2.6 Extended reality in daily life 64
What have you learned? 68

3 Computational thinking: Artificial intelligence 70
3.1 Make decisions 72
3.2 Heuristics 76
3.3 Machine learning 80
3.4 Train the computer 84
3.5 Natural language 88
3.6 Generate natural language 92
What have you learned? 96

4 Programming: The fish pond plan 98
4.1 A model pond 100
4.2 Make the model 104
4.3 Fill the pond 108
4.4 Evaporation and rainfall 112
4.5 Use the model to help solve a problem 116
4.6 Boolean operators 120
What have you learned? 124

5 Analysing data: Managing a project 126
5.1 What is a project? 128
5.2 Plan a project 132
5.3 Understand requirements 136
5.4 Plan a project timetable 140
5.5 Work on an agile project 144
5.6 Test and feedback 148
What have you learned? 152

6 Understanding technology: Inside the CPU 154
6.1 The computer system 156
6.2 The fetch-execute cycle 160
6.3 The computer and logic 164
6.4 Complex logical statements 168
6.5 Logic gates 172
6.6 Robots in the real world 176
What have you learned? 180

7 Creating web content: Use JavaScript 182
7.1 User control over text size 184
7.2 Add night mode 188
7.3 Flip a card 192
7.4 An e-commerce web page 196
7.5 Improve the colour menu 200
7.6 Complete your web page 204
What have you learned? 208

Glossary 210
Jobs for the future 216

How to use this book

Welcome to your Student Book

This introduction shows you all the different features *Oxford International Computing, Lower Secondary* has to support your learning of computing. This book is the first of three in the series. Each book is divided into seven units. In each unit, you will find: a unit introduction, six lessons, and a unit summary ('What have you learned?').

</> Wherever you see this symbol, you will learn essential coding skills (in the Computational thinking and Programming units).

Wherever you see this symbol ⬇, you will need a 'Digital Activity File' to use as the starting point for an activity, for example, Python programming files or images to edit. To download the files, go to: www.oup.com/OI-Computing-3e-teacher

Key words

Key words for each lesson are highlighted in **bold** in the text. They are also included in alphabetical order in this box. You can find their definitions in the glossary at the back of this book.

Stop, think

This box will help you develop your online safety skills.

Spiral back

This box will remind you what you already know about a topic.

Think maths

The 'Think maths' and 'Think science' boxes highlight links with learning in maths and science.

Activity

Practical activities allow you to apply your knowledge and skills.

Case study

The case studies help you to practise new computing skills in real-life contexts.

✓ Test

Each lesson contains a test which includes questions to help check you have understood the key learning from the lesson.

Stretch zone

The 'Stretch zone' activities suggest ideas for how to take your learning further and discover something more.

Digital citizen

The 'Digital citizen' discussion activities encourage you to think about the responsible use of technology now and in the future.

Be creative

The 'Be creative' activities encourage you to use your creative skills.

Unit introduction
These pages include an activity and a class discussion to help you think about the topic.

The introduction activity can always be carried out without using a computer.

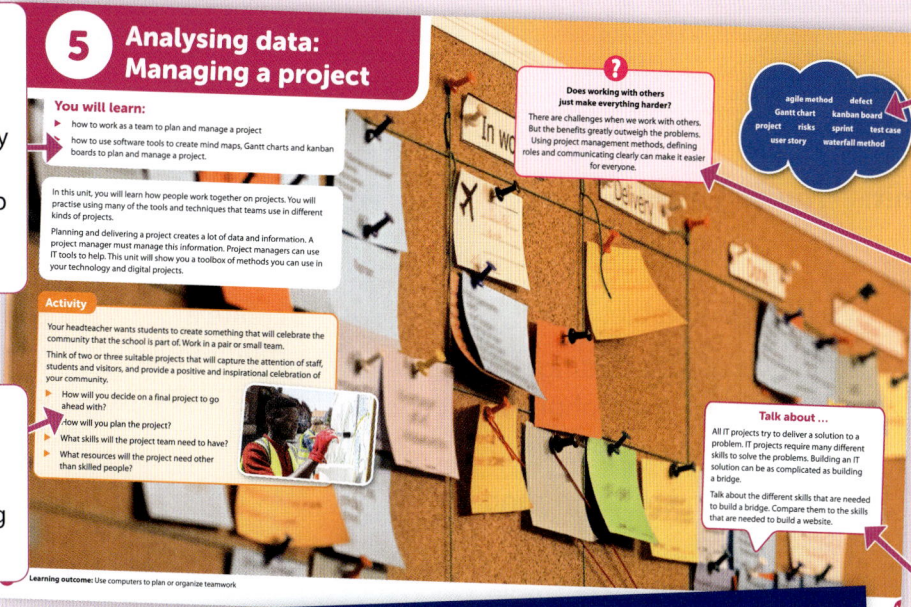

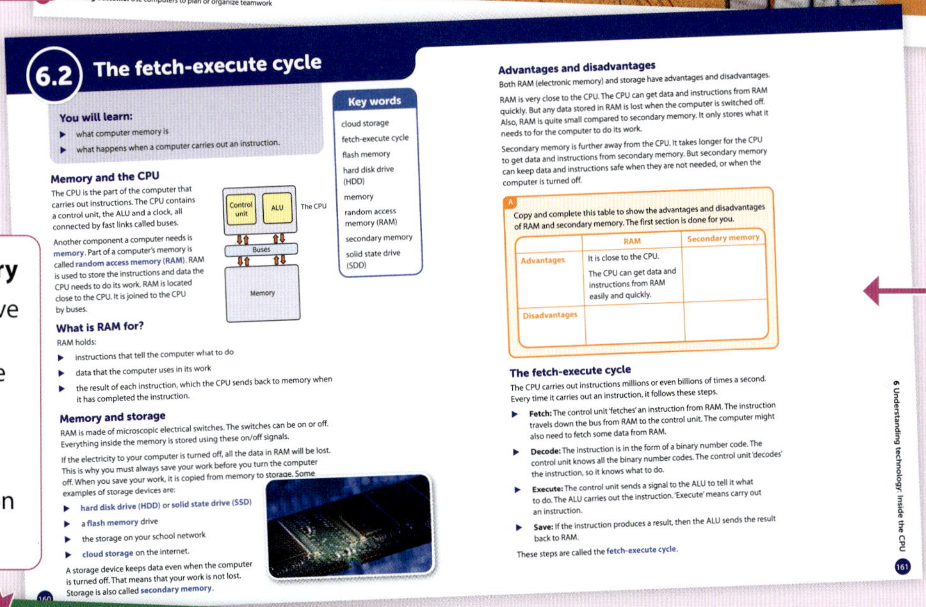

Unit summary
The 'What have you learned?' pages include a review test, review activity and self-evaluation table.

The word cloud builds vocabulary by identifying key terms from the unit.

The 'Big question' encourages you to discuss real-life contexts linked with key content in the unit.

The 'Talk about …' speech bubble contains a discussion starter.

Lessons
Each four-page lesson guides you through activity-based learning. The learning objectives are clearly set out at the start of each lesson.

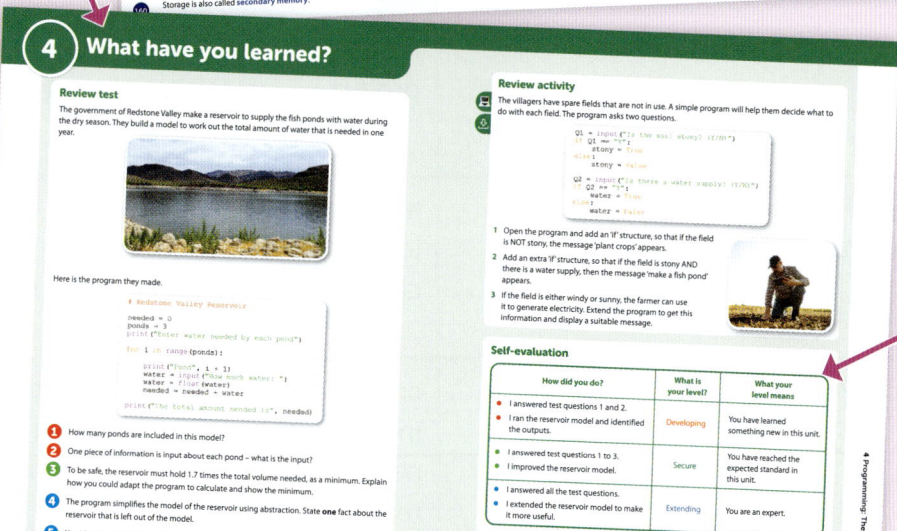

The self-evaluation table allows you to assess what level you are working at by the end of the unit:

Developing You are working at this level if you have found the content challenging but have made progress.

Secure You are working at this level if you have achieved all of the learning objectives.

Extending You are working at this level if you have developed additional skills and a deeper understanding.

5

Your learning journey

Complete this unit:	You will need …	You will …	By the end of the unit, you will be able to …
1 Creative media	a laptop/PC/tablet digital sound recording hardware, for example, microphone input and headphones digital sound recording and editing software a web browser, for example, Google Chrome	create a multimedia web platform	plan, create and refine digital content to a high quality
2 Digital literacy	a laptop/PC/tablet a web browser, for example, Google Chrome	work online in a responsible way	use social media safely
3 Computational thinking	a laptop/PC/tablet Scratch, Python	write software for a radio operator to process signals	explain how AI makes decisions
4 Programming	a laptop/PC/tablet Scratch, Python	write software to manage water resources	create an abstract model and use it to solve problems
5 Analysing data	a laptop/PC/tablet spreadsheet software, for example, Microsoft Excel/Google Sheets	manage a team project	use software to support teamwork
6 Understanding technology	a laptop/PC/tablet with a network connection	analyse the logic of digital circuits	say how a computer processor works
7 Creating web content	a laptop/PC/tablet a web browser, for example, Google Chrome a text-only editor, for example, Microsoft Notepad	create interactive web pages that respond to user input	write and edit web pages using HTML and JavaScript

Creative media

Creative media is about creating new multimedia content to share with others, for example, audio and video recordings. It develops creative skills that enable you to communicate effectively and deliver clear, attractive content.

Planning
- Designing, scripting and storyboarding media projects
- Choosing the right hardware and software with care

Critical thinking
- Engaging with real-world challenges

Learning skills (metacognition)
- Using feedback to reflect and improve
- Designing content that suits an audience

Professional skills
- Understanding the standards and techniques used by professionals in multimedia production

Software skills
- Recording original digital content
- Using professional software to edit multimedia content
- Using different types of software to generate new content

Creativity
- Creating attractive and interesting content
- Making something completely new
- Expressing your individual ideas
- Using your taste and judgement

Digital literacy

Digital literacy is about knowing how to find and use information. It also means being safe and polite when we use technology.

Wellbeing skills

- Respecting the environment and sustainability
- Knowing how your use of technology can affect your own physical and emotional wellbeing
- Being a positive social presence online

Personal safety skills

- Recognizing online risks and knowing how to stay safe
- Understanding the importance of personal privacy and your online identity

Research skills

- Using online research to create new content
- Using content responsibly and avoiding plagiarism
- Understanding that AI-generated content needs to be checked for accuracy

Computational thinking

Computational thinking is about developing problem-solving skills. These skills help you to write programs and to make good decisions in other subjects and outside school.

Evaluation skills
- Testing, checking and improving software in a cycle of development
- Knowing how to ensure the readability and usability of your programs

Coding
- Understanding how input and output are handled in professional text-based languages
- Storing and processing data of different types using variables
- Making changes to values using operators and functions
- Creating and using data structures with multiple values

Problem solving
- Developing a thoughtful understanding of the latest developments in software, such as machine learning and natural language processing
- Understanding the limitations of computer-based decision-making and when decisions need to be human-based

Maths skills
- Understanding mathematical operations and using operators to transform values
- Understanding precedence and the use of variables in calculations

Programming

Programming is about writing instructions (code) that tell the computer what to do, using programming languages that are block-based (for example, Scratch) or text-based (for example, Python).

Critical thinking
- Comparing different ways of solving computational problems
- Understanding what causes program errors and learning to write error-free programs

Problem solving
- Writing programs that tackle and solve real-world problems
- Thinking logically and using logical programming methods
- Evaluating AI techniques, such as the use of expert systems
- Building abstract models of real-world systems and using them to create solutions

Maths skills
- Understanding Boolean logic and Boolean expressions
- Using abstraction to simplify a complex problem to logical and quantified values

Coding
- Writing text-based programs using a range of structures, including iteration and selection
- Designing and writing programs to meet given requirements
- Checking programs against requirements and making changes as required
- Writing modular programs, and understanding the advantages of modular programming

Self-regulation skills
- Persisting with problems until they are solved, for example, to fix bugs in code
- Checking and improving a program until you are happy with what it does

Analysing data

Analysing data is about using software to input, store, and process data. By analysing data, you will get information that is useful for a purpose and that you can use to answer questions.

Maths skills
- Understanding and using numerical data
- Selecting and developing numerical formulas

Decision-making
- Understanding how 'big data' and AI are used to support decisions in the modern world
- Processing data to make complex decisions
- Selecting software and information to meet business challenges

Collaboration
- Using communication technology and communication apps to work as a team
- Managing a project using professional project management techniques and software
- Using project management software to organize, plan and track deliverables

Software skills
- Using spreadsheet software to collate and organize data in a structured form
- Using software formulas and functions to process and transform data values

Professional skills
- Using professional applications from the start
- Processing data to solve realistic and challenging problems

Understanding technology

Understanding technology means knowing how computers work, what they can and cannot do, and how using technology can help you to solve real-world problems.

Understanding digital processes

- Understanding what digital data is and how it is processed and transmitted between devices
- Explaining how all types of data can be held in electronic digital form inside the computer
- Knowing how data is processed inside the CPU using electronic digital circuits

Professional skills

- Troubleshooting devices and ensuring that technology works as intended
- Using cloud services and remote storage knowledgeably and securely
- Understanding why digital technology works well with some problems – those involving mathematical and logical processes – and not with others

Technology skills

- Understanding the technical principles that have created modern technologies
- Understanding that data is held and processed in digital electronic form
- Understanding the underlying technology that enables modern robotics
- Understanding the structure and function of the processor and the fetch-execute cycle

Maths skills

- Knowing how to calculate the capacity and power of computer systems using relevant digital units
- Knowing the difference between digital values and other types of information
- Understanding number bases, and the conversion of numbers between base 10 and base 2
- Understanding the Boolean operators and how they transform data values

Creating web content

Creating web content is about using text-based markup languages to make web pages with accessible and engaging content.

Reasoning and coding
- Learning new programming languages
- Combining a range of techniques to create new content

Consideration and cooperation
- Using feedback to reflect and improve
- Reflecting on accessibility and clear communication
- Working with others on team projects

Design and development
- Researching and choosing assets to use in a web project
- Designing the layout and format of web content

1 Creative media: Multimedia content

You will learn:

- how to apply the media skills you have learned in this course in a real-world project
- how to combine different kinds of media using a multimedia platform
- how to extend your media skills with new technologies like VR (virtual reality) and AR (augmented reality).

Multimedia projects combine different kinds of media. They provide an audience with information in the way that best meets their needs. Multimedia is used in journalism, entertainment and education, usually by delivering content on the web.

For example, many teachers create online courses that include audio and video presentations. Now learners can access their teaching from anywhere in the world and learn at their own pace.

Emerging technologies create opportunities to create new kinds of content. The exciting world of extended reality helps content creators engage with their audiences in new ways.

In this unit, you will create a multimedia project that combines text, images, audio and video. You will consider how new technologies like virtual reality and augmented reality could be used in your project.

You will create a school media project that informs and entertains students, staff and parents at your school. This could be:

- an online product like a blog website, featuring media hosted on streaming services
- an offline product like a newsletter, containing links and media content in a file that you can share.

The examples show an online product, using a blogging platform.

Learning outcomes: Create and combine multimedia content; Explain the meaning and use of virtual reality (VR) and augmented reality (AR)

Is VR (virtual reality) better than real life?

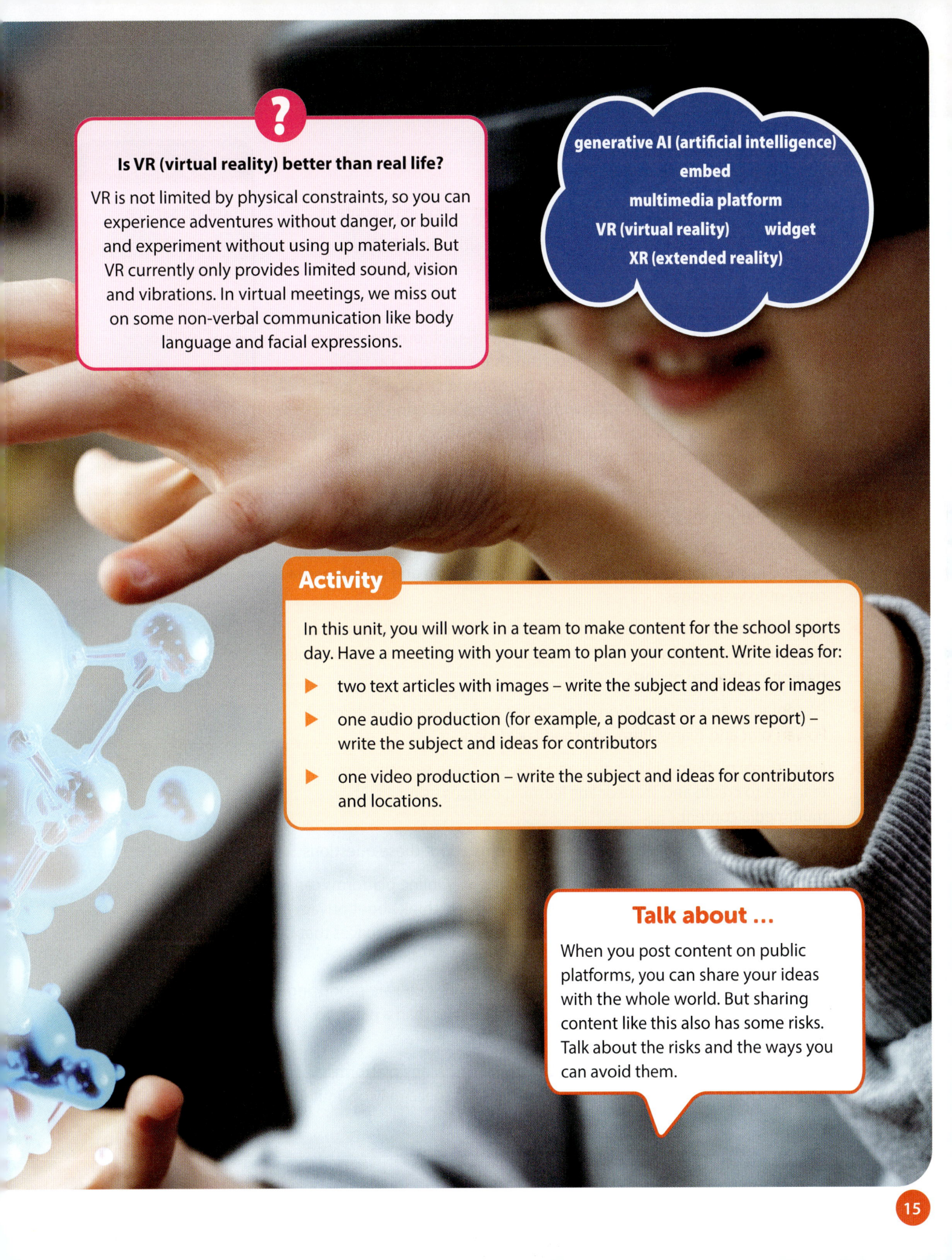

VR is not limited by physical constraints, so you can experience adventures without danger, or build and experiment without using up materials. But VR currently only provides limited sound, vision and vibrations. In virtual meetings, we miss out on some non-verbal communication like body language and facial expressions.

---

generative AI (artificial intelligence)
embed
multimedia platform
VR (virtual reality)   widget
XR (extended reality)

Activity

In this unit, you will work in a team to make content for the school sports day. Have a meeting with your team to plan your content. Write ideas for:

- ▶ two text articles with images – write the subject and ideas for images
- ▶ one audio production (for example, a podcast or a news report) – write the subject and ideas for contributors
- ▶ one video production – write the subject and ideas for contributors and locations.

Talk about …

When you post content on public platforms, you can share your ideas with the whole world. But sharing content like this also has some risks. Talk about the risks and the ways you can avoid them.

1.1 Create a multimedia platform

You will learn:
- how to choose and set up services to present multimedia content
- how to bring content together through a multimedia platform.

Key words

hosting service
multimedia platform
page
post (online)
social media
widget

Choose a platform

Multimedia is any digital content that combines different forms of media, such as text, image, sound, and video. You can share content you make directly, by sending files or giving access to file-sharing storage or cloud storage. To share your content with a wider audience and bring together the different content types to make a true multimedia product, you need to use a **multimedia platform**. These are the tools you can use to make, share or view multimedia content.

Examples of multimedia platforms include:

- Website **hosting services** that provide easy templates for text and image pages. They often include **widgets** to add audio, video and **social media** content to web pages.

- Social media services that allow you to add text, image and video content. These platforms might restrict the way you can show content, for example, by limiting the size of posts.

- Presentation and collaboration applications and services like Microsoft PowerPoint and Teams, Prezi, Miro and Lucidspark.

- Educational platforms like Canvas and Moodle. These services allow teachers to create and share online learning courses using multimedia content.

When you are choosing a platform, you need to think about these questions:

- **Who is your audience and what is your content?** Online platforms can help you reach a wide audience. But you should also think about privacy and security. You can choose platforms that provide 'private' spaces that only friends can see.

- **How well will your content work on the platform?** If you are producing long text articles then a blogging site will work better than a platform that specializes in short-form content.

- **What is the cost and availability of the platform?** Many platforms provide a free service, but the features and storage space may be limited.

The examples in this unit use WordPress. It provides free website themes. You can also add audio, video and social media content.

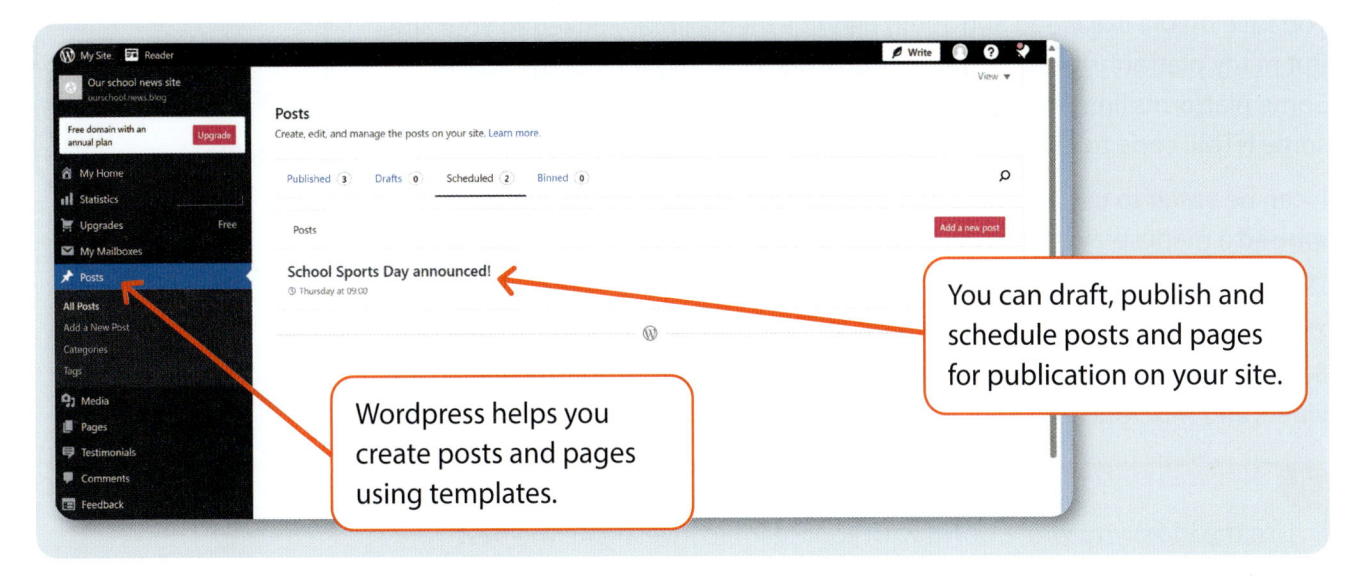

Wordpress helps you create posts and pages using templates.

You can draft, publish and schedule posts and pages for publication on your site.

Set up a multimedia platform account

You will need to use an email address to set up an account for a multimedia platform. Each service will have a sign-up page that will ask for details about you and the way that you want to use the service. Some services will also ask you about the service level you want. The examples in this unit use the service levels that are free of charge.

Services like WordPress, Blogger and Wix let you choose a template. You can start with a simple template that allows you to add **posts** and **pages**.

▶ Posts are items you can add on a scrolling page of a social media or blog site. Usually, the newest post appears at the top.

▶ Pages are for content that you want to keep separate. Readers use the site menu or links to navigate to pages.

The examples in this unit use a theme called 'Friendly Business' in WordPress.

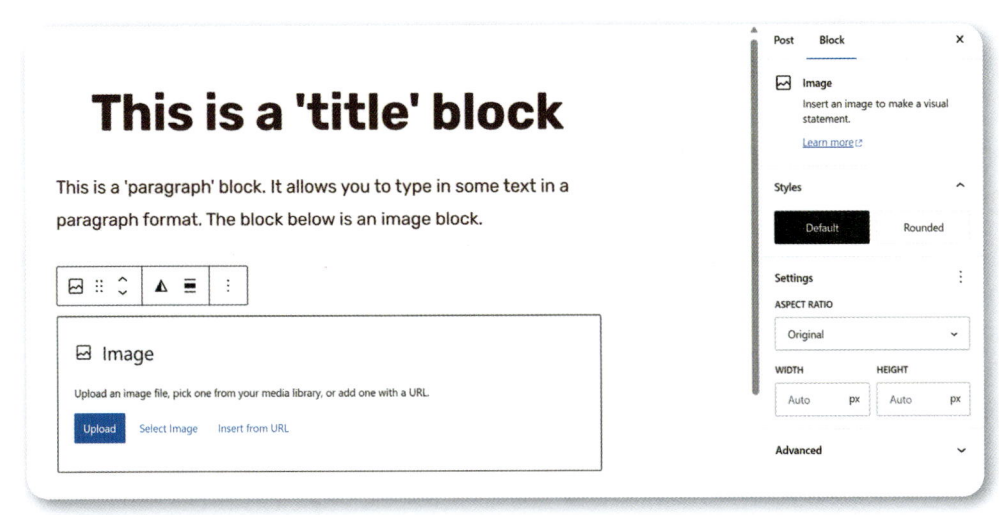

This image shows the 'Friendly Business' theme template.

1 Creative media: Multimedia content

17

1.1 Create a multimedia platform

Choose services for media content

Some platforms let you upload content other than text and images. They let you save media like video and audio files in a media library linked to your site. But many platforms give you this option only if you pay for storage space. Some platforms limit the file size for your media. You might also need to use some HTML code to make media players work on pages on the platform.

It can be easier to use a hosting service for some types of media. You can **embed** a media player from the hosting service in a page on your site. This way you can benefit from the hosting service's **streaming** capacity and features.

There are many hosting services for media files. The examples in this unit use SoundCloud for audio content. Other options include YouTube and Vimeo for video, and Mixcloud and Podbean for audio.

> **A**
> Use the ideas you wrote down with your team to investigate the best multimedia platform and media-hosting services for the content you plan to create.

Key words
compression

embed

stream

Set up a media-hosting service account

When you have decided on which media services to use, you can sign up using an email address. Most services provide a free option that lets you upload media files for streaming. You can upload media files to the service. Then you can embed the audio content in your platform page using a link.

Our School
My Podcast - Episode 1
🔒 Private

Upload complete. Go to your track.

Share your new track

https://soundcloud.com/user-244

By uploading, you confirm that your sounds comply with our Terms of Use and you don't infringe anyone else's rights.

Use an offline platform

If you are not able to use an online platform and online media-sharing services, you can still create a multimedia project. You can use any application that lets you combine text, images, audio and video on pages that can be displayed on a computer, tablet or smartphone. For example, you can use Microsoft PowerPoint, Microsoft OneNote or another presentation or content-sharing application.

Stop, think
Consider the needs of your audience. For example, young users might feel safer using an offline platform.

This example shows a video embedded in a Microsoft PowerPoint slide.

The embedded media content is saved inside the project file. This can create large file sizes that are difficult to share. Think carefully about what media to include. You should use **compressed** media files.

> **B**
>
> 1. Create one or more accounts with the services you need, or familiarize yourself with the offline alternatives.
> 2. Follow the set-up instructions of your online services to create a simple platform that contains at least one main page for posts.

Stretch zone

Test your media-hosting services. Create or find a small audio or video file and upload it to your service. Check that the content uploaded successfully. Check that you can copy a URL (a web address beginning with 'http' or 'https') for the content you uploaded.

✓ Test

1. What is a 'multimedia' project?
2. Name three things you need to think about when choosing a platform for a project.
3. Explain the benefits of using a specialist streaming service to host video and audio content.
4. Write a short paragraph describing how you decided on the best platform for your project. What options did you consider? Say why you made your choices.

1.2 Create text content

You will learn:
- how to collaborate on writing and editing text content
- how to use AI to create text content
- how to add your content to an online platform and publish it.

Key words
AI (artificial intelligence)
AI hallucinations
final proof
generative AI
global
publish

Create text for your project

In the opening activity, you created ideas for the text content for your project. In this lesson, you will create the text. You can write the text individually and then collaborate with classmates to edit the text until you all agree on a final version. You can then **publish** this final version on your platform.

Professional writers call the text they write their 'copy'. You can create the copy for your project directly in your multimedia platform application or interface. If you are using an online service like WordPress, you can type your copy directly into the page templates provided. If you are using an offline platform like Microsoft PowerPoint, you can type directly into the slide templates.

Working with platform templates is usually fine for small pieces of text. But you might find it easier to type longer pieces into a word-processor document. A word processor may have more powerful editing capabilities than other applications.

Spiral back
In Book 4, you learned how to use collaborative editing tools. You can use these skills in this unit to create the content for your project.

Use AI to create copy

A lot of website text content is created using a type of **AI (artificial intelligence)** called **generative AI**.

AI platforms like ChatGPT or Microsoft Copilot create text content based on the prompts you give, for example, any specific details to include, the style, and the length of the copy. The app you use may look different to this example.

You can use AI tools to help you write your content for this project. This example shows a prompt for a new story about a school sports day. You can copy the text created by the AI and edit it as you want.

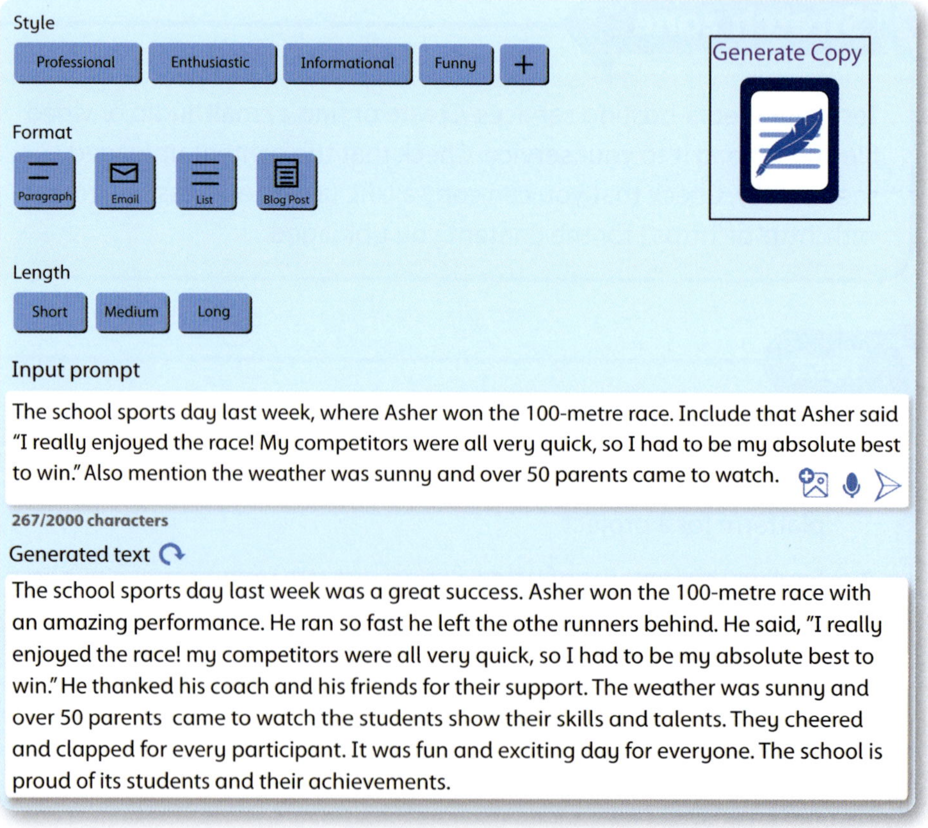

Style: Professional | Enthusiastic | Informational | Funny | +

Format: Paragraph | Email | List | Blog Post

Length: Short | Medium | Long

Input prompt

The school sports day last week, where Asher won the 100-metre race. Include that Asher said "I really enjoyed the race! My competitors were all very quick, so I had to be my absolute best to win." Also mention the weather was sunny and over 50 parents came to watch.

267/2000 characters

Generated text

The school sports day last week was a great success. Asher won the 100-metre race with an amazing performance. He ran so fast he left the othe runners behind. He said, "I really enjoyed the race! my competitors were all very quick, so I had to be my absolute best to win." He thanked his coach and his friends for their support. The weather was sunny and over 50 parents came to watch the students show their skills and talents. They cheered and clapped for every participant. It was fun and exciting day for everyone. The school is proud of its students and their achievements.

Generate Copy

🌐 Digital citizen

AI generates text based on the content it has access to. It tries to make the text it creates sound real, by making it similar to the content it knows about. It often contains mistakes or facts that are not true. These are called **AI hallucinations**. Always check the text produced by AI carefully. Check that any facts it contains are true, and edit or delete them if they are not.

Edit as a team

You can use your word processor to collaborate with others. In previous books, you learned how to use collaborative editing tools. You can use some of these tools in this project.

▶ Track changes can help you make suggestions for changes to a shared document. Changes are shown as mark-up so that you can see what the reviewer or editor is suggesting. You can choose to accept or reject suggested changes.

▶ Comments can help you share ideas and thoughts about parts of the text. A reviewer or editor can add comments to the page margin.

▶ Find and replace can help you quickly make **global** changes to words or phrases.

A

In the introduction to this unit, you wrote some ideas for a short post or page. Now write the text for the post or page.

Proof your text

When you have finished editing your text, you can do a **final proof**. This means that you check the spelling and formatting of the final version. You can use your word processor's proofing tools to do this.

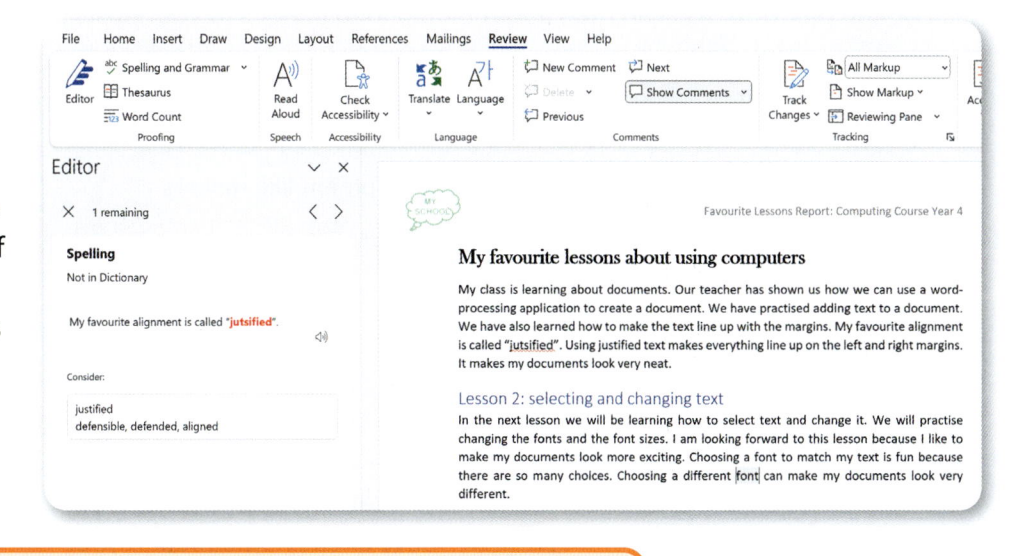

B

Ask your team members to review your text. They can suggest changes and corrections using collaboration tools.

1 Creative media: Multimedia content

21

1.2 Create text content

Add content to the platform

When you have a final version of your text, you can add it to your project. If you are using an online platform, you can add the text as a new post or as a page.

Use a post if the text is a news item. It will appear at the top of the site's main page. Any new posts published later will appear above it.

Use a page if the item is something you want to keep separate from the main page. For example, if it contains background information like an 'about us' or 'contact us' page.

This example shows how content is added to a post in a WordPress theme.

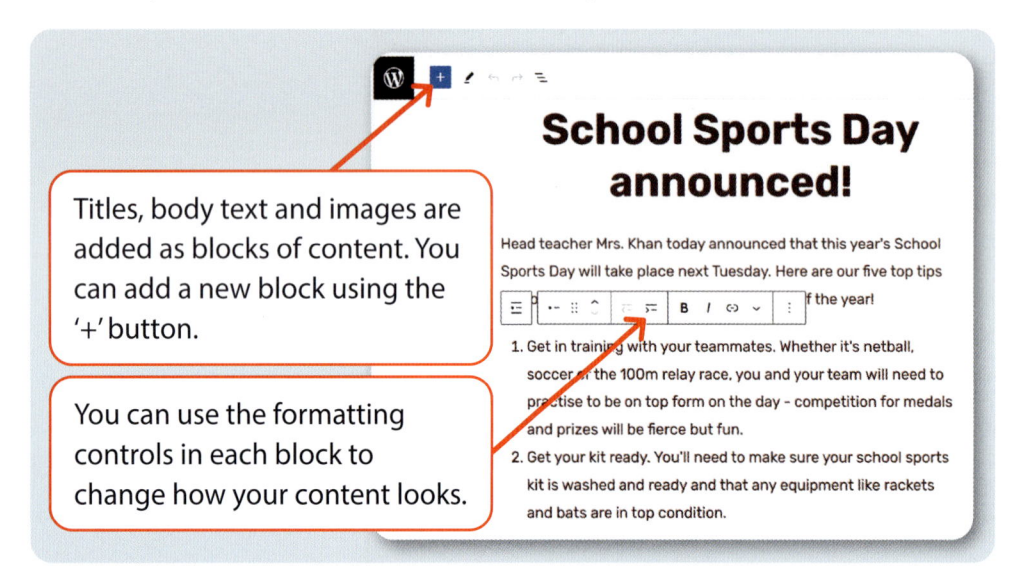

> **Key word**
>
> preview

Titles, body text and images are added as blocks of content. You can add a new block using the '+' button.

You can use the formatting controls in each block to change how your content looks.

School Sports Day announced!

Head teacher Mrs. Khan today announced that this year's School Sports Day will take place next Tuesday. Here are our five top tips if the year!

1. Get in training with your teammates. Whether it's netball, soccer or the 100m relay race, you and your team will need to practise to be on top form on the day - competition for medals and prizes will be fierce but fun.
2. Get your kit ready. You'll need to make sure your school sports kit is washed and ready and that any equipment like rackets and bats are in top condition.

Add images to your text

You can add images to your text by uploading them to the media library of your online platform. You can then add the uploaded images to your posts and pages. The example shows how images are added to an image 'block' on the WordPress platform.

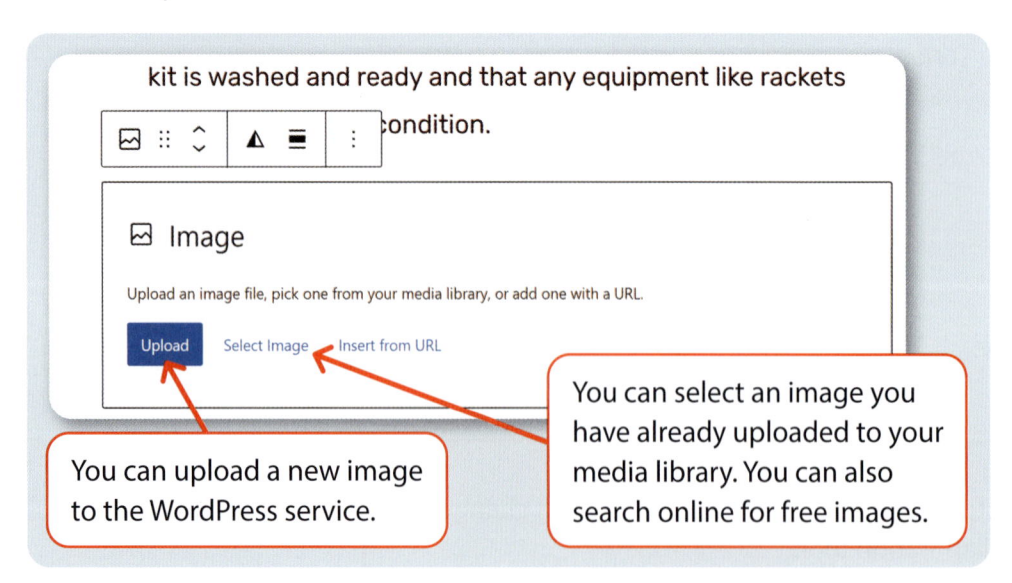

kit is washed and ready and that any equipment like rackets condition.

Image
Upload an image file, pick one from your media library, or add one with a URL.
Upload   Select Image   Insert from URL

You can upload a new image to the WordPress service.

You can select an image you have already uploaded to your media library. You can also search online for free images.

Preview and publish your content

When you have created your post or page, you can **preview** it before you publish it. This helps you spot any mistakes. When you publish it, the content will be visible on the world wide web.

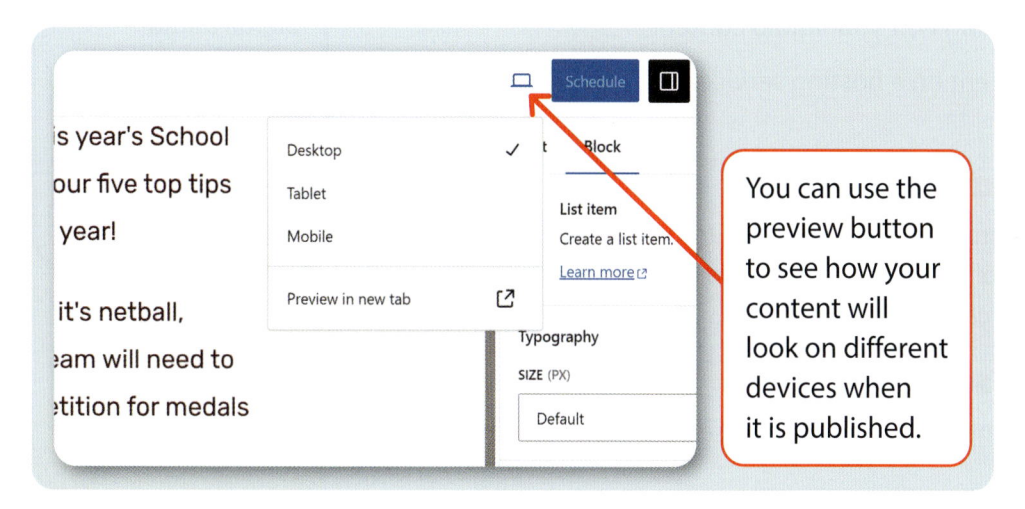

You can use the preview button to see how your content will look on different devices when it is published.

C

Copy the final text to your platform. Add any images to the post or page.

Stretch zone

Explore how AI services like ChatGPT or Microsoft Copilot could help you create or improve your content. Use a prompt that includes subject, style and length to ask AI to suggest content. What do you think about the content the AI generates? How does it compare to what you created?

✓ Test

1. What does 'proofing' a document mean?
2. Explain the difference between a post and a page on a blogging platform.
3. Explain the benefits of using a word processor to create content, rather than entering text directly in a website template.
4. Describe some of the advantages and disadvantages of using AI to help create content.

1.3 Create audio content

You will learn:
- how to plan, record and edit your audio content
- how to publish content on a hosting service.

Key words
digital audio workstation (DAW)
outline plan
script
segment

Plan your recording

Even a short audio programme needs to be structured. You need to plan the order of the different parts of the content. In media production, the parts of a programme are sometimes called **segments**.

Make an outline plan and script

An **outline plan** lists the content of each segment and places them in order. Segments can include:

- **an intro:** a short segment explaining what the programme is about
- **a jingle:** a short piece of music to help the audience recognize and remember the programme
- **topic segments:** the main content of the programme, such as presentations or discussions
- **closing remarks:** a summary of the content and a thank you to the audience and contributors.

Some segments of your programme might need a **script**. A script can help you remember exactly what you want to say. If you are using a script, think about the style of presentation of your content. Write the script to match the style you want, for example: formal, informal or exciting.

Spiral back

In Book 7, you learned how to make an outline plan for a podcast and how to use a DAW. You will use these skills again in this unit.

A

Review your audio ideas from the activity at the start of the unit.

It is time to plan your audio content. You can download an outline plan template to help you plan.

Now create an outline. The outline should show:
- the aim of the content
- a brief description of the content in each segment
- a more detailed script for any segment that needs to be scripted.

Record audio content

In Book 7, you learned how to set up and make recordings using devices like smartphones or laptop computers. You can remind yourself about the process by reviewing Unit 1 in Book 7.

9:1.3 Podcast Outline: Digital Activity File

Make sure you check your recording levels – this is the most important part of getting a good quality recording. If you have the time, it is always a good idea to make a short test recording to check for distortion and background noise.

The example below shows the recording features and process using simple **digital audio workstation (DAW)** software.

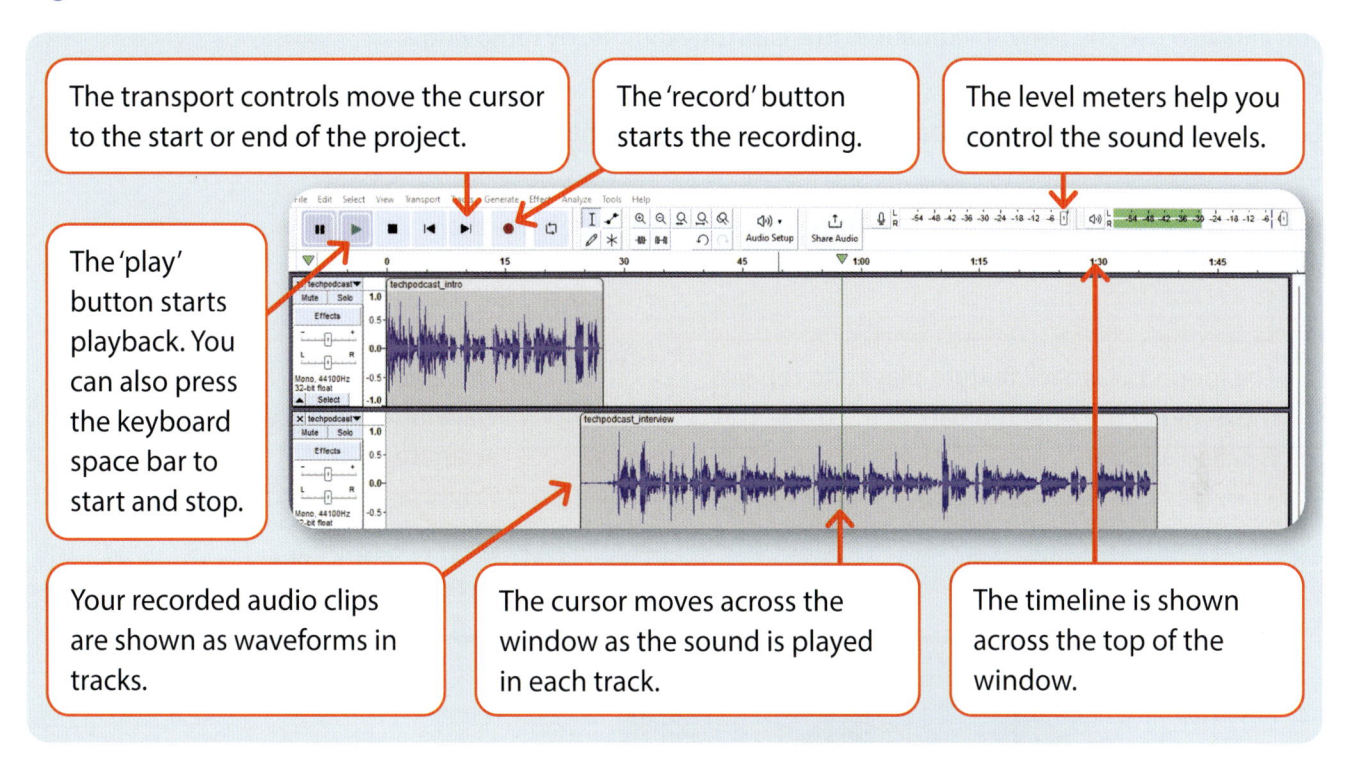

The transport controls move the cursor to the start or end of the project.

The 'record' button starts the recording.

The level meters help you control the sound levels.

The 'play' button starts playback. You can also press the keyboard space bar to start and stop.

Your recorded audio clips are shown as waveforms in tracks.

The cursor moves across the window as the sound is played in each track.

The timeline is shown across the top of the window.

You can also make a simple recording using a handheld device like a smartphone. Most devices have a voice recorder application. It will allow you to record audio without any other equipment. You can export your recordings to a DAW and edit them there.

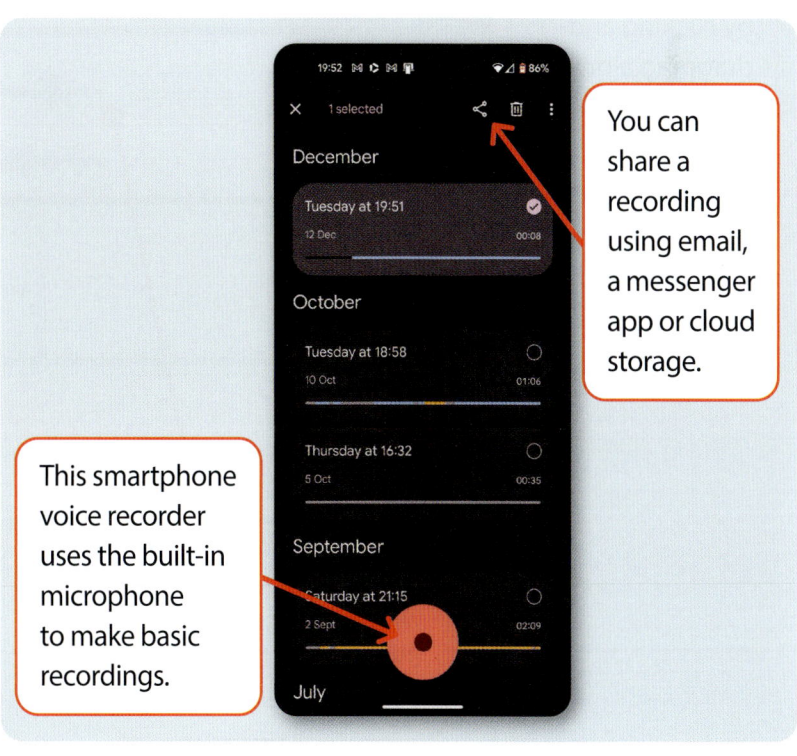

You can share a recording using email, a messenger app or cloud storage.

This smartphone voice recorder uses the built-in microphone to make basic recordings.

1 Creative media: Multimedia content

25

1.3 Create audio content

Edit and mix your audio content

You can use your DAW to assemble the final programme. If you have more than one audio file or clip, you can arrange them on the timeline so that they fit together without gaps. You can trim the start and end of clips to remove any unwanted audio or any gaps.

You can also use the DAW to edit audio in a clip, for example, by removing a part of a clip.

Using features like looped playback and the 'zoom' tool will help you make precise edits.

If you are using more than one audio track, use the mixer to balance their levels, so that the tracks are the same volume.

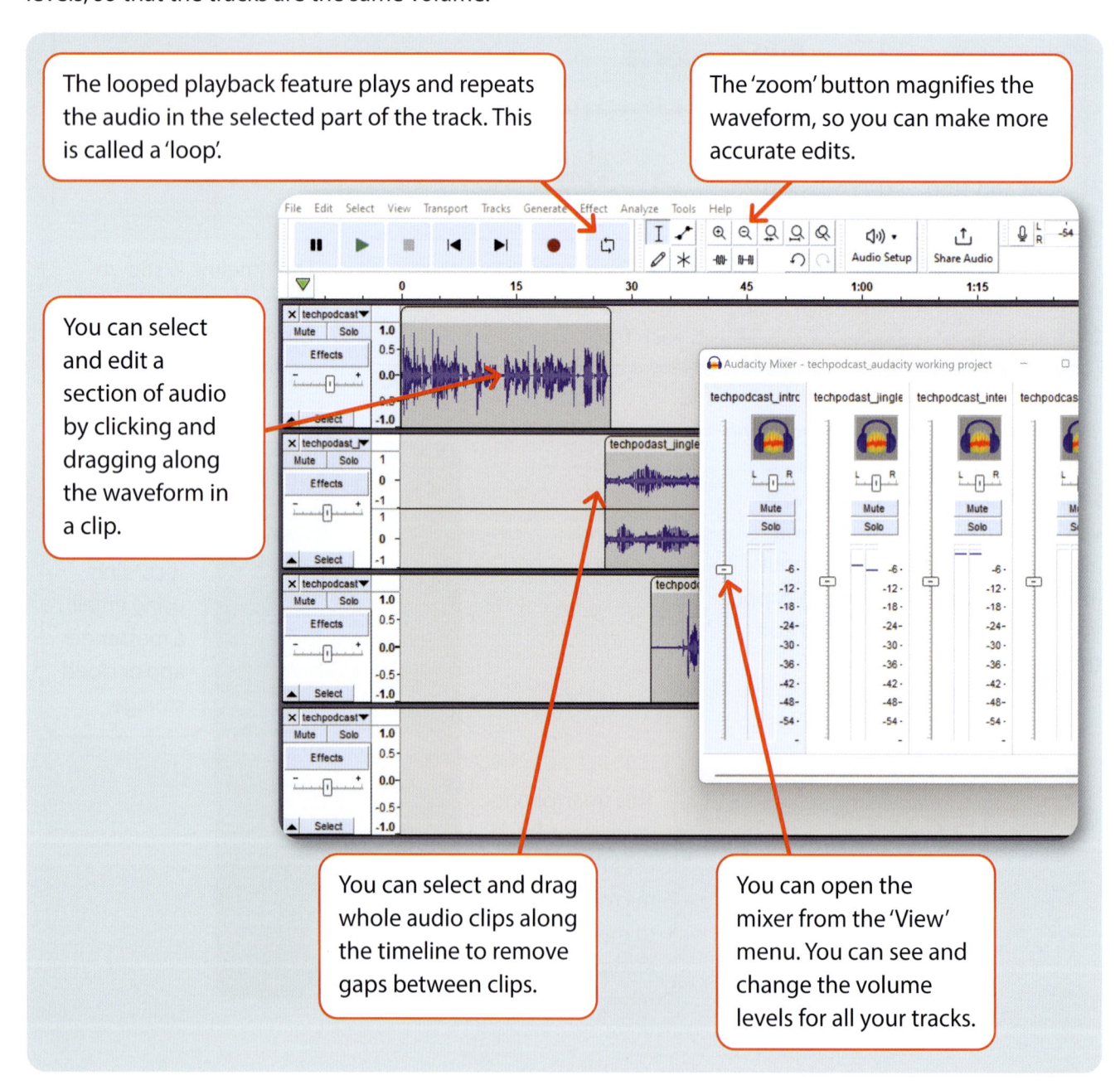

The looped playback feature plays and repeats the audio in the selected part of the track. This is called a 'loop'.

The 'zoom' button magnifies the waveform, so you can make more accurate edits.

You can select and edit a section of audio by clicking and dragging along the waveform in a clip.

You can select and drag whole audio clips along the timeline to remove gaps between clips.

You can open the mixer from the 'View' menu. You can see and change the volume levels for all your tracks.

B

1. Record your audio content in your DAW or on your handheld device.
2. Use separate tracks (or files) if you are recording more than one segment.
3. Combine the segments using a DAW and export the complete programme as an audio file (for example, an MP3, MP4 or WAV file).

Be creative

Make a jingle for your podcast. You could use musical instruments, or software that allows you to create music. Write some lyrics for your jingle.

Stretch zone

Make a list of material you think will be useful to include on your multimedia platform with the audio file. Think about other types of content that can help the audience understand and engage with your audio content.

Test

1. What do the letters 'DAW' stand for?
2. What is the purpose of a test recording made before the actual recording session?
3. Explain the difference between an outline and a script for audio content.
4. Describe some of the ways that other types of content can work together with audio to help an audience engage with your content.

1.4 Create video content

You will learn:
- how to collaborate on a video project by agreeing content and style
- how to edit together clips to create a finished video.

Key words
- brief
- file format
- orientation
- resolution
- rough cut
- screen format
- shot type

Agree content, style and technical standards

In the planning session at the start of this unit, you agreed the theme of your video content for your multimedia project. In this lesson, you will create the content.

Media professionals often work in separate teams to create different parts of the content. When you work like this, you need to agree:

- **the technical standards:** how the content should be recorded
- **the content:** what should be recorded
- **the style:** how the content should look.

Technical standards

The team needs to agree the technical standards for the content they create, so that the editor can work with the material in the next stage of production.

- **Screen format** (or 'aspect ratio') and **orientation** should be the same for all clips. Most cameras can record in different formats. 16:9 is a common widescreen format that works well for most content. But some social media platforms use different formats, for example, a 1:1 ratio, which creates a square image. Teams should also agree on using landscape (horizontal) or portrait (vertical) orientation.

- **Resolution** and **file format** should also be consistent. Modern smartphones and cameras can record in 4K 'ultra-high definition'. But this creates very large file sizes and may not work on all sharing platforms. A 'high definition' setting like 1920×1080 pixels (for a 16:9 aspect ratio) is more suitable.

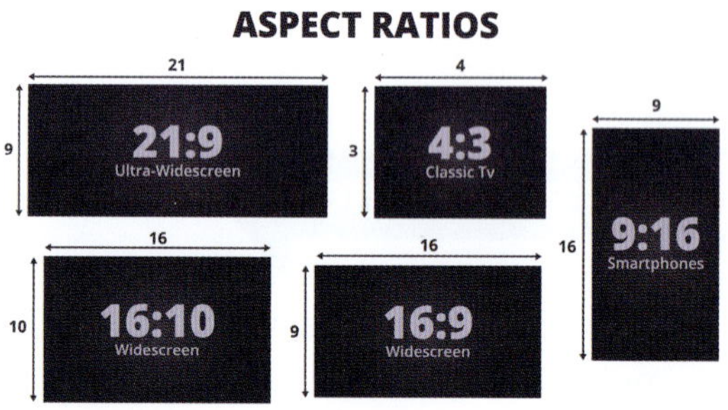

ASPECT RATIOS

21:9 Ultra-Widescreen
4:3 Classic Tv
9:16 Smartphones
16:10 Widescreen
16:9 Widescreen

8K ULTRA HD | 4K ULTRA HD | 1080p FULL HD
5K ULTRA HD | 2K QUAD HD | 720p HD

Content and style

To make sure that teams create content that meets the original plan, they decide on a division of work. Each crew needs a **brief** for their work, which tells them what they need to do. The brief can include a shot list that shows a list of specific scenes or items that the crew needs to record. The example shows a shot list for a team filming the exterior of a school.

Shot no.	Scene no.	Camera movement	Camera angle	Description	Notes
1	1	Pan	Wide	Day time exterior of school building (front). No students.	
2	1	None	Wide	Day time exterior of school building (front). Students leaving at home time.	At least 20 seconds duration.

You can use the shot list to help teams achieve a consistent look in all the clips they record. You can add instructions about:

▶ **shot type:** a combination of wide-angle and close-up shots will make your video more interesting

▶ **camera movement:** tracking or panning movements can add interest and excitement to your video

▶ **framing:** you can include suggestions of where to place a subject in the frame.

A

1. Plan and record your video content. You could use the Video Shot List template to help you with the planning.
2. Record your content using your smartphone, tablet, camera or other device.
3. Record separate clips (or files) if you are recording more than one segment.

wide-angle shot

Assemble and edit

You can use the shot list to bring together all the clips recorded. You can put them in order in your video-editing application. This early version of a video or film is called a **rough cut**. The rough cut helps you review the material and make decisions about the final edit.

During the rough cut stage, you can explore some ideas to help improve the final edit. For example:

▶ Change the order of the scenes to see if they work better. You do not have to tell a story step by step in time order. You can break up the structure of a video by using flashbacks or cutaways.

▶ Use still images in different places, for example, between interviews. You can use your own images or you can search for images on the web. Remember to look for content that is free to use, for example: public domain, royalty-free or licensed under Creative Commons.

close-up shot

9:1.4 Video Shot List: Digital Activity File

1.4 Create video content

▶ Insert a **cutaway** for added detail. A cutaway is a short shot of something in the environment where the scene is happening. It does not show the subject. You can insert a cutaway into the middle of a scene by splitting it. Cutaways can be wide shots or close ups. They can add interest and context to a scene.

Scene	Cutaway ideas
An interviewee talking on camera	Extreme close-up of subject's hands as they talk
A student walking along a school corridor	Close-up of a poster on the wall

Key words

auto-caption

caption

cutaway

Stop, think

Make sure that everybody appearing in your video has given permission for you to include them.

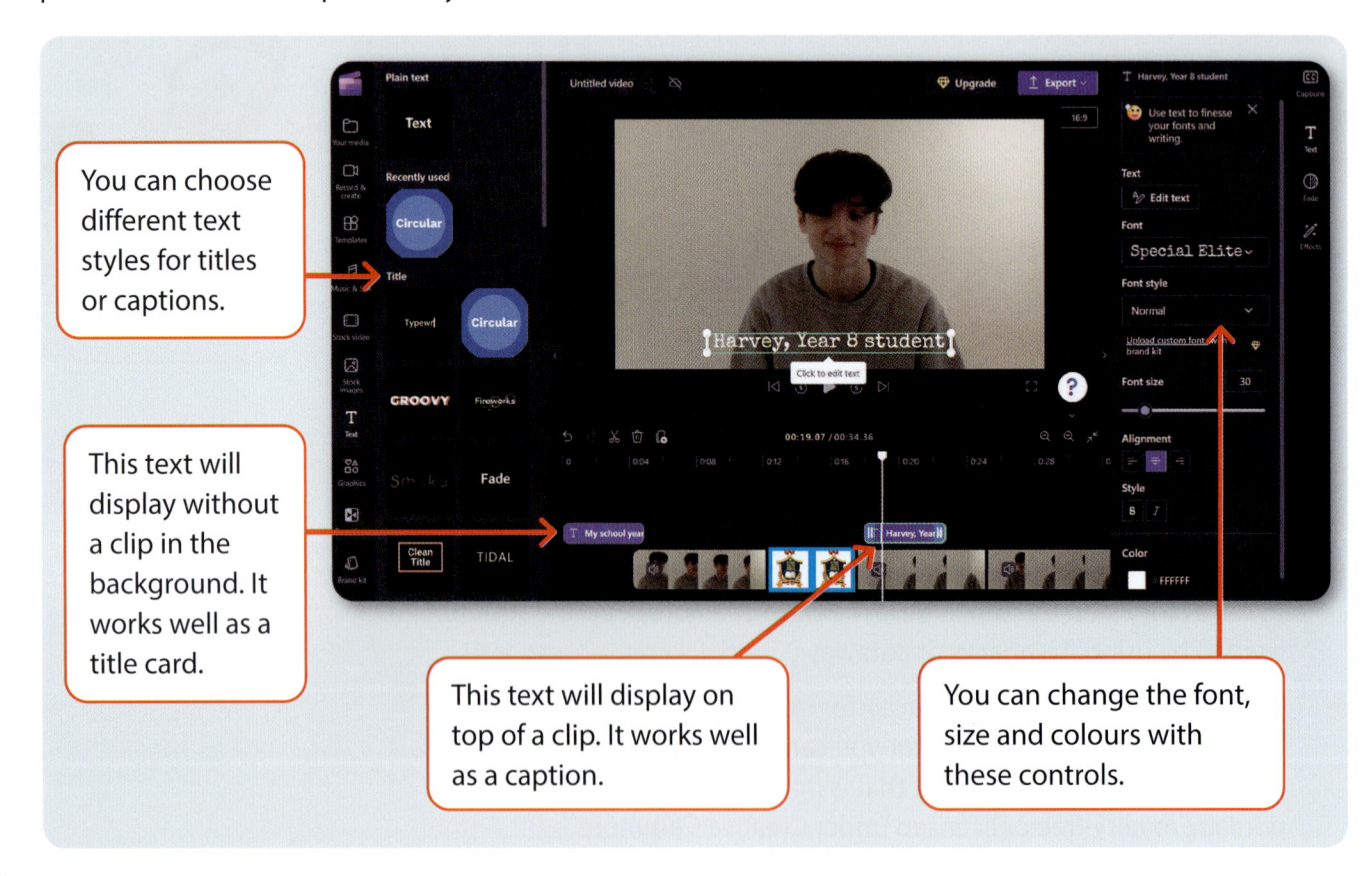

Add titles and captions

Your video-editing application may allow you to add titles and **captions** over any image or clip. Think about how to:

▶ use a main title card at the start of your video

▶ use subtitles for each segment of your video, for example 'Interviews with classmates'

▶ add captions, for example, to name the subject in a shot.

Use the text feature of your editing application to choose fonts, styles, placement and other options for your on-screen text.

You can choose different text styles for titles or captions.

This text will display without a clip in the background. It works well as a title card.

This text will display on top of a clip. It works well as a caption.

You can change the font, size and colours with these controls.

B

1. Assemble and edit your video content.
2. Combine all the clips into a rough cut and review it.
3. Make any edits you think are needed to create the final cut.
4. Add titles and captions.
5. Save the final edited version of your video.

Stretch zone

Does your video-editing app have an **auto-caption** feature? Explore how modern applications use AI and voice recognition to turn audio into speech. In Microsoft's Clipchamp application, for example, select it from the captions menu. Play back your video and read the captions – are they correct?

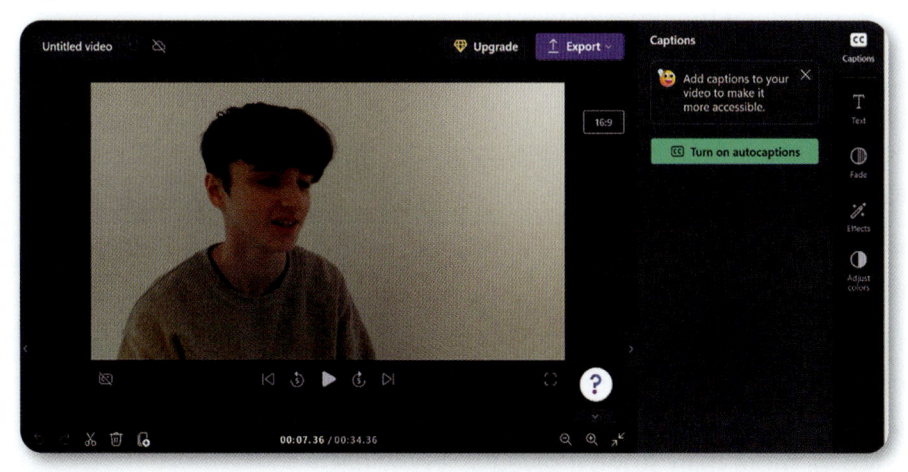

✓ Test

1. What does 'rough cut' mean?
2. Explain how you can use on-screen text to improve your video content.
3. What is a cutaway shot?
4. List the types of shot you used in your video (for example: wide, close-up). Explain how you used them to create a more interesting final edit.

1.5 Host and embed content

You will learn:
- how to publish content on streaming platforms
- how to add metadata to support your content
- how to embed published content in websites or other platforms
- how to embed content into offline files.

Key word

metadata

Export your content

In 1.1–1.4, you created new audio and video content. In this lesson, you will upload the content to online services. In 1.1, you reviewed the available services for your type of content and made some decisions about where to host your content. These hosting services will have their own requirements for your content. Usually, these requirements limit things like:

- the format of your content, in particular the types of files that you can upload
- the size of your content, usually either by limiting the length of a piece of content (for example, no longer than 10 minutes of video), or by limiting the file size you can upload.

Before publishing your content to your chosen host, you should check that the content you have exported meets all the requirements.

Remember to use compressed file formats where possible. These files are easier and quicker to export and upload. The file size depends on the format of file used. A 3-minute audio clip saved as a MP3 might be 3 MB. The same clip saved as a FLAC file could be 15 MB, or more than 30 MB if saved as a WAV file.

The size difference of different video file formats can be even greater. An uncompressed .avi file can be 50-times larger than a compressed MP4 file.

Upload files to hosts and streaming services

If you are using an online platform, you can upload the file using its website or app. When you log in to the service, you can choose to upload a file that is stored on your device.

UPLOAD   **CLOUD UPLOAD**

The example shows the upload feature of the SoundCloud service for audio streaming.

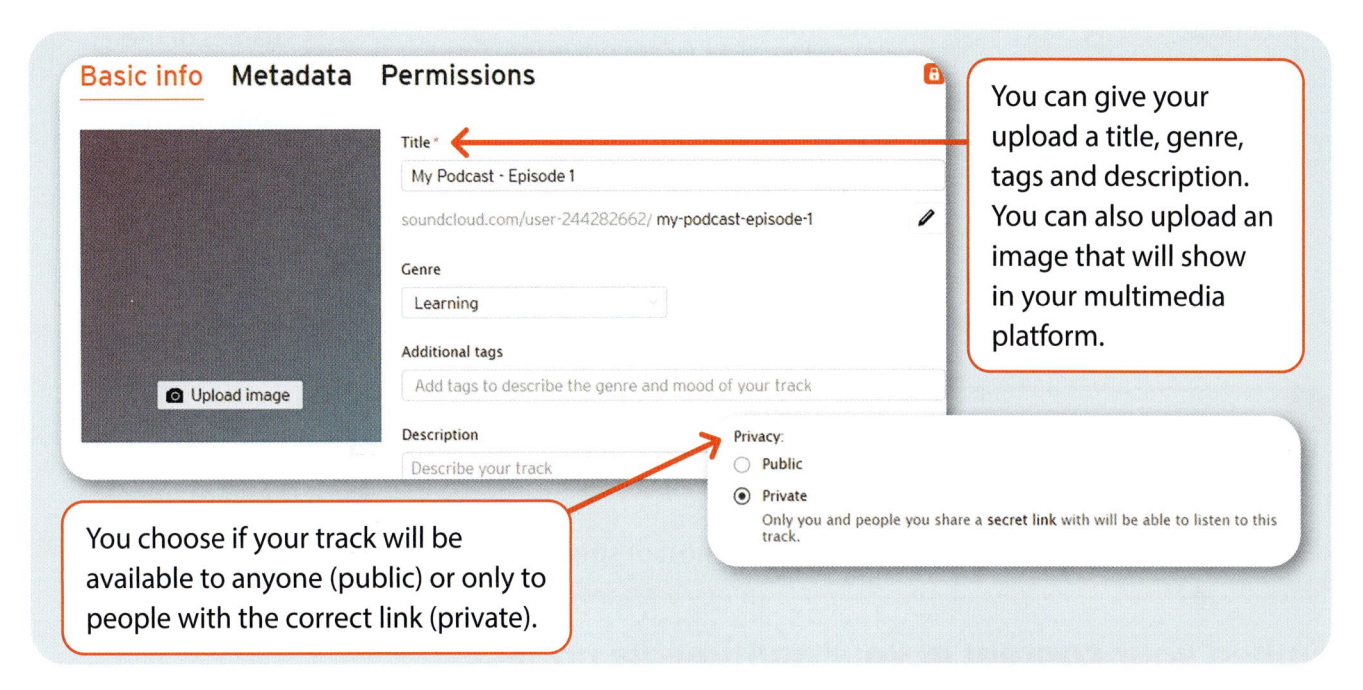

You can give your upload a title, genre, tags and description. You can also upload an image that will show in your multimedia platform.

You choose if your track will be available to anyone (public) or only to people with the correct link (private).

This example shows the upload screen for YouTube, from a smartphone device.

The hosting or streaming service will usually give you some options to control who can find and view the content. Setting your content to 'public' view means that anyone on the web can find and see your content. Setting your content to 'private', 'followers only' or a similar restriction will mean that people can only see your content with your permission. However, these settings may prevent you from embedding the content in your multimedia platform later.

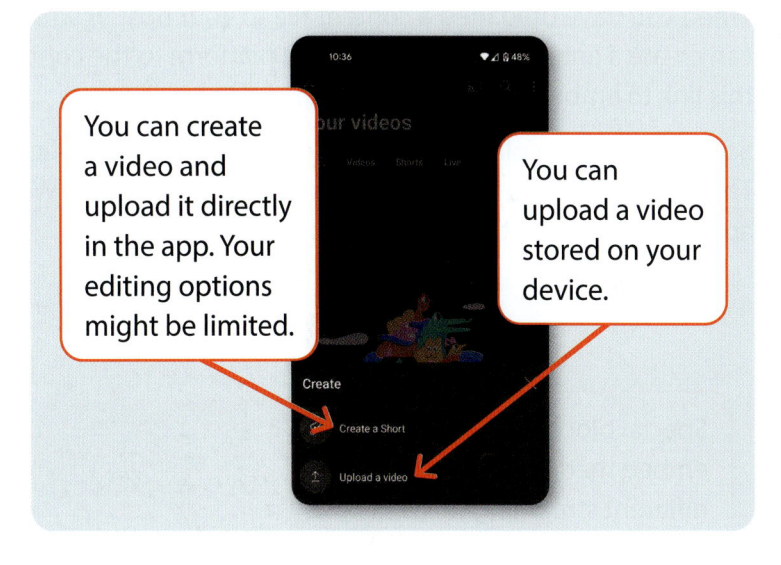

You can create a video and upload it directly in the app. Your editing options might be limited.

You can upload a video stored on your device.

Add metadata

Metadata is data that describes other data. For media content, this usually means that it is a set of values about the form and technical standard of the content in your media files. Media players often display metadata to the user when your content is played back. The data might include:

- ▶ the length (in hours, minutes and seconds) of the content
- ▶ the title of the content, for example, a podcast and episode name, or a song title
- ▶ the name of the creator of the content
- ▶ the resolution or quality of the recording, for example, the bitrate of any audio or the compression type used.

1.5 Host and embed content

> You can choose how to license your content when it is published.

> You can add the names of the creators and the content. This data will become part of the content when it is published.

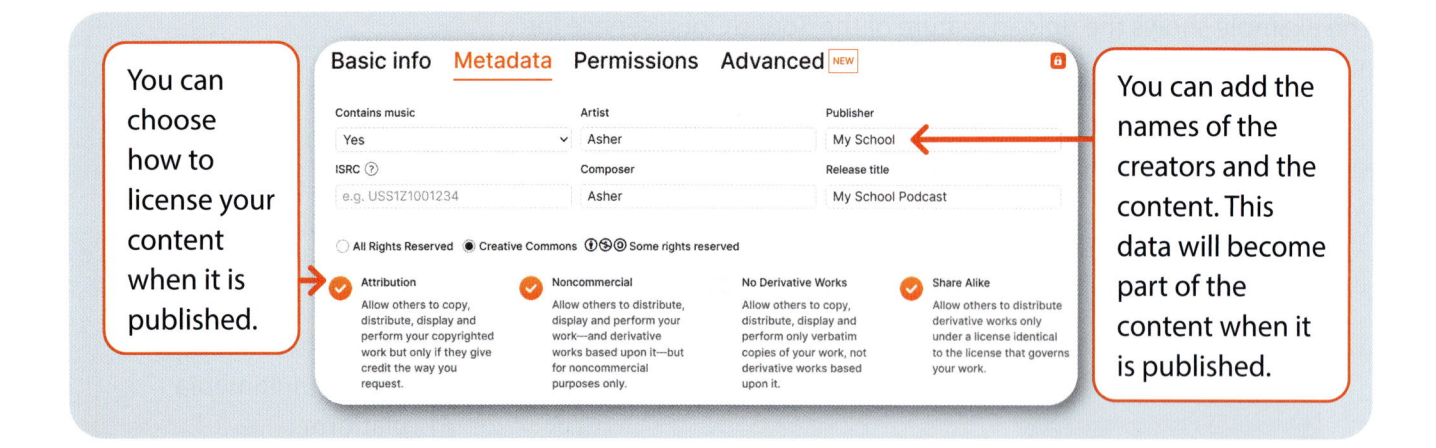

A

1. Export your audio and video content to create files that you can upload to your multimedia platform.
2. Upload your media content to your chosen host or streaming service.

Embed your content in your multimedia project

When you have uploaded a content file to your host or streaming service, you can create a link from your multimedia platform to the content. You can use this link to embed the content in a page or post.

Some multimedia platforms have media players for specific streaming services. This example shows how you can use a content block on WordPress to embed audio content from the SoundCloud streaming service.

> Special block types embed media from different streaming hosts. Use the URL from the host when you create the new block.

> The new block shows the embedded player for the streaming site. Visitors to your site can play your content with the embedded player.

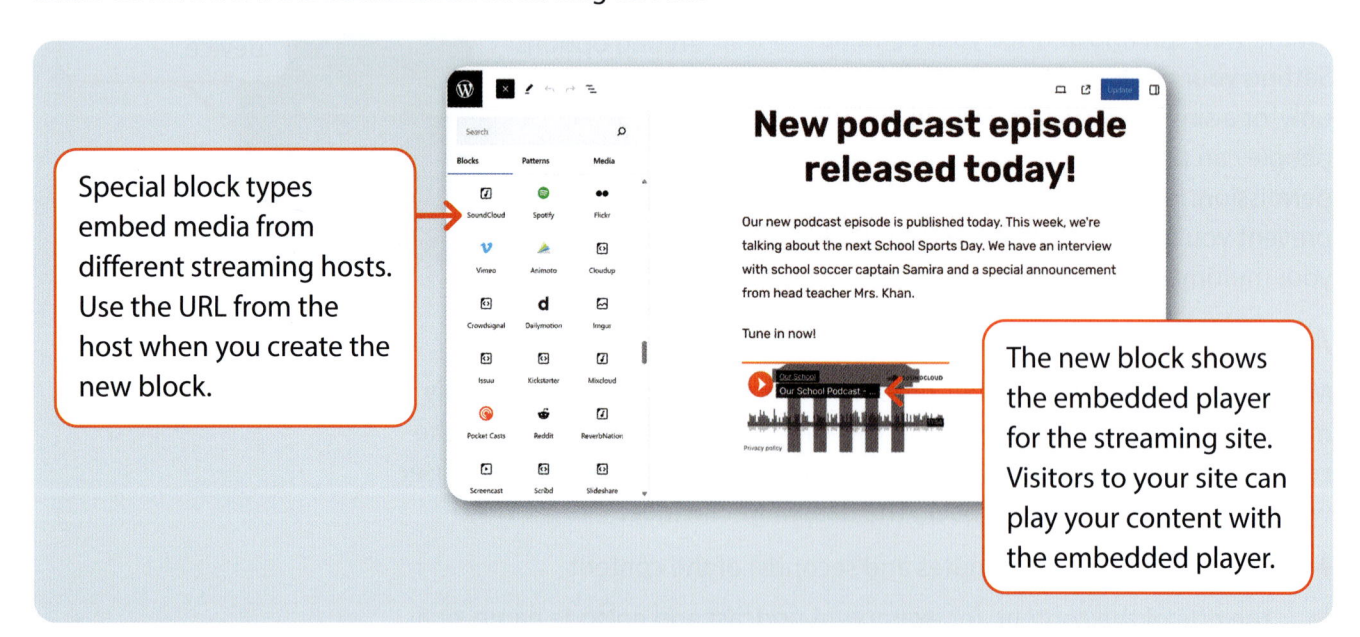

After you have embedded the content, you can preview the page or post. You should see that a media player appears on screen. When you click 'play', the media should start.

34

Embed content in an offline presentation

If you are sharing your content in an offline presentation, you can embed files directly into a document. This example shows a video file embedded in a slide of a Microsoft PowerPoint presentation. Users can click the player controls to start and stop the video.

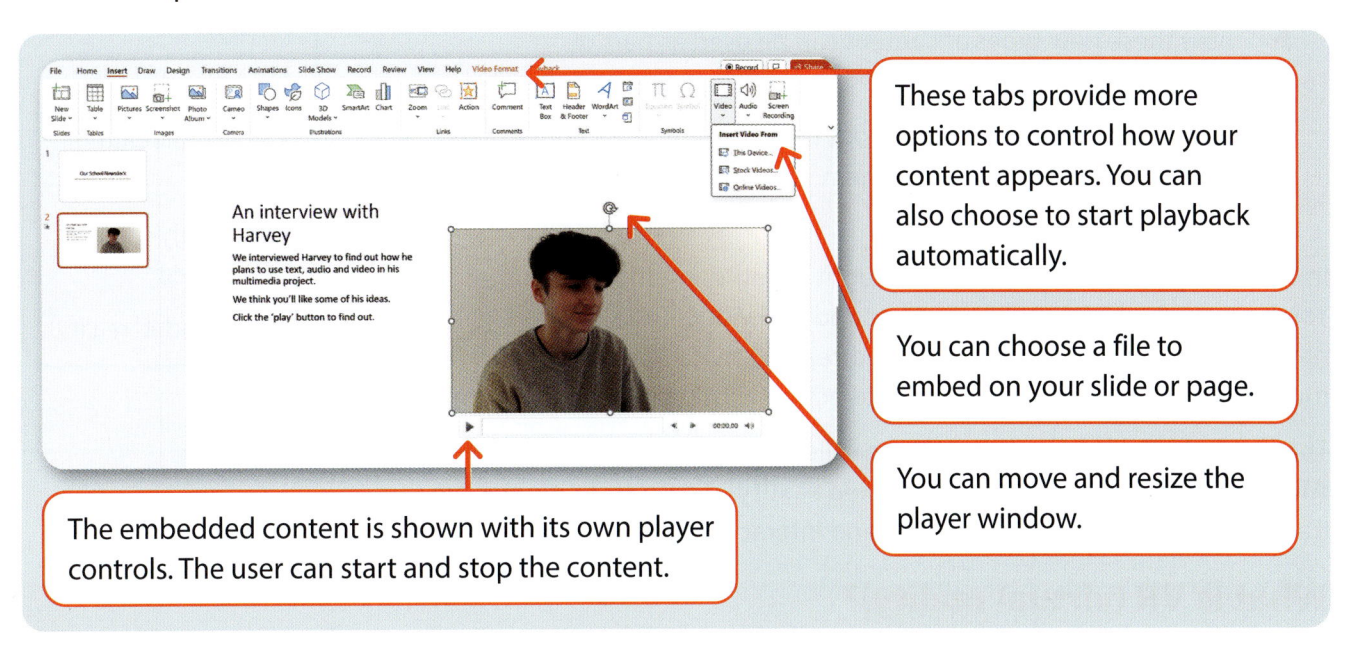

These tabs provide more options to control how your content appears. You can also choose to start playback automatically.

You can choose a file to embed on your slide or page.

You can move and resize the player window.

The embedded content is shown with its own player controls. The user can start and stop the content.

B

1. Embed the content on a post or a page on your platform.
2. Use the preview feature to check that your media plays correctly.

Stretch zone

Find some examples of metadata in files on your computer. Open a file in an application like a word processor or drawing programme. What metadata can you find? Look for menus with names like 'Properties'. What does the metadata tell you about the content you find?

✓ Test

1. What does 'publishing' digital content mean?
2. Explain what metadata is.
3. Which of these types of data in a text document file is NOT metadata?
    a name of author   b date last saved   c the document text
4. Describe how an embedded media player works on a multimedia platform.

1.6 Extended reality: new kinds of content

You will learn:
- what mixed reality, augmented reality and virtual reality are
- how these new types of content can be used as part of multimedia productions
- how you can find out more about these new types of content and the technology that enables them.

Key words
AR (augmented reality)

MR (mixed reality)

VR (virtual reality)

wearable technology (wearables)

XR (extended reality)

In this unit, you have created and brought together multimedia content. You have worked with text, images, sound and video. Today, there are new technologies called **XR (extended reality)** that extend the world of multimedia. They add new ways of interacting with content you can create.

The technologies that make up XR are called **VR (virtual reality)**, **AR (augmented reality)** and **MR (mixed reality)**. These technologies are transforming the way we experience and interact with the world around us.

What is VR (virtual reality)?

VR creates a simulated environment using 3D models. This environment is completely separate from the real world. Users wear a VR headset that has screens and headphones to create an experience you are part of. VR headsets also have a range of sensors that respond to movement of the wearer's head or eyes. This allows the user to move and look around the 3D simulated environment. For the user, VR is like stepping into another reality.

Examples include VR games, educational simulations and virtual tours.

Students can use VR to learn skills like industrial design.

Doctors can use VR to help patients understand their conditions.

VR provides a more exciting experience for gamers.

Think science

VR headsets and smartphones include motion sensors. They detect movement and adjust what you see to match the movement. Motion sensors can include an accelerometer or a gyroscope – find out how they work.

What is AR (augmented reality)?

AR enhances the real world by overlaying digital information onto it. Unlike VR, AR does not replace the real environment. Instead, it adds a digital layer to it. AR is typically presented to the user through a device like a smartphone or through **wearable technology (wearables)** like AR glasses.

Because AR experiences are available through smartphones, this form of content is more accessible to users and more suitable for use in a real-world environment. For this reason, the typical applications of AR are different to VR.

Some AR games use smartphones to place animated objects and characters in the real world.

Google Glass is a wearable computer that supports AR. The built-in screen can overlay digital content in the wearer's view.

A 'head-up display' can project digital information into a driver's field of view. Now they can see data and warnings without taking their eyes off the road.

Google Lens can translate text on labels. It uses optical character recognition to read the original text. It uses a translation engine with artificial intelligence (AI) to translate the text into your chosen language.

Google Lens can then use AR to overlay the translated text directly onto the image as you look at it on your device.

1 Creative media: Multimedia content

37

1.6 Extended reality: new kinds of content

What is MR (mixed reality)?

MR is an extension of the ideas and technology of AR. In MR, digital objects are still added to the real world – but now the digital object can interact with the real world, not just with the user.

For example, you might use MR to place a virtual ball on a real table and then play with it as if it were a real ball. In this game, you are interacting with the ball, but the ball is also interacting with other objects in the real world, for example by 'bouncing' against a real table.

MR applications need to model the real-world environment. They need to be able to detect real-world objects and determine how the simulated objects should interact with them. To do this, they need to detect things like the edges of objects and boundaries of spaces. They also need to model characteristics from physics, like gravity. This kind of application needs a lot of computing power. Typically, an application might use real-time cloud-computing and AI to create an MR environment.

In an MR application, the digital object interacts with the real-world objects around it. In this example, the computer must recognize the real-world table and place the cup on it.

> **A**
> 1. Research how XR technology and content is being used in one of these areas: education, gaming, healthcare or architecture.
> 2. Write down your favourite uses of XR. Explain how you think it makes content more helpful and engaging.

XR applications

Some applications of XR need specialist equipment and very powerful computing. The technology to deliver XR experiences is developing all the time. Your school may already have some equipment that can demonstrate the XR experience to you.

Apps you can try

If you have a smartphone or tablet, you can already use some XR applications to experience this new world of content. You can search your device's app store for free applications that include XR features.

> This example shows an AR app that allows visitors to the Parthenon in Athens to see – and interact with – a 3D model of the building as it would have looked 3,000 years ago. You can also use this app without travelling to Athens.

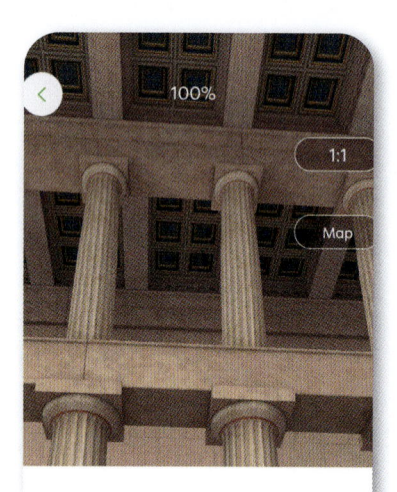

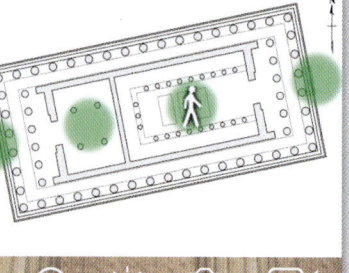

Information you can search

You can explore websites that feature XR content and technologies, like Oculus (for VR) and ARCore (for AR). These sites often have demos that can help you understand how the technology works.

You can search for reviews and tutorials on technology websites, social media and video-sharing platforms like YouTube.

B

Write down some ideas about how you could use XR for your school sports day multimedia project. Download the worksheet for this lesson to help you get started.

This example shows an AR design app. It includes some 3D models that you can place in your real-world environment.

Stretch zone

Review the list of your favourite XR uses. You have already written down what you like about them. Every technology choice we make has benefits and limitations. Limitations are things that the technology cannot do. Write down some limitations of XR technology against each of your examples.

✓ Test

1. Explain the difference between VR and AR.
2. Describe an example of AR that you have seen.
3. Explain how VR or AR could be used in education or training. What are the benefits of using the technology in this way?
4. Describe the role of sensors in VR or AR. Why are they needed?

9:1.6 XR Ideas: Digital Activity File

1 What have you learned?

Review test

1 What is a multimedia project?

2 Write a sentence describing the steps you took to create and edit digital content in your project.

3 Describe at least **two** tools you can use to plan audio or video content for a project.

4 Explain what extended reality technologies like VR and AR do.

5 Write a short paragraph describing how you made sure that the content in your project was right for your audience.

6 Explain how you think AR or VR content could be used in your project in the future.

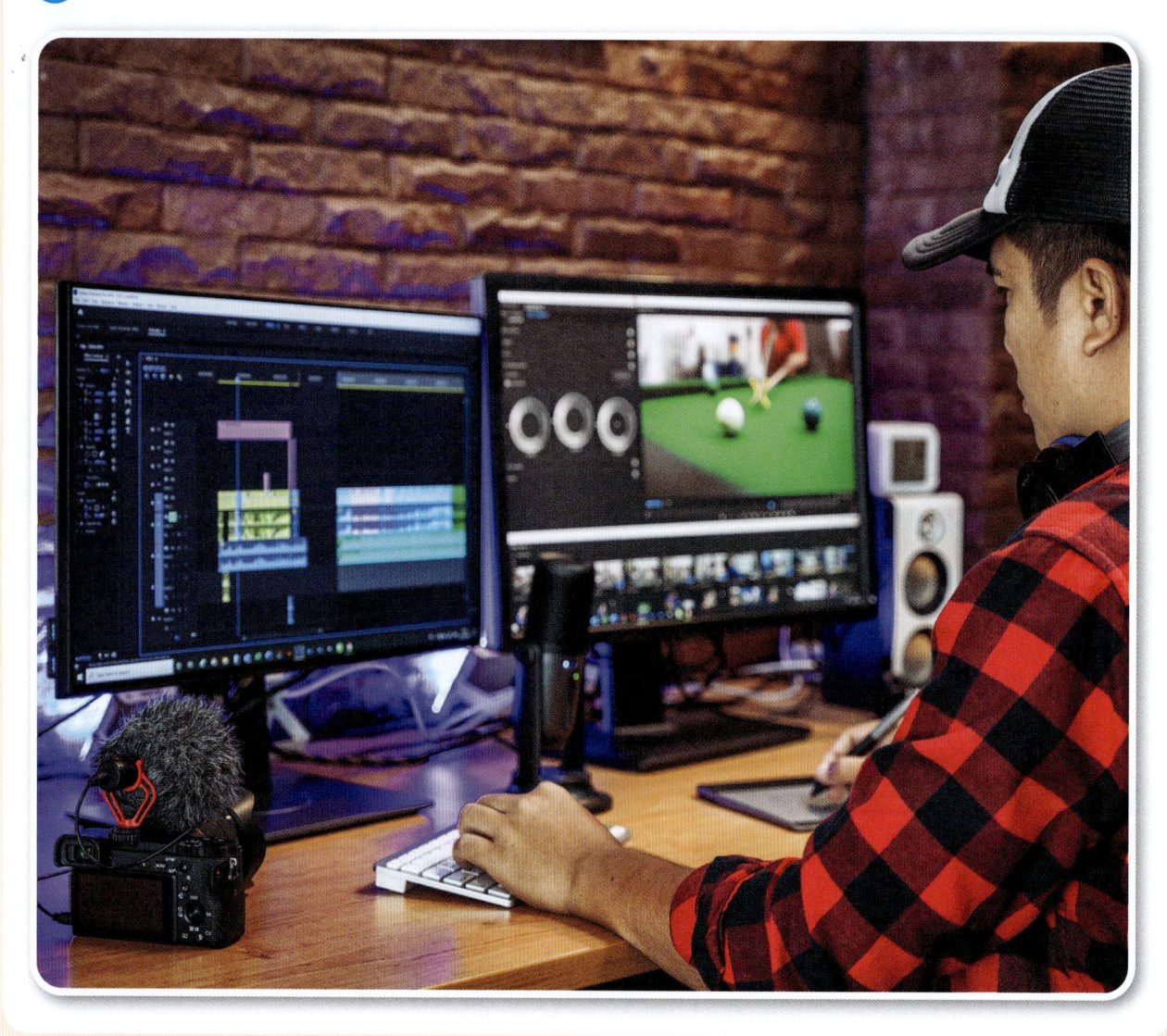

Review activity

1 Open the worksheet for this lesson. It contains a brief for a multimedia project for the Tropical Beach Dive Shop.

2 The brief asks for your ideas and proposals about:
- media content such as text, images, audio and video
- platforms that could be used to share the content
- using XR content to engage with users.

3 Read the project brief then fill in the form on the worksheet.

Self-evaluation

How did you do?	What is your level?	What your level means
• I answered test questions 1 and 2. • I described ideas for multimedia content. I gave an example of VR.	Developing	You have learned something new in this unit.
• I answered test questions 1 to 4. • I proposed a combined multimedia project using text, images and other types of media.	Secure	You have reached the expected standard in this unit.
• I answered all the test questions. • I evaluated the benefits of AR and VR.	Extending	You are an expert.

What next? To improve your level you can go back and repeat some of this unit.

2 Digital literacy: Make good choices

You will learn:

- how to use social media in a way that keeps you and others safe
- how to report concerns and ask for help
- to explain what virtual social spaces are
- to explain the benefits and risks of using virtual social spaces.

Everyday life is full of dilemmas. A dilemma is a situation where you have to make a difficult choice between two or more things. Sometimes all of your choices are great options. Sometimes all of your choices are challenging.

In this unit, you will learn about the dilemmas you might face when you use social media. In each lesson, you will be given a different dilemma to think about. You will learn how to use social media safely and responsibly.

? Are the friends you make online as good as friends you meet face-to-face?

People you meet online may not be what they seem to be and it can be harder to feel empathy for people we do not meet, which can make friendships problematic. But if we are careful, we can make good friends who will support us in difficulties.

Learning outcomes: Use social media safely and with regard to others; Describe the remote social space created by new technology ('the metaverse')

addictive design   empathy
ethics of care   follower
humane design   metaverse
obligation   post
social media

Talk about …

What social media sites can you think of? Make a list of names as a class. Draw the logos of as many sites as you can. Next time you go online, check whether you got the logos right.

Activity

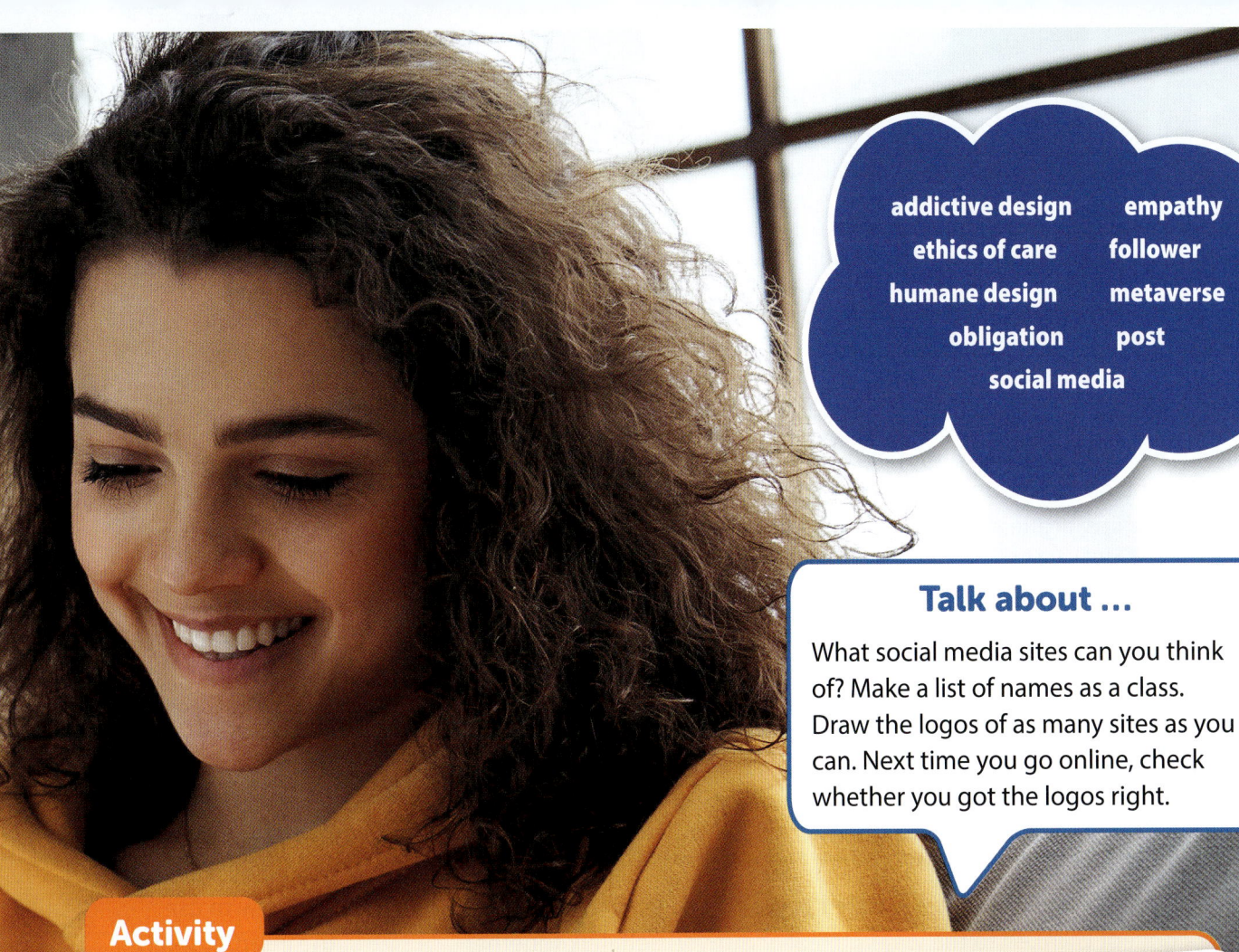

Some people have lots of 'followers' on social media. This means that lots of people see the content they produce. These people are called influencers. People who follow influencers tend to think that influencers are relatable and trustworthy (even if they are not).

Companies often pay influencers to advertise their products for them. This can be in the form of:

▶ competitions where the influencer gives away product samples

▶ giving influencers free products or services so that they say positive things about them online

▶ giving influencers money to make social media content, such as videos, blogs, vlogs or posts, about a product

▶ giving the influencer a small amount of money every time a follower clicks on the link to a company's website or uses a special code – this is called affiliate marketing.

Imagine you are an influencer who is asked to promote information about a new clothing brand in your country. Make a list of the dilemmas you might face. For example, do you know whether the clothing is made ethically, or using forced labour? Share your list with a group and discuss.

43

2.1 Your online self

You will learn:
▶ why people might make fake social media accounts.

Key words

social media

What does it mean to 'be yourself'?

Humans are complicated living things. We change as we grow. We work together and alone. We understand the world around us in different ways. We start friendships, argue and make friends again. We want to make a difference in the world. We want to be treated with respect.

> **A**
> 1. Work with someone in your class. Talk with each other about these topics. Make notes about each other's answers.
>   - I am good at …
>   - I would like to be better at …
>   - I am happy when …
>   - I worry about …
>   - At home I enjoy …
>   - At school I enjoy …
> 2. The way you see yourself is called your self-concept. Your self-concept is linked to the way you feel about yourself. Talk together about what your answers might tell you about your self-concept.

Spiral back

In previous years, you have learned how to use content from online sources and how to use the internet safely and fairly.

How do you present yourself online?

What do you think could be inside each of these boxes? Perhaps it is something nice. Perhaps it is something unpleasant. Perhaps it is nothing. The outside of the box tells us very little about what is inside.

Our digital lives are bit like these boxes.

> **B**
>
> Imagine a box which contains all of your digital life.
>
> 1. Write or draw about what the outside of your own 'digital life box' looks like. What faces, feelings or shapes do you choose to show online?
> 2. What is inside your own 'digital life box'? How do you choose to communicate online? How do you choose to behave online?
> 3. Is there anything you would like to change about your 'digital life box'?

Fake social media profiles

Some people set up more than one **social media** profile. They have more than one 'box' they choose to show others online. There are many reasons why you might set up a fake social media profile.

▶ To protect yourself.

▶ To allow you to express your individuality without being criticized by others.

▶ To try out different types of personality or sides of your own personality.

▶ To post content that is personal for friends or family. For example, you might have had a bad grade at school. You might need to talk to someone about it, or ask for help to improve the grade.

▶ To post private thoughts. Some people even post rude or worrying content. If the profile is fake, then nobody in everyday life will be able to link the profile with the person who posted the content.

▶ To share, or post, content that only certain people will be interested in, for example, hobbies.

An affinity group is a group for people who like a certain thing. Affinity means that you like something. For example, you might really like a book. You could find other people who like the book on social media. You could communicate about the book with other fans using a website or app. But you might be embarrassed about liking the book. You might not want anyone else to know. So you might set up a fake profile. Then you could post without other people knowing who you are.

Some people set up fake profiles in affinity groups for more serious reasons. They might want to gather information about the things people like so that they can target adverts at them. They might want to influence people to change their minds about the things they like. They might want to involve other people in dangerous or harmful activities.

2.1 Your online self

Risks of fake social media profiles

Some reasons for setting up a fake social media profile are positive. But a fake social media profile could harm you or other people.

> **Key word**
> follower

- ▶ When you use a fake social media profile, nobody knows who you are.
- ▶ You might see content that is not appropriate.
- ▶ It can be hard to keep track of which profile you are using.
- ▶ You might accidentally upset people if you post a comment from the wrong profile.
- ▶ Many fake social media profiles are trying to get personal or private information from you or people close to you, or take money from you.
- ▶ Some fake social media profiles might try to influence your views on important issues.

Many people and organizations use fake social media profiles. This makes it very difficult to know who to trust online.

Types of fake profile

You will find different types of fake profile on different apps. One common type of fake profile is a 'finsta'. This is a fake Instagram account used for posting to one specific group of people, or to post anonymously.

For example, Johannes loves cooking and uses a finsta 'chef_food_delights' to share his cooking tips, photos and videos. Johannes does not want his friends and family to know about his cookery yet.

You need to think about three things before you create a fake profile.

1. **Trust your instinct:** Ask yourself if you feel good about making the account. Perhaps it feels a little bit wrong. Ask yourself why you might be feeling that way.
2. **Act right:** Ask yourself whether you are likely to use the account to post something that is harmful, hurtful, or a lie. Ask yourself if you would say the same things if you were face-to-face with another person.
3. **Make a positive difference:** Ask yourself if you are staying true to who you are as a good person when you post to a fake profile.

How to spot a fake social media profile

▶ **The content does not make sense.** For example, the person might share very different views over a short period of time. They might use language that does not make sense.

▶ **The profile picture looks fake.** Some browsers have a reverse image search function. Use this to see if the photo came from a real person.

▶ **The profile has very little activity.** If the only content on the profile is a picture, then it is likely that the profile is fake.

▶ **They follow a surprisingly large number of people.** If someone has only a few **followers**, but is following thousands of people, be on your guard.

How can I spot a fake social media profile?

C

1. Create this table using a word processor or spreadsheet app.

Fake accounts can be harmful	Fake accounts can be useful

2. Complete the table. Why can fake accounts be both harmful and useful?

Stretch zone

Discuss the following question in a group. When you 'go online', are you really going to different places?

✓ Test

1. Name three different types of content that could be posted on social media.
2. What sort of person would you like to be seen as online?
3. Amanda has set up three different social media profiles. Give a possible reason for each of the three social media profiles Amanda has set up.
4. Explain the risks Amanda faces by setting up so many different social media profiles.

2.2 Types of social media

You will learn:
- about different types of social media
- about what information is safe to share with people online
- how to recognize warning feelings and how to act on them.

Key words

curate
GIF
infographic
meme

Types of social media

There are lots of different types of social media.

Social networking sites

Social networking sites help you to connect with family, friends, new people and businesses trying to sell you things. They try to make you feel like you are connecting with real human beings. On a social networking site, you can share your thoughts, images and videos. You can join groups to connect with people with similar interests. You can share your achievements, education and work history. You can look for new jobs.

Social review sites

On a social review site, people post comments about experiences they have had and things they have bought. You can read their thoughts about these things. You can share your own experiences with others.

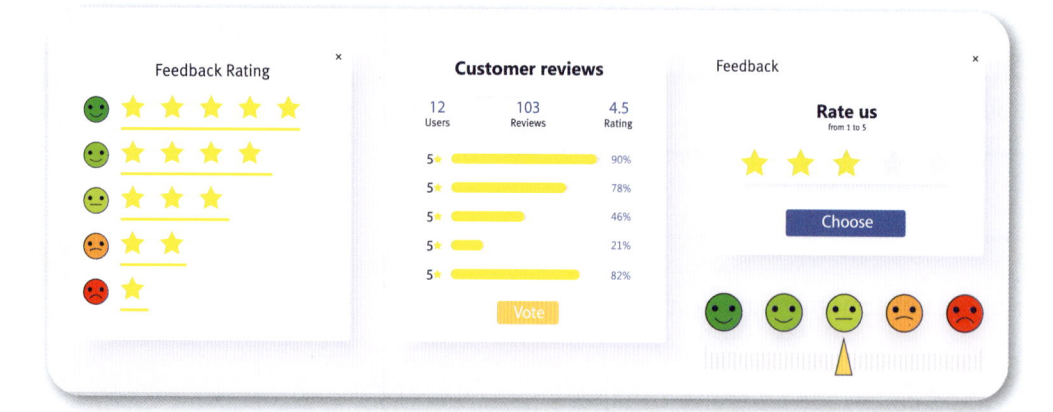

Image-sharing and video-hosting sites

People use image- and video-sharing sites to create and share images and videos. The companies that run the sites can **curate** the content. This means they select what to show first and how to group the content. The users of the site can also do this.

Different types of images can be shared using social media sites.

▶ An **infographic** is a quick, visual way of representing data or information.

▶ A **meme** is an image format that is adapted by different people to show different short messages. Memes are shared very quickly across the internet.

▶ **GIF** stands for 'graphics interchange format'. It is a basic single image with a message or very short animation.

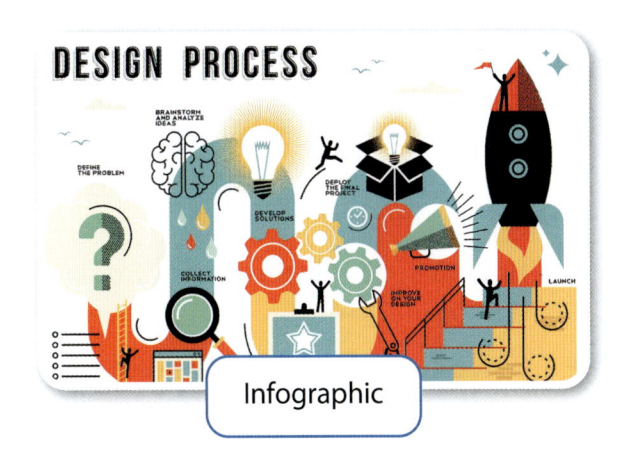

Infographic

GIF

Meme

Game-based social media

Many computer games let you connect and communicate with other players online. This is also a form of social media.

A

If you plan to use social media, you will need to decide which type of social media you would most like to use. Most social media sites have age restrictions, so you might have to wait before you are allowed to set up an account – this is to protect you.

What type of social media is best for me?

1 Use the internet to find one example of each type of social media you can access in your country.

2 Find the part of the website that tells you how old you have to be before you are allowed to use the site.

2.2 Types of social media

Your social media communities

When you use social media, you can communicate with many people. It is important to think about how well you know someone online, so that you can be safe and responsible. To work out how well you know someone, ask yourself the following questions:

- How often do I see the person? Do I know the person in real life or only online?
- How often do I communicate with the person?
- How do we communicate?
- How long have I known the person?
- How did I get to know the person?
- Have I seen the person communicate with other people I trust?
- Has the person ever said or done anything that makes me feel uncomfortable?

B

1. On a large piece of paper, draw a set of rings like this.

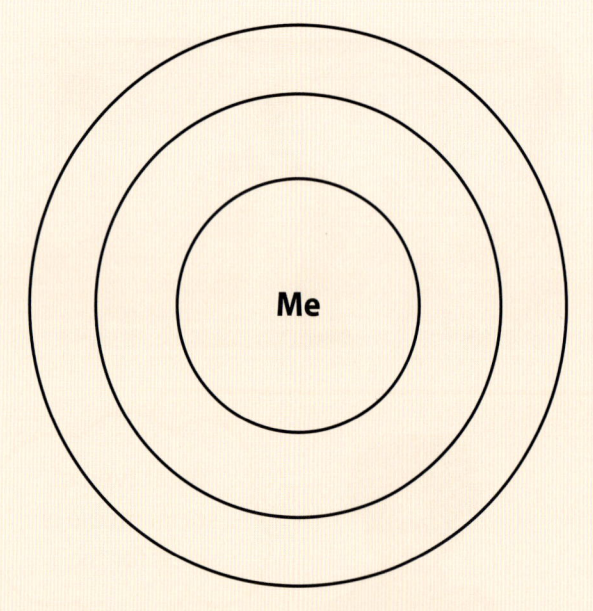

2. Put your name in the centre of the circle.

3. Think about the people you interact with most days. How well do you know them? If you know them extremely well, write their names in the middle circle with you. If you know them less well, put them in the next circle. If you do not know them well, put them in the last circle.

4. Make a similar diagram for people you interact with using social media, text messaging or online gaming. What differences are there between your diagrams?

Warning feelings

No matter which type of information you are sharing with which group, remember that social media content lasts a long time. Think about whether you would want other people to see that information in many years.

Sometimes people do not behave well on social media. Bad behaviour can make social media risky or unsafe. When you see bad behaviour, you might feel uncomfortable, scared or upset. You should always listen to these kinds of warning feelings.

Can you think of any examples of behaviour that could cause a warning feeling?

When you have a warning feeling:

- **slow down**
- **think about the situation** – what caused you to have the feeling?
- **consider your actions** – what are your choices?
- **act** – make a good choice, or ask an adult for advice.

Stretch zone

Imagine you posted an image like this on your social media site. Look at the comments.

What might each of the posters be thinking?

What impact do these comments have on your feelings?

34 likes

John: That looks amazing.

Seth: How can you drink that stuff?

Arjun: Whaaaaat? I thought you said you were going to the library to study!

Add a comment...   Post

✓ Test

1. Give an example of a type of social media.
2. What steps should you take if you have a warning feeling when using social media?
3. Choose a type of social media you have used, or would like to use. Write about why this would be a good choice of social media for you.
4. What risks do you face when you use social media?

2.3 Ethics of care

You will learn:
- about the responsibilities that come with using social media
- how to care for yourself and others online.

Key words

empathy

ethics of care

Ethics of care

Social media can be a place where people are kind and creative, and connect to each other. It can also be a place where people say or do hurtful things. We all need to be responsible when we use social media.

When you are using social media, remember these three ideas.

1. **We depend on each other.**

   As human beings we often learn and grow together. We sometimes help each other out when times are difficult. We make friends and argue with each other. Our societies need us to make things and give things to each other. Some communities need us to sell things to each other.

   We also need each other on social media. We want other people to hear what we have to say. We want to communicate with our friends and family. Companies need us to use social media.

2. **No one feels strong and positive *all* the time.**

   When you respond to something on social media, try to remember that the other person might be feeling vulnerable, scared, worried or sad. Only write something you would say to their face. Try to remember that what you post will probably make a difference to the person reading the post. Think about how you would like the person seeing your post to feel.

   Imagining how others are feeling is called **empathy**. We do not often think about it, but empathy is a really important part of keeping the internet a safe and positive place for everyone.

3   **What we say, type, share and do every day on social media should aim to protect and promote better lives for everyone.**

We each have the power to do these positive things, even when we do not have power in other aspects of our lives.

These ideas together mean you can develop digital **ethics of care** that will make your experiences on social media helpful and positive.

A

Is social media good or bad?

1   Do you have any experiences with social media? If so, have your experiences been good, bad or a bit of both?

2   Work in a group to make a list of the useful and problematic things about social media. Think about the many types of social media you can use. What are the useful and problematic things about each? Write down your thoughts in two columns like this:

Useful	Problematic

3   Share your list with the rest of the class. Does everyone agree?

2 Digital literacy: Make good choices

53

2.3 Ethics of care

Obligations

An **obligation** is something you do because it is a tradition in your society. You do it because you feel it is the right thing to do. Obligations are like responsibilities or duties. Our obligations bind us together. Understanding your digital obligations can help you be part of making digital society a good place to be.

Key word

obligation

What would you do if your friend shared too much on social media?

▶ Not react to their post.
▶ Send a private message suggesting your friend removes the post.
▶ Comment on the post and laugh at your friend for sharing it.

What is your obligation to your friend? What is your obligation to your own digital footprint?

Hani has shared photos of his new friend. Sam sees the photos. Sam knows it is important to ask permission before sharing any photos of someone else online.

Sam talks quietly to Hani about his post.

I am glad you have a new friend, Hani. Did your friend give you permission to post the photo of them online?

Thanks, Sam. Yes, he did say I could share the photos.

B

1. Draw a picture of yourself in the middle of a piece of paper. Write down up to three obligations you have for looking after your own digital footprint.
2. Now draw a group that is important to you somewhere else on your page. It could be your family, your friends, or your community. Write down up to three obligations you have for looking after their digital lives.

Be creative

Create a poster for your school that helps other people remember the three ethics of care ideas. If you use social media, you could post an image of your poster with the hashtag #DigitalEthicsOfCare.

By using the hashtag symbol in this way, all posts with that hashtag can be seen together. Remember to keep your personal information safe.

Digital citizen

Some people use software called a screen reader to read social media posts out loud. The words in a hashtag are joined together with no spaces. This makes it hard for the screen reader to read them properly. You can use a capital letter for the first letter of each word in a hashtag, like in #DigitalEthicsOfCare. Then the screen reader can separate the words and read them properly. It makes your hashtag more accessible.

> I try to make my posts positive and only post things I would say to someone's face.
>
> Try to remember that the person reading your post might not be feeling good.

Stretch zone

You have thought about your obligations to yourself and people you know.

Think about your obligations to people online that you have never met, and may never meet. What are your obligations to these people?

> What are my obligations?

✓ Test

1. What are the three main ideas of digital ethics of care that you should remember to apply to yourself and others?
2. Which of the three ethics of care ideas means most to you? Explain your thinking.
3. Sarah wants to post some pictures of a family celebration on social media. Some of the pictures include her young cousins. They are aged 1 and 4. What should Sarah do?
4. a Name one obligation you have to yourself to look after your digital footprint.
   b Name one obligation you have to others to look after their digital footprints. They can be people you know well or strangers.

2.4 Healthy balance

You will learn:
▶ how to keep a healthy balance between screen time and offline time.

Key word

addictive design

Know when to stop

Using social media can be fun. It is designed to draw you in. It links you with lots of people and keeps you interested. Sometimes people enjoy using technology so much they find it hard to stop. Some people even believe they are addicted to their phones or other computing devices. Addiction means that they do not think they could stop using their technologies.

Sometimes we do not use technology because we need to connect with someone, make something, or find something out. Sometimes we use technology because it is a habit.

Your brain is built for you to have some habits. These could be simple habits like getting dressed or greeting a family member.

Many types of social media are designed to make using the software a habit. This is called **addictive design**. Addictive design aims to use the pleasure your brain gets from succeeding at something or carrying out a habit to get you to feel good. The good feeling means you will probably use that social media again.

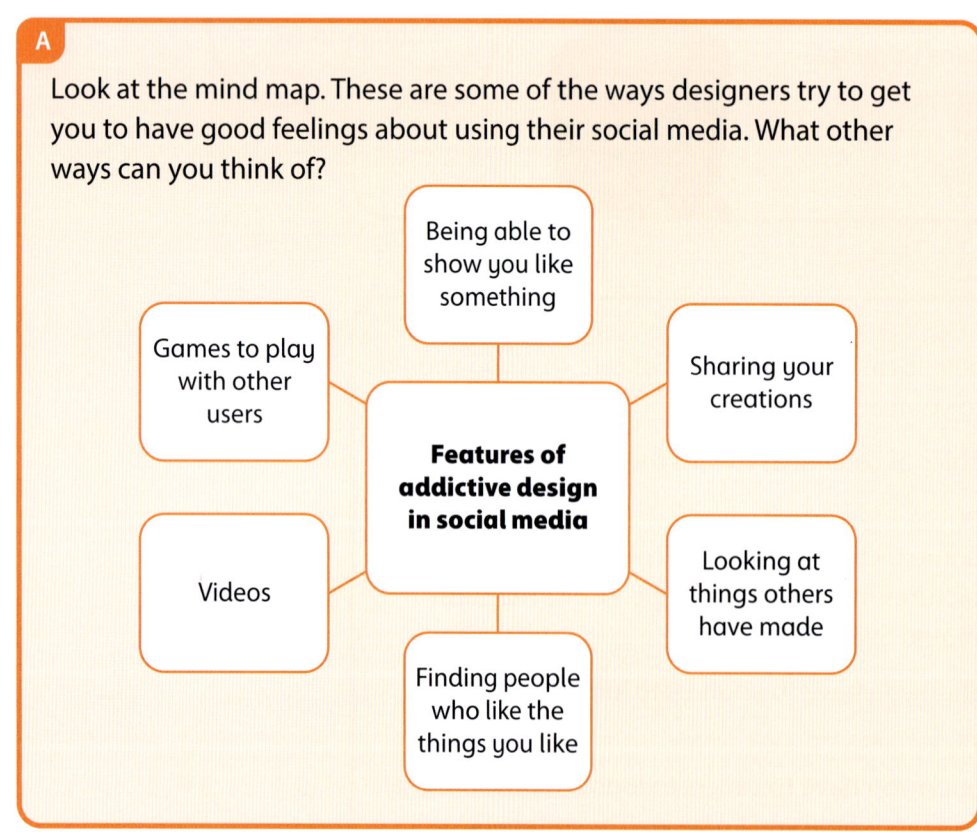

A

Look at the mind map. These are some of the ways designers try to get you to have good feelings about using their social media. What other ways can you think of?

Features of addictive design in social media
- Being able to show you like something
- Games to play with other users
- Sharing your creations
- Videos
- Looking at things others have made
- Finding people who like the things you like

Design tools

Designers use lots of different features to make social media addictive.

Some apps make it easy for you to use filters to make simple photos look amazing very quickly.

Some apps use push notifications to tell you that something new has happened in the app. Seeing the notification might make you want to visit the app.

Some apps use loading screens and adverts to make you wait for new content. They might even reward you in some way for waiting. Most apps will not reward you every time you use the app. They will reward you to keep you interested.

B

Am I addicted to social media?

If you use social media, make a list of all of the addictive design features you have used over the past week. Which features do you like best? Which are you not interested in? Which are annoying?

Find a healthy balance

There are lots of ways to recognize that you need to take a break from using social media.

▶ You might get a sore head and neck.
▶ You might start to feel grumpy, moody or sad.
▶ You might find it hard to get to sleep.
▶ Your family might say you spend all your time online.
▶ You might get hungry or thirsty, and realize a lot of time has passed.

Your digital ethics of care mean you need to look after yourself. If you notice any of these signs, do something else for a while. Maybe you could plant something, take some exercise, do some craft, do a chore, talk with someone or play an instrument.

2.4 Healthy balance

Humane design

Some technology design companies try to help you to keep a healthy balance between your social media use and other activities. Making software that tries to make lives better for people is called **humane design**. Humane design works well when designers think about the meanings people get from using social media, rather than just the product they are buying. Some apps and software have both addictive and humane design features.

> **Key word**
>
> humane design

In humane design, the software should show that the designer:

- understands the real problems of everyday lives
- pays attention to the history, culture and environment of a place; the people using the software are more important than the software itself
- understands that people do not use social media alone; social media is used together with face-to-face conversations and people's complicated lives
- knows how to iterate (change) the design to make it better.

There are many examples of humane design. Humane design means being able to:

- turn off any notifications or reminders that come from the software, rather than from people
- make your screen change to black and white after a certain amount of time using social media, to give a signal that you should stop
- make your screen change from bright blue to orange as the evening approaches, to help your brain to settle down for rest
- put addictive design apps in a separate place on your device
- set your phone to silent when you sleep so it does not wake you up
- avoid difficult feelings like envy and promote positive feelings like self-respect.

C

Use the internet to find out the goals of humane design. Reflect on each thing you find out. Do you agree with the goal? Why, or why not?

1. Think of two design features that you would think of as humane design. For example, your phone might alert you if you have been using an app for too long.
2. Share your humane design features with your class. Make a class list of humane design features.
3. Which types of social media that you know about have humane design features?

Stretch zone

Get your brain into a new habit. Set one rule for yourself for a month to help you keep a healthy balance between your social media use and other activities. Write down your rule and how you think it will help you.

Test

1. Write two things that would help you notice if you are using too much social media.
2. Why is it important to keep a healthy balance between how much social media you use and other activities you do?
3. Write an example of a type of social media that uses addictive design. Write one addictive design feature it uses.
4. Draw a table like this:

Addictive design	Humane design

Put each of these design features into the correct column.
- Keeps track of how long you have been using social media.
- Makes it very difficult to leave the social media platform.
- Makes it possible to hide or remove your social media profile.
- Gives you rewards for spending more time or money using the social media platform.
- Automatically plays content such as videos.

2.5 You, money and the internet

You will learn:
- ▶ the risks of spending money online
- ▶ how to protect yourself against spending money in dangerous ways
- ▶ what to do if you need to report a website online.

Key word

self-regulation

Risks and opportunities

Everything you do on the internet offers risks and opportunities. To use the internet safely, you need to understand and manage the risks, and make the most of the opportunities.

A

1. Open the Web Risks worksheet for this lesson. Look at the list of activities. Put them in order from most to least risky. There are no right and wrong answers. Discuss your views with others in your class.

2. Now look at the graph on the worksheet. The *y*-axis represents how bad the harm is that you could experience if something goes wrong. The *x*-axis represents how likely it is that something could go wrong.

3. Choose four of the activities and put them on the graph. For example:

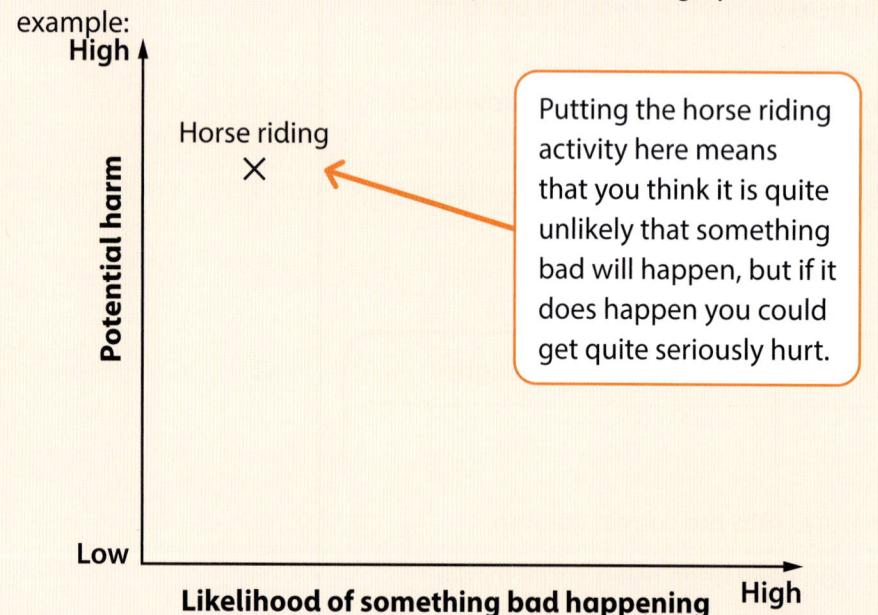

[Graph: *y*-axis labelled "Potential harm" from Low to High, *x*-axis labelled "Likelihood of something bad happening" from Low to High. "Horse riding" marked with an X in the upper-left area.]

> Putting the horse riding activity here means that you think it is quite unlikely that something bad will happen, but if it does happen you could get quite seriously hurt.

Using social media and being online has lots of risks. You can use a risk graph to help you work out whether something is too risky for you. Being able to stop when you might be doing something risky is called **self-regulation**.

Think maths

A risk graph is a type of graph called a scatter plot. Find out more about this type of graph and the use of *x*- and *y*-coordinates.

60   9:2.5 Web Risks: Digital Activity File

Spend money online

You already know that you can use the internet to buy and sell things. You know how to do this safely, and to keep information about your money and yourself as safe as possible, for example, by using strong passwords and trustworthy websites.

Some computer games give you the option to spend real money.

Amaya is playing a puzzle game on her phone. Her friend Nora has reached the level above Amaya. Amaya wants to play at the same level as Nora. Amaya needs 100 stars to reach the next level.

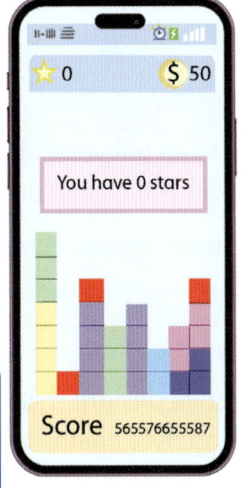

Stop, think

Remind yourself of how to make a strong password. Use numbers and symbols as well as letters. Do not use words, dates or names that could be easy to guess.

Amaya has 50 'coins' in the game. This is not real money.

In this game, you can either earn stars by playing, or you can 'buy' extra stars using virtual 'coins'. 1 star costs 1 'coin'. Amaya needs 100 stars to reach the same level as Nora. She decides to use her debit card to make an in-game purchase for 50 'coins'. She will then have 100 'coins', which she can use to buy 100 stars, allowing her to progress to the next level immediately.

Amaya has saved her debit card details in the app. She will now be able to buy extra points with a single click whenever she wants. She risks spending much more money than she can afford without realizing it.

You can often spend real money to buy virtual tokens/credits to spend in a game. Sometimes it can be difficult to separate real money from 'virtual' coins (credits) in a game, as you can see in the example above. When you are enjoying a game, it can be very easy to forget that you are spending real money whenever you buy something from the shop in a game. Remember that spending low amounts lots of times can add up to a lot of money.

61

2.5 You, money and the internet

B

1. There are lots of ways you can help yourself to make sure you do not spend money online without realizing. For each of the ways below, write an example of how you could do this in your everyday online life.

   Avoidance: When you do not play games too much, you are not so tempted to spend money.

   Making the reward unimportant: When you focus on a reward, it becomes difficult to self-regulate.

   Distract: Do something else.

   Self-directed speech: If you tell yourself 'I have to wait until this evening or tomorrow', you will be less impulsive.

2. Share your ideas with others in your class.

Addiction online

In 2.4, you learned about addictive design. This is when software is designed to make you want to use it over and over again.

Some researchers think that people are more or less likely to be addicted to something because of the way their bodies react. This is called the biological approach to addiction.

Other researchers think that people are more or less likely to be addicted to something because of the way they think. This is called the cognitive approach.

Other researchers think that people are more or less likely to be addicted to something because of patterns in the way they behave and the things they use. This is called the behavioural approach.

Whichever approach you think is right, we all have a choice in how we behave online.

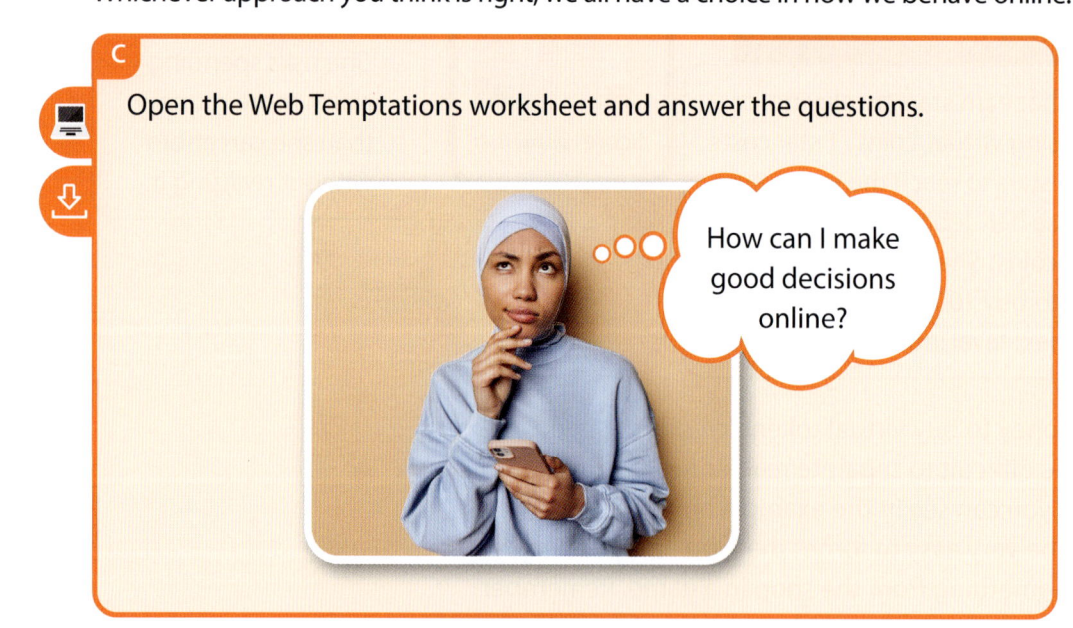

C

Open the Web Temptations worksheet and answer the questions.

How can I make good decisions online?

9:2.6 Web Temptations: Digital Activity File

Report dangerous sites and content

You already know that it is important to talk with a trusted adult if you come across something online that disturbs or upsets you.

Sometimes a website is so addictive that it leads to someone behaving in a dangerous way that could harm them or other people. Sometimes you might not feel able to talk to anyone. In this case, you can report the website that is concerning you to an organization that is trained to work out whether the website is dangerous. You can report websites via most search engines. The Internet Watch Foundation https://www.iwf.org.uk/ specialize in websites that involve child abuse of any sort, including financial abuse.

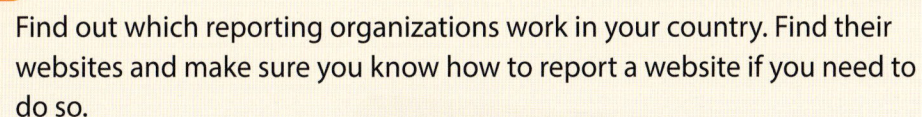

D

Find out which reporting organizations work in your country. Find their websites and make sure you know how to report a website if you need to do so.

Stretch zone

'Skins' are decorations, outfits or accessories that you use in digital games. In some games, skins can be bought, traded and sold for real money. Zara wants to make and sell skins in the game she plays. She cannot know if the money she gets from selling skins is legal or illegal.

Answer the questions on Zara's situation in the Web Temptations worksheet.

✓ Test

1. What are two risks of spending money online?
2. Name one organization you can report a website to in your country.
3. What are the four ways you can stop yourself being tempted to spend money online?
4. Draw a risk graph. Write one activity in the graph where something bad is very likely to happen, but the potential harm is low.

2.6 Extended reality in daily life

You will learn:
- what the metaverse is
- about different social aspects of using XR in daily life.

What is the metaverse?

The word **metaverse** was originally made up by a science fiction author named Neal Stephenson in 1992 in his book *Snow Crash*. In the book, people interact with virtual environments to learn, socialize and be entertained. They use headsets, phones and other technologies to go into these environments and interact with other people from anywhere in the world.

'Meta' is the Greek word meaning 'beyond', and 'verse' means 'reality'. So 'metaverse' means 'beyond reality', or more precisely, beyond *physical* reality.

Some people think that the metaverse is the next version of the internet.

Right now, the metaverse is mainly made up of immersive technologies such as **AR (augmented reality)**, **MR (mixed reality)** and **VR (virtual reality)**. Together, we call this **XR (extended reality)** and sometimes it is called computer-mediated reality.

Key words

AR (augmented reality)

metaverse

MR (mixed reality)

VR (virtual reality)

XR (extended reality)

Spiral back

You learned about XR in 1.6.

A

Open the XR in Daily Life worksheet for this lesson. Use the internet to help you complete the worksheet with more information about each aspect of XR.

When should XR be used?

A researcher called Jeremy Bailenson made up an acronym, DICE, to remember good reasons for using XR in daily life.

Dangerous: If it would be too dangerous to do or practise the activity in real life, learn how to do it in XR first. For example, you could learn to deep sea dive in VR before braving the ocean.

Impossible: If it is impossible to do something, it might be possible to experience it a little in XR. For example, you could visit another planet, go inside a human body or visit an ancient site that is now a ruin.

Counterproductive: You can use XR to work out the consequences of actions that are dangerous or prohibited in real life. For example, you could learn about air pollution by creating a very polluted atmosphere and seeing what happens to the environment.

Expensive: If you could not afford to do an activity in the real world, you could perhaps try it in XR. For example, you could visit a distant city.

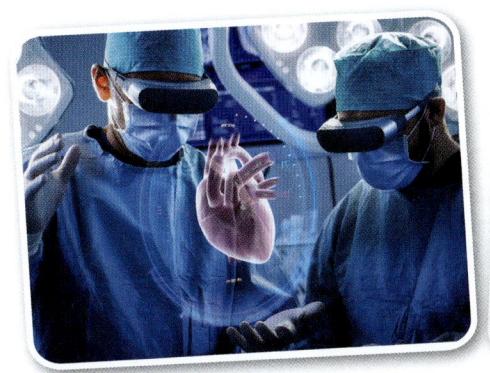

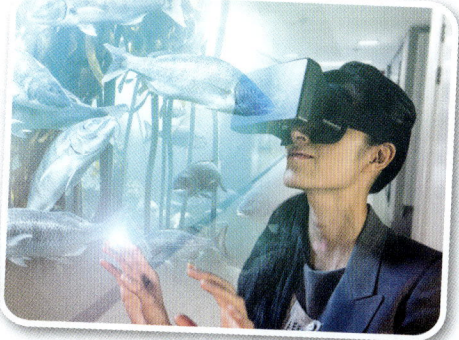

When should XR *not* be used?

There are no laws making sure that metaverse design is humane. The metaverse has just as many risks as any other type of technology.

Over-stimulation: XR experiences give users a lot of stimulation to senses including sight, sound and smell. We do not yet know exactly what this means for people who struggle with lots of stimulation, and what it means for how people learn, grow and sleep.

Feelings: Some people feel like they will be physically sick when they use VR headsets. Some people find that being in the metaverse makes them feel very emotional.

9:2.6 XR in Daily Life: Digital Activity File

2.6 Extended reality in daily life

Accessibility: Many people with physical and other forms of disability cannot use the hardware needed for XR. There are currently very few VR apps that are accessible to people who have a limited range of movement. For example, bed-bound patients cannot use VR apps where the virtual horizon cannot be adjusted.

Privacy: Some companies making XR technologies gather a lot of data about users, including about emotions and movements. It is difficult to manage data in the virtual world, and even more difficult to make companies stop using that data in problematic ways.

Safety: Because you can still interact with other people in the metaverse, you are still at risk of people behaving badly towards you. This includes cyberbullying, abuse, or being tricked in some way.

Affordability: Both the hardware and software for XR are still extremely expensive. This means not everyone can afford to use it.

Key words

cryptocurrency

non-fungible token (NFT)

B

Should school take place in the metaverse?

Some people think that when the technology has developed, students could attend school entirely in XR. Other people think this would be a bad idea. Current guidance from health experts and the makers of VR headsets is for children to not use them before the age of twelve.

What do you think? Write a report about the potential advantages and disadvantages of attending school in XR.

Money in XR

Just like other aspects of human life, XR has led to people developing new forms of money. These are not very stable – this means that you cannot be sure whether this type of money will still be around next year or in the next ten years, or whether digital 'coins' you own now will be worth the same amount tomorrow as it is worth today. This is a risk.

Cryptocurrencies are digital money. They are not coins or notes you can hold in your hand. Cryptocurrency is not well-regulated – this means that governments or banks do not control how this money is used. When you use cryptocurrency, the movement of money is secure and anonymous.

Non-fungible tokens (NFTs) are digital items that are unique. They are an exclusive digital collectible with a special code that shows it is the only authentic copy. They are bought and sold using cryptocurrency.

> **C**
>
> Use the risk graph from 2.5 to work out what some problems and opportunities of using cryptocurrencies and NFTs might be.

Stretch zone

You now know that XR offers lots of risks and opportunities. Have a polite debate in a group on one of the following topics:

- ▶ Does crime committed in XR count as real crime? For example, if someone punches someone else in the virtual world, does it count as a real punch?
- ▶ Because XR is expensive, lots of people cannot afford to use it in their daily lives. Is this creating serious divisions in society? If so, what are the consequences of those divisions likely to be?
- ▶ What can be done to make XR a place where humane design is strong? Who needs to do that work?

✓ Test

1. Write one paragraph about what the metaverse is.
2. Explain the difference between AR, MR and VR.
3. Write four ways in which XR could be used for good purposes.
4. Write four problems with XR.

2 What have you learned?

Review test

1. Why is it important to care for yourself and others online?

2. Why would someone set up a fake social media account?

3. Write about the difference between addictive and humane design. Give at least **two** examples of each type of design in your writing.

4. Elena has joined a new social media site. She notices that her brother is also using the site. Elena sees that her brother has posted some hateful messages to other people about what they look like. What do you think Elena should do? Explain your thinking.

5. Write about the ways you can stop yourself from spending money online in a problematic way.

6. Write an explanation of what the metaverse is. Explain the difference between AR, VR and MR.

Review activity

1. Make a poster or video that explains the three main ideas of digital ethics of care.

2. Include one example of social media in your poster or video. Explain how each of the three ideas of digital ethics of care applies to your example of social media.

3. Include examples of obligations to yourself and to others in how you behave, what you do and say, and how you interact with others online.

Self-evaluation

How did you do?	What is your level?	What your level means
• I answered test questions 1 and 2. • I explained the three main ideas in digital ethics of care.	Developing	You have learned something new in this unit.
• I answered test questions 1 to 4. • I applied my understanding of digital ethics of care to social media.	Secure	You have reached the expected standard in this unit.
• I answered all the test questions. • I described my obligations in online interactions.	Extending	You are an expert.

What next? To improve your level you can go back and repeat some of this unit.

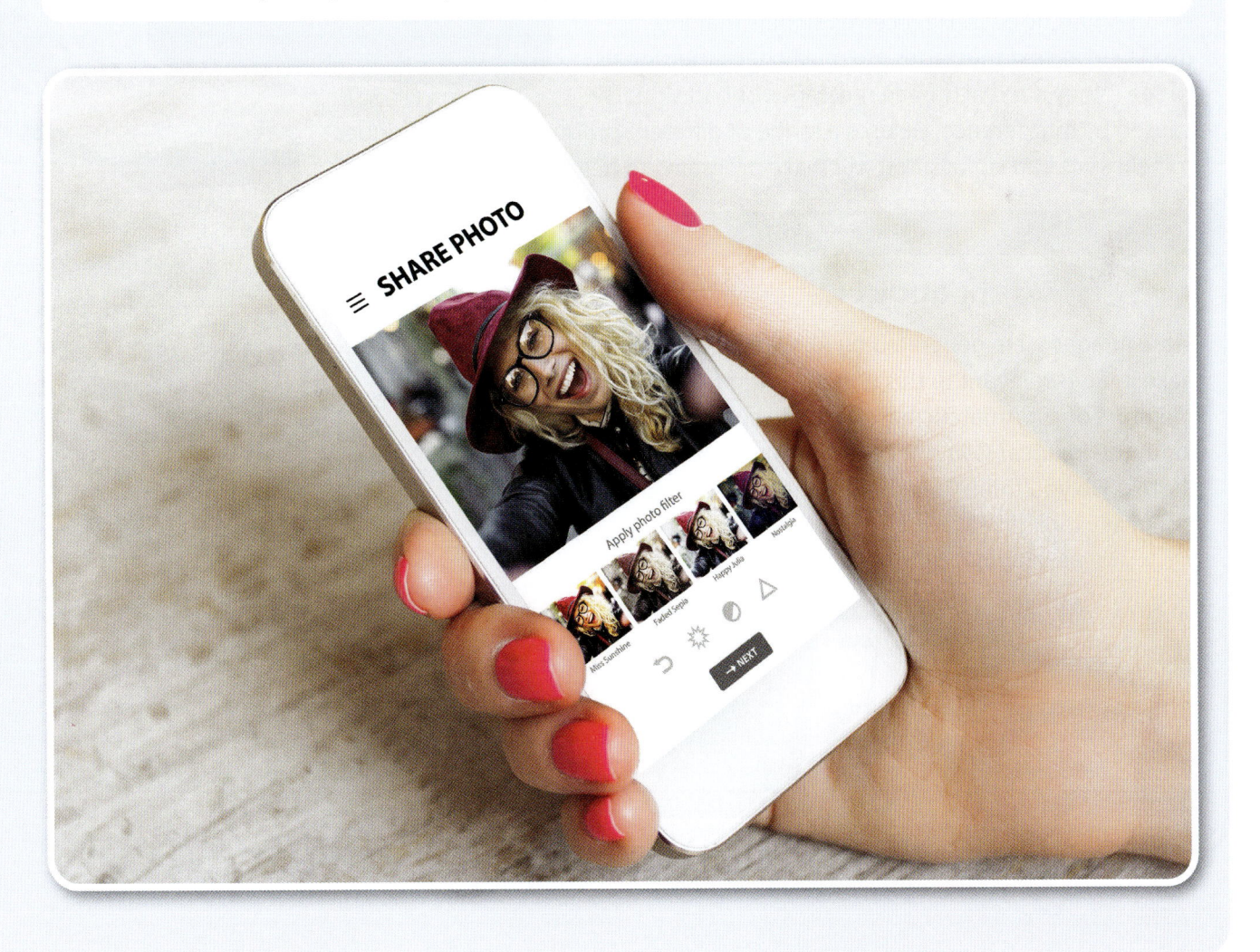

3 Computational thinking: Artificial intelligence

You will learn:

▶ the meaning of artificial intelligence (AI) and natural language processing (NLP)

▶ how AI and NLP are used in real life.

In this unit, you will learn about artificial intelligence (AI). You will explore some programming methods used to develop artificial intelligence. You will learn the advantages and disadvantages of different AI techniques.

This unit uses a case study. Taz is a radio operator on an Antarctic base. He receives signals that are displayed as text messages. He must check the signals to see if they are real human messages or bad signals caused by interference. He uses a range of different programming techniques to help spot bad signals. You will make programs to help with this task.

Talk about ...

These images were generated by AI. We asked it to make images relevant to this unit, showing radio operators on an Antarctic base. How do you feel about the images? Could they be mistaken for photos? Do you think they show what an Antarctic base really looks like?

Learning outcomes: Describe the uses of machine learning in AI; Explain the meaning and use of natural language processing (NLP) in AI

? Can a computer think like a person?

At this time, no computer has the ability to think like a person. Even AI can only currently do a limited range of things, for example, generate new content based on human-created material.

AI (artificial intelligence)
heuristics
large language model (LLM)
machine learning
natural language processing (NLP)
reinforcement

Activity

AI can make and recognize images. In this activity, you will see how an image can be made with feedback from an observer. This is called reinforcement learning.

Here is a grid shape. The rows and columns are numbered.

Set up: Make two copies:

- a small copy on an ordinary-sized piece of paper
- a much larger copy on a poster-sized sheet.

Rules: One student is the designer. They create an image by shading some of the cells on the small sheet. They keep the image secret.

1. Pin the large grid up where everyone can see it. Students pick cells at 'random'. Students can either point to a cell on the big sheet or call out its position ('row 3 column 7').

2. The designer says if the chosen cell is part of the design or not. If it is, colour in that cell in the big grid. Gradually, the image will appear. As more of the image appears it will be easier to guess the right cells.

3. See how quickly you can recognize or complete the design.

3.1 Make decisions

You will learn:
▶ how decisions can be made without the use of AI
▶ how AI may be used to help with decisions.

Case study

Antarctica is a large continent at the far south of the globe. It is very cold. The scientists who live there receive messages by radio. In this unit, you will write programs to process the signals received at an Antarctic base. The signals are text strings. This is a simplified version of a real-life task.

Taz is a radio operator. He must check each signal. He must only pass on good signals. He must delete bad signals. You will write a program to help Taz.

Spiral back

In Book 8, you made Python programs to work with lists. In this lesson, you will traverse a list and append items to a list.

Good and bad signals

The base receives good signals such as this one:

```
"Weather warning: there is a storm approaching"
```

It also receives bad signals such as this one:

```
"asjdha## djhaidj# ddjiadj#",
```

Taz has to pass on the good signals to the people who work on the base. He has to block the bad signals, or ask for the signal to be sent again.

A

1. Open the program for this lesson. It includes a list of example signals. The program traverses the list of signals one by one.

```
for i in range (len(signals)):
    item = signals[i]
    print(item)
```

Remember that traversing a list means visiting the items in a list one by one. In this example, the counter loop counts through the list of signals. Each item is printed out.

```
.
Weather warning: there is a storm approaching
~
Helicopter arriving McMurdo station 10:00 Tuesday
**
First aid kit needed at far camp
*&_)*&^%^&*%^$~@:~
Food delivery drop will be delayed by 48 hours
Repairs needed at the observation platform
Urgent - update all anti-virus systems
Please re-send meteorological data
234724u2u23u888
..asjdha## djhaidj# ddjiadj#
Medical officer requested at main base
%
43umcu3rg0ucthgm@:;<
Penguin migration has begun 2 weeks early
Solar flare may affect radio communication
-
```

2. Run the program and make sure it works. Look through the list of signals. Can you tell which are the good signals?

A list of good signals

Taz decides to amend the program so he can check each signal one by one. First, he makes an empty list to store the good signals. This command goes at the start of the main program.

```
good_signals = []
```

Identify the good signals

Taz makes an input command. This command goes inside the loop. The prompt asks Taz if the current item is a good signal. His answer is stored as a variable called 'good'.

```
good = input("Is this a good signal? (Y/N) ")
```

If the answer is 'Y', then the item is appended to the list of good signals. Remember that 'append' means 'add to the end'.

```
if good == "Y":
    good_signals.append(item)
```

Print the good signals

Taz adds a final command at the end of the program to print out the list of good signals. This command belongs after the loop, not inside the loop.

```
print(good_signals)
```

9:3.1 Show Signals Program: Digital Activity File

3.1 Make decisions

B

1. Extend the program. Add commands that allow Taz to check each signal one by one and add them to a list of good signals.
2. Run the program, and complete the task. Identify all the good signals.

```
good_signals = []

for i in range (len(signals)):
    item = signals[i]
    print(item)
    good = input("is this a good signal? (Y/N) ")
    if good == "Y":
        good_signals.append(item)

print(good_signals)
```

Key words

AI (artificial intelligence)

expert system

Problems that are hard for computers

In real life, a radio operator receives a lot of signals. There could be hundreds per hour. Checking them is a lot of work for Taz. Could a computer help to do this work?

Computers can help with many tasks. They can follow clear logical and mathematical instructions. They can do calculations and comparisons very quickly and accurately.

But computers are not so good at other tasks. Checking messages in human language is an example of a problem that is hard for a computer to do. That is because this problem does not have clear steps to a solution. The messages are varied and unpredictable.

Artificial intelligence

AI or **artificial intelligence** means computers that can solve difficult problems using judgement. This includes tasks such as:

- recognizing faces
- diagnosing illness
- driving cars
- speaking in a realistic way
- solving complex problems.

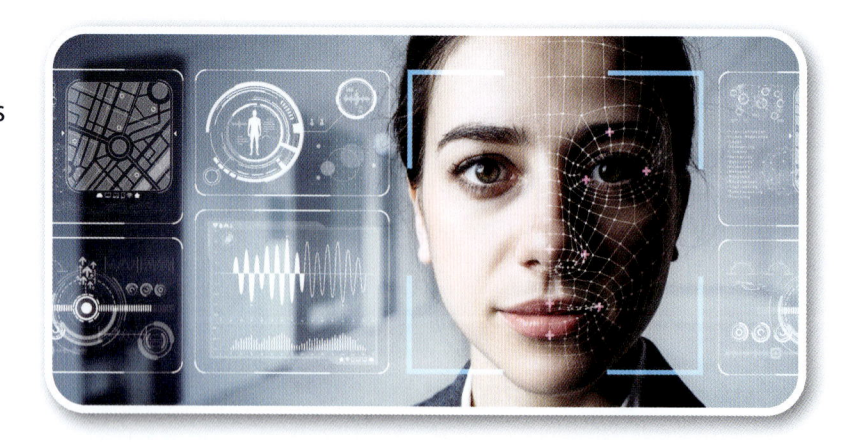

In this unit, you will learn about some of the methods used to make computers solve more problems and work in more intelligent ways.

C

1. What are the advantages of using AI for tasks such as those listed? Work with a partner and note any you can think of.

2. Now repeat the task, thinking of any disadvantages or risks when AI is used for tasks like these.

Methods

An **expert system** is a form of AI. You learned about the use of expert systems in Book 7. This unit will introduce some new AI methods:

- heuristics
- machine learning
- natural language processing (NLP).

You will not create real examples of AI. But you will learn about some of the ideas that are used in AI. If you want to find out even more, work hard at computer science and maths, and you could be involved in developing the next generation of AI.

D

Write an email from Taz to the commander of the Antarctic base. The email should explain what AI means and how Taz could use it to help with his work. What are the advantages for Taz and for the people who work on the base?

Stretch zone

Create a second list called `bad_signals`. Add extra lines of code to the program so that every bad signal is copied to this list.

Print out both lists. Add messages to explain which list is which.

Test

1. What does 'AI' stand for?
2. Give one example of how AI might be used in everyday life.
3. In the example in this lesson, the human user made a decision that would be hard for a computer to make. What was the decision?
4. What might happen as a result of the decision made by the human?

3.2 Heuristics

You will learn:
- what 'heuristics' are
- how heuristics can be used in programming.

Key word

heuristic

Heuristics

Some problems are difficult to solve. Getting them right takes a lot of steps and a long time. Programmers may use **heuristics** to speed up problem solving. A heuristic is a rule that helps you to make a decision. It is like a guess, or a rough estimate. But it is a guess based on experience and rational thinking. Heuristics are not always completely accurate. But they provide a useful way to simplify difficult problems.

Here are some examples of heuristics we might use in everyday life.

- If you see or smell smoke, there may be a fire.
- Food that is not a normal colour may be bad to eat.
- A broken ladder might not be safe to use.

These rules help us to make sensible decisions and stay safe. They are not always accurate, but they are helpful. We use heuristics to make good decisions if we do not have full information.

A

Open the program you made last lesson. Check the list of good signals. What is the shortest length of a good signal? What is the shortest length of a bad signal?

Case study

Some of the bad signals are just one or two random characters. None of the good signals are this short. Taz decides to use this fact to help pick out the good signals.

Here is the heuristic Taz chose:

```
good signals have more than three characters
```

This heuristic is not perfect. It will not remove all bad signals. But it will simplify the task. It will remove some of the bad signals. Taz will not need to check so many signals.

This heuristic will definitely save me some time. — Taz

9:3.2 Check Signals Program: Digital Activity File

B

If you are a confident programmer, try to change the program by working independently. Use the heuristic that Taz chose. Make and print a list of signals with more than three characters. If you need support, look at the next section.

Repurpose a program

Taz alters the program to use the heuristic. He carries out these steps.

- Delete the code that prints the signal.
- Delete the input command that asks for his decision.
- Add a command to check if the signal is more than three characters long.

Delete commands

The old program has these commands. They are inside the loop.

```
print(item)
good = input("Is this a good signal? (Y/N) ")
```

The commands are:

- print the item
- ask Taz for a Y/N answer.

Taz does not need these commands in the heuristic program. The computer will make its own decision.

New commands

The 'if' statement in the old program looks like this:

```
if good == "Y":
    good_signals.append(item)
```

The command checks if Taz has input the answer 'Y'. The new program will not use this test. Instead, the program will check if the string is longer than three characters.

```
if len(item) > 3:
    good_signals.append(item)
```

C

Change your program to use the heuristic. Run the program to make sure it works.

Here is the completed program.

```
good_signals = []
for i in range (len(signals)):
    item = signals[i]
    if len(item) > 3:
        good_signals.append(item)
print(good_signals)
```

77

Evaluate the heuristic

The heuristic has made a list of good signals. It has run quickly, and without any input from the user. This program could check hundreds of signals in the time that Taz would take to check one or two.

Here is the output of the heuristic program.

> **D**
>
> Look at the new list of good signals. Has the heuristic worked?
>
> ▶ Many of the bad signals have been removed from the list.
>
> ▶ All the good signals are still in the list.
>
> ```
> ['Weather warning: there is a storm approaching',
> 'Helicopter arriving McMurdo station 10:00 Tuesday
> ', 'First aid kit needed at far camp', '*&_)*&^%^&
> *%^$~@:~', 'Food delivery drop will be delayed by
> 48 hours', 'Repairs needed at the observation plat
> form', 'Urgent - update all anti-virus systems', '
> Please re-send meteorological data', '234724u2u23u
> 888', '..asjdha## djhaidj# ddjiadj#', 'Medical off
> icer requested at main base', '43umcu3rg0ucthgm@:;
> <', 'Penguin migration has begun 2 weeks early', '
> Solar flare may affect radio communication']
> ```
>
> The heuristic has helped a lot. But it missed some bad signals.
>
> The heuristic has not completely solved the problem. This is a common feature of heuristics. Heuristic results are not always perfect.

Real-life uses of heuristics

Virus-checking software uses heuristics. Computer viruses have common features. Programmers can catch viruses by checking for these common features.

Heuristics and AI

One aim of AI is to make computers that can solve human-type problems. This often requires complex decision-making. Making accurate decisions can be difficult.

Heuristics offer a short cut to simplify a difficult decision. Humans use heuristics in real life. By putting heuristics into programs, we can help computers to make human-like decisions.

Your work in this lesson is a very simple example.

Summary

Using heuristics in a program has some advantages.

▶ A heuristic can solve a problem quite quickly.

▶ A heuristic can mean less work for the user.

▶ A heuristic gives a 'good enough' result.

Using heuristics has some limitations.

▶ The heuristic is not always accurate. It might produce some incorrect results.
▶ The heuristic may provide a solution, but it might not be the best solution.

Usually, we combine heuristics with other methods of problem solving.

> **E**
>
> Create a poster setting out what you know about heuristics in a lively format. Your poster should say what a heuristic is, and the advantages and limitations of heuristics.

Stop, think

Online health advice apps use heuristics to give you health advice based on what information you give. The advice could be wrong. Always go to a human doctor if you are worried about your symptoms.

Stretch zone

Taz notices that good signals are always made of words with spaces in between. He makes a second heuristic:

```
if a signal has no spaces in it then it is a
bad signal
```

Add this heuristic to the program. For example, add a nested `if` statement inside the `for` loop. Has this heuristic improved the accuracy of your program?

Digital citizen

Some people think that computers are always right. But computer systems often use heuristics and other short-cut methods. Heuristics are estimates. Remember that information and advice from a computer is only as good as the program that controls it.

✓ Test

1. What is a heuristic?
2. State one advantage to Taz of using a heuristic to spot bad signals instead of checking them himself.
3. State one possible disadvantage of using a heuristic.
4. Taz spotted that some bad signals contain the symbol #. Write code to:
   - traverse the signals list
   - identify signals that contain #
   - copy these signals to a list called bad_signals.

3.3 Machine learning

You will learn:
- what machine learning is
- how machine learning is used in AI.

Key words
cluster
deep learning
machine learning
reinforcement learning
supervised training
training
unsupervised training

Case study

Taz works with many scientists at the Antarctic base. A scientist called Sara tells Taz about **machine learning**.

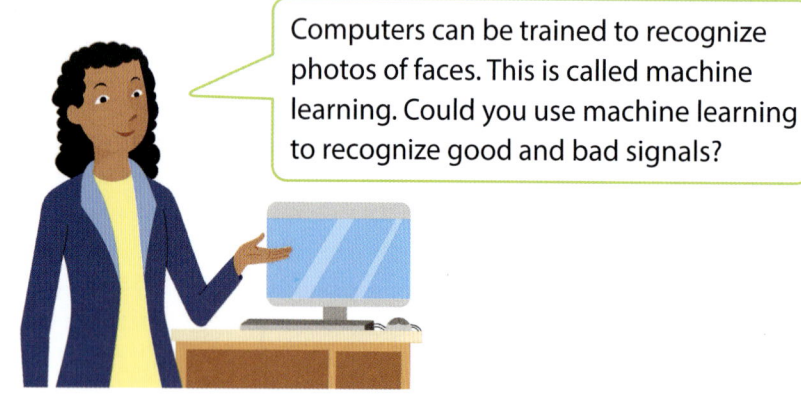

> Computers can be trained to recognize photos of faces. This is called machine learning. Could you use machine learning to recognize good and bad signals?

In this lesson, you will find out if machine learning methods could be used to help Taz.

What is machine learning?

You have learned how to make programs by writing algorithms. An algorithm sets out the steps to solve the problem. You turn the algorithm into a program. The computer carries out the commands in the program.

Machine learning works differently. You do not make an algorithm. The computer learns how to solve a problem for itself. This is called **training** the computer.

There are several types of training. For example:

- **supervised training**
- **unsupervised training**
- **reinforcement learning**
- **deep learning**.

Train the computer

Machine learning is used to train computers to recognize objects, such as faces in images.

The computer can recognize where people appear in an image.

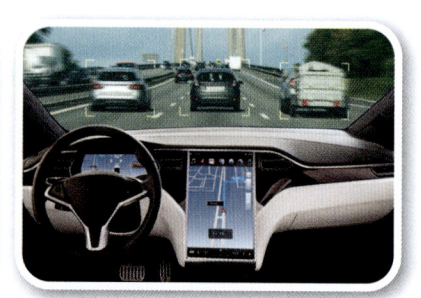

A self-driving car uses AI to work out where the road, other cars and other obstacles are.

Supervised training

In supervised training, the computer is given a lot of data that has already been organized and labelled. For example, the computer might be given millions of images that have been labelled to say if they show faces or not. The computer will learn to tell the difference between images that contain faces and other images.

Unsupervised training

In unsupervised training, the computer is given a lot of data. It is not sorted or organized. The computer has to find the patterns for itself.

For example, the computer might be given millions of images of many types. The computer will put the pictures into groups that are similar. One of those groups will be pictures of faces.

Groups are called **clusters**. All the images in a cluster will have a lot in common.

This means the computer can use data that has not been labelled. There is lots of this type of data on the internet. It is easy to find billions of images.

Digital citizen

Websites that allow you to upload content might use that content for training AI. Not everybody wants their writing, pictures and videos to be used in this way. Many websites have a setting that allows you to opt out.

Reinforcement learning

In reinforcement learning, the computer starts by producing random or undirected outputs. Reinforcement is feedback that tells the computer if the output is good or not, a bit like when your schoolwork is marked by a teacher. Gradually, the computer learns to produce output that is closer to the right result.

For example, a computer generated random patterns of light and dark squares on a grid. A human user told the computer which one looked more like a face. Gradually, by getting lots of feedback, the computer learned to make patterns that looked a lot like a face, like the second pattern below.

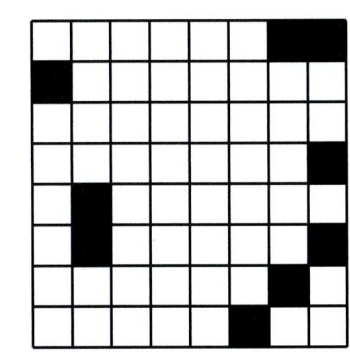

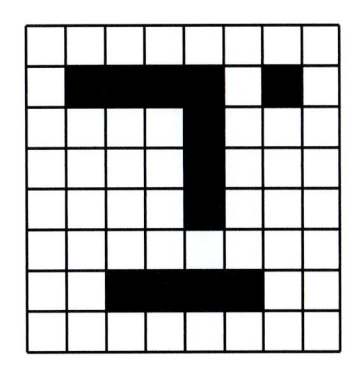

Deep learning

Deep learning combines all the other methods into a highly complex learning process. Deep learning typically uses an advanced type of computer structure called a neural network.

Deep learning can produce very powerful results. Computers can make images that look exactly like photos of real people and meet other image requests.

Key words
AI hallucinations
bias
prejudice

Real-life uses

You have seen how machine learning is used to recognize faces and make images of faces. It can be useful for other purposes, for example:

- diagnosing illnesses
- weather forecasting
- understanding speech
- spotting computer viruses.

By looking at lots of real-life examples, the computer can learn to make predictions. A weather computer could recognize the early signs of a hurricane, so people have time to take shelter.

Summary

Machine learning has big advantages:

- We do not need to tell the computer how to solve the problem.
- We give the computer a goal and it will work out its own solution.

But machine learning has limitations:

- The computer needs a lot of data.
- The data must be diverse and varied.
- Machine learning can go wrong.

For example, a scientist wanted to train a computer to recognize images of bacteria. He showed the computer lots of examples. But all the pictures of bacteria were taken on a black background. The computer learned to recognize the colour black. That was not what the scientist wanted.

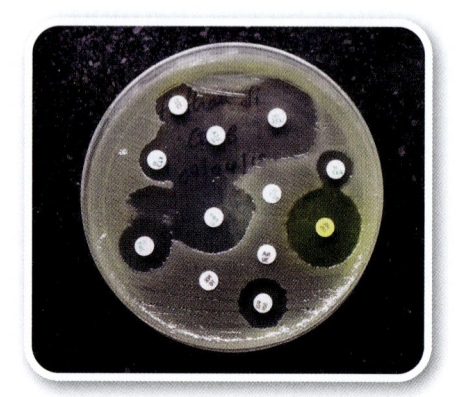

1   Read the descriptions of different types of machine learning.

> The computer is given data that has not been labelled or sorted. The computer finds clusters or groups in the data by looking for similarities. It learns how to sort the data into clusters.

> The computer generates random or undirected output. Feedback tells the computer if it has produced the right output. It learns how to produce the right output.

This method requires a complex type of computer system called a neural network. It combines the other methods to produce the most powerful type of machine learning.

The computer is given lots of data. The data is labelled and classified. The data is already organized into groups. The computer learns what the members of each group have in common.

2   Match each description to one of these terms:
- supervised training
- unsupervised training
- reinforcement learning
- deep learning.

Stretch zone

Write a brief description of how each type of learning might be used to teach the computer to recognize good and bad signals. The first one is done for you.

▶ Supervised training: The computer is given lots of example signals. The example signals have been labelled as good or bad signals. The computer learns what the different types of signal have in common.

▶ Unsupervised training:

▶ Reinforcement learning:

Digital citizen

Prejudice (**bias**) in training data can lead to mistakes in the AI trained on that data. Mistakes made by AI are called **AI hallucinations**. For example, an AI program trained to recognize pictures of doctors might be shown images of doctors of European heritage. The AI would not learn to recognize doctors from other ethnic groups. But of course, in real life there are doctors from all ethnic groups.

Test

1   What does 'machine learning' mean?
2   State one advantage to Taz of using machine learning to spot bad signals.
3   In both supervised and unsupervised training, the computer gets lots of data. What is the difference between the two?
4   What type of computer system is needed for deep learning?

3.4 Train the computer

You will learn:
▶ to recognize some features of reinforcement learning.

This lesson uses programming commands that you have used before. It will test your understanding of programming. It will also demonstrate some features of machine learning in a simplified way.

Supervised training 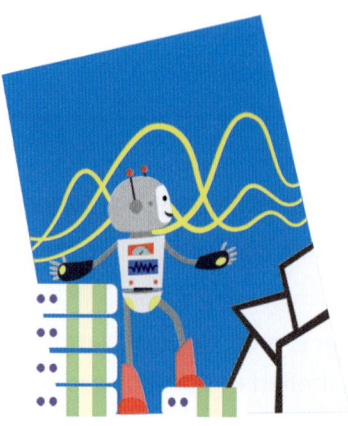 | Unsupervised training 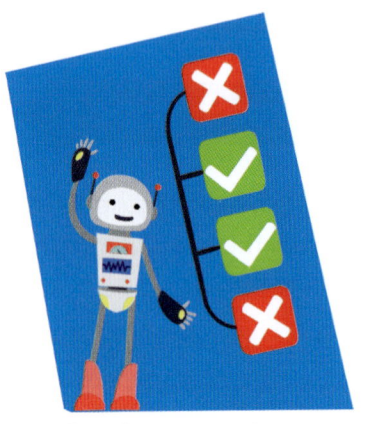 | Reinforcement learning

Feedback

Remember the features of reinforcement learning:

▶ The computer makes random or undirected output.

▶ Feedback tells the computer if the results are good.

▶ The process is repeated many times until the computer reliably reaches the goal every time.

Feedback is input from the user. The feedback tells the computer whether the result is correct or not. The computer uses the feedback to learn.

🌐 Digital citizen

Generative AI can be trained using feedback from humans. It will favour answers that get positive feedback. If the feedback is wrong, then the AI will learn to give responses that are wrong. For example, a medical AI got feedback from users who thought antibiotics can cure a cold. Then the AI recommended antibiotics to a user with a cold. This advice is wrong – antibiotics cannot help fight a virus. Errors like this, whether in text, image or video, are examples of AI hallucinations.

Spiral back

In this lesson, you will use skills you learned in Books 7 and 8, including using the Python shell, using loops and making random numbers.

> **Case study**
>
> Taz has to check text strings to see if they are bad signals. Good signals are made of valid characters, such as letters of the alphabet and punctuation marks.
>
> Bad signals contain other random characters. For example:
>
> ```
> ʽHZɲÔ;>ℏɟ¿☐åØϒŋ、
> ```
>
> In this lesson, you will look at a simple example of 'training' the computer to recognize valid and invalid characters.

A simplified example

In this example, you will create a simple program showing how a human can 'teach' a computer. This task is not real machine learning, just a simplified exercise.

Your program will 'train' the computer to recognize valid text characters. The program will have these features:

- generate ten random characters
- identify if characters are valid
- make a list of all valid characters.

Make random numbers

To make a random number, you must 'import' a module called `random`. This will do all the work for you. The random module was created by Python programmers. They have made it freely available to anyone who wants to use it.

```
import random
```

You give this command once at the start of a program or work session.

The random module includes a command called `random.randint`. This will give you a random integer. For example, this command will make a random number between 1 and 999:

```
random.randint(1,999)
```

A

Work in the Python shell. Practise making random numbers from 0 to 999.

```
>import random
>random.randint(0,999)
860
>random.randint(0,999)
754
>random.randint(0,999)
142
>
```

3.4 Train the computer

Use Unicode to make a character

You will try out the commands to make a random character in the Python shell. Then you will make a computer program.

Unicode is a number code system. Every text character has a number code. Unicode includes thousands of different characters, including different alphabets and other symbols. You learned about Unicode in Book 8.

This Python function makes a Unicode character. It will make the character with code number 65. That is the letter 'A'.

```
chr(65)
```

You can put any number into the brackets. The computer will create the Unicode character that matches that number.

> **Key word**
>
> Unicode

B

Try out the chr() function in the Python shell. Use a range of different numbers.

```
>chr(62)
'>'
>chr(65)
'A'
>chr(199)
'Ç'
>chr(441)
'ƹ'
```

Make random characters

You have learned to make random numbers. And you have learned to make numbers into characters. You can combine these skills to make a program that creates ten random characters. Here is the program plan.

Repeat ten times:

▶   make a random number

▶   turn the number into a character

▶   print the character.

C

Combine the commands you have learned this lesson. Make a program that prints ten random characters.

```
import random

for i in range(10):
    number = random.randint(1,999)
    character = chr(number)
    print(character)
```

'Teach' the computer

Taz wants to use this program to create a list of valid text characters. He amends the program to add these features. Here is the program plan:

Create an empty list called `valid`.

Repeat ten times:

- ▶ print a random character
- ▶ ask the user if the character is valid (Y/N)
- ▶ if the answer is 'Y', append the character to the `valid` list.

At the end of the program, print out the list of valid characters.

D

Use your Python skills to create a program to match the program plan.

```python
import random

valid = []

for i in range(10):
    number = random.randint(1,999)
    character= chr(number)
    print(character)
    check = input("Is this a valid character (Y/N)? ")
    if check == "Y":
        valid.append(character)

print(valid)
```

Save for later?

To make this program more useful, Taz should save the list of valid characters to a text file, stored on the computer. Then he can use the list of valid characters in other programs, for example as part of a heuristic. Saving text in a file is a more advanced Python topic.

Stretch zone

Carry out your own investigation into Python commands that allow you to store data in a text file. Can you extend the program to store the list of valid characters?

✓ Test

1. Reinforcement learning uses feedback. What does 'feedback' mean?
2. Which line of the program gets feedback from the user? Write that line.
3. This program lets you check ten random characters. Explain how you would change it so you can check more characters.
4. How could a list of valid characters help Taz to identify good and bad signals?

3 Computational thinking: Artificial intelligence

3.5 Natural language

You will learn:
- what natural language processing (NLP) means.

Key word

natural language processing (NLP)

Case study

Taz sometimes has to leave the radio room to do other tasks. He is worried that he might miss an important message. So Taz has installed a voice recognition system. The computer monitors voice messages. It can recognize key words such as 'fire' or 'danger'. Then it sends an alarm call to bring Taz to the radio to deal with the emergency. This is an example of **natural language processing (NLP)**.

What is natural language processing?

The way a computer uses words is quite different from human language. Computers generally produce a limited range of text. The goal of NLP is to create a computer program that can use language in a more 'natural' way – like a person does.

- **NLP inputs:** The computer can understand the full range of human speech.
- **NLP outputs:** The computer can produce words as if a real person is talking or writing.

In this lesson, you will look at some of the challenges in writing a program that understands natural language input. In 3.6, you will learn about natural language output.

Understand natural language

One goal of NLP is to make a computer that recognizes all types of written or spoken words. That includes:

- Reading different sorts of handwriting. This is difficult because people write in very different styles. Some writing is very untidy.
- Understanding spoken words. This is difficult because people's voices differ a lot. Some speak less clearly than others.
- Understanding all the different ways of saying the same thing. For example, a computer must understand that 'Yeah', 'OK' and 'I agree' are different ways of saying 'Yes'.

Achieving these NLP goals requires a powerful computer and complex software.

A

Open the program for this lesson and run it. This program allows the user to call for the emergency helicopter.

```
location = input("enter your location: ")
answer = input("do you need the emergency helicopter? ")
if answer == "Y":
    print("helicopter sent to",location)
print("goodbye")
```

To call for the helicopter, the user has to type 'Yes'. If they type anything else, the helicopter will not come. That is not very useful, because in an emergency people might not be so careful with their typing.

B

1. At the top of the program, make a list of things people might type for 'Yes'. You can call it 'yeslist'.

   ```
   yeslist = ["Yes", "yes", "Y", "y", "OK", "agree"]
   ```

   If you can think of any other words that mean 'yes', perhaps in different languages, add them to the list.

2. The program has an 'if' structure. Change the 'if' structure so that it accepts any answer in 'yeslist'.

   ```
   if answer in yeslist:
       print("helicopter sent to", location)
   ```

3. Run the program now. Any of the answers in 'yeslist' will call the helicopter.

   ```
   yeslist = ["Yes", "yes", "Y", "y", "OK", "agree"]
   
   location = input("enter your location: ")
   answer = input("do you need the emergency helicopter? ")
   if answer in yeslist:
       print("helicopter sent to",location)
   print("goodbye")
   ```

C

Make a list of words that mean 'No' and call it 'nolist'.

▶ If the user gives an answer in 'nolist', output a message saying that no helicopter will be sent. Here is the code you will need.

```
if answer in nolist:
    print("no helicopter will be sent")
```

▶ A user could give an answer that includes a word that means 'yes' and also a word that means 'no'. Or they could give an answer that is not included in either list. A more complicated program would be needed to deal with this type of answer. These are typical problems when writing programs for natural language processing. If you have time, add extra code to your program to solve these problems.

9:3.5 Helicopter Call Program: Digital Activity File

3.5 Natural language

Machine learning and NLP

In your program, you made a list of all possible answers. This is a slow way of teaching the computer to recognize language. There are too many different styles of speech and writing. Instead of writing all the possible answers, programmers may use machine learning. That means the computer will process large amounts of data. The computer will review many examples of different voices and writing. The computer will learn to recognize a wide range of different words and phrases. Look back at 3.3 and 3.4 for more information about machine learning.

Real-life uses of NLP

In this program, the computer needed to understand a command or request from the user. Understanding written or spoken commands is a very common use of NLP. For example, you can buy voice recognition devices for the home. The device will perform tasks such as playing music or turning on the lights. It will understand the words you speak.

Key words

speech emotion recognition (SER)

Giving voice commands has many advantages. You can control the computer when your hands are not free to type. For example, if you are driving. It helps people who cannot write for any reason, for example, because of a visual impairment.

Another common use of NLP is translation from one language to another. The computer takes input in one language and produces output in another language. Many search engines offer a translation service.

D

Find an internet site that offers translation from one language to another. Enter a sample of text in a language that you know. Translate it to another language, then back into the language you know. Evaluate the result. Has the translation service done a good job?

Recognize emotions

As well as understanding commands, people sometimes want the computer to recognize emotions in speech. For example, a company might analyse social media messages to see if people like their product. Or an advice program might respond to happy or sad messages from the user with different types of advice. The name for this is **speech emotion recognition (SER)**.

E

Discuss with a partner what you think the advantages and disadvantages are for teaching AI systems SER.

Stretch zone

This program checks for happy words in a sentence.

```
happylist = ["good", "glad", "happy", "like", "pleased", "enjoy"]

happy = False
sentence = input("How do you feel today? ")

for word in happylist:
    if word in sentence:
        happy = True

if happy = True:
    print("I think you are happy today")
```

1. Make this program and try it out with some example sentences. Does it work well?
2. Extend the program by adding a 'sad list' to check if you are sad.

In real life, SER is much more complex than this.

Stop, think

Always think carefully about what information you are sharing with an AI app. Do you know if your information will be stored, and if it will stay secure or be sold to other companies?

✓ Test

1. Give an example of a computer application that uses voice input.
2. Why is it harder for a computer to read handwriting than printed text?
3. Explain why it is challenging to write a program that recognizes human speech.
4. Explain how machine learning could help to improve speech recognition.

3.6 Generate natural language

You will learn:
- how computers create natural-seeming language.

Key words

large language model (LLM)

syntax

Case study

Taz sends radio messages about weather conditions. He uses software that reads numerical weather data and outputs natural language messages (for example, 'it is very cold' or 'the wind is stronger than usual'). The creation of human-style speech output is an example of NLP.

How can we teach the computer to 'speak'?

The rules of language are called **syntax** or grammar. A computer must make sentences with the right syntax. For example, this sentence has the right syntax:

> Taz sends messages by radio.

This sentence does not have the right syntax:

> The sends messages radio by Taz.

Different languages have different syntax. So how can we make sure the computer makes good sentences? There are two ways.

1. Program the rules of syntax when you make the software.
2. Use machine learning and probability.

In this lesson, you will look at both methods.

Rules-based NLP

Programmers will study the rules of language. They will make sure their programs make output that has good syntax. For example, we can pick out three parts of a sentence:

- **the verb:** the action that happens
- **the subject:** the person or thing that does the action
- **the object:** the person or thing that is affected by the action.

English sentences usually have the structure:

> subject – verb – object

For example, 'Sam owns a bike'. Other languages have different syntax. There are lots of very complex rules in any language. It is hard to make a program to cover all the rules.

A

Open the program for this lesson. This program has lists of subjects, verbs and objects. The program picks a random word from each list.

```
subjects = ["my cat", "my brother", "the teacher", "Taz", "a dinosaur"]
verbs    = ["makes", "breaks", "eats", "draws", "sings"]
objects  = ["a pizza", "the school", "a car", "a song", "the moon"]

import random

subj = random.choice(subjects)
verb = random.choice(verbs)
obj  = random.choice(objects)

print(subj)
print(verb)
print(obj)
```

1. Delete the lines that print out single words. Add this command to print a sentence with subject, verb and object in the right order.

   ```
   print(subj, verb, obj)
   ```

2. Add new values to the three lists. For example, put your own name and your classmate's names into the subjects list.

3. Put the program into a loop so that it makes lots of sentences. How many are realistic sentences?

Large language model (LLM)

Instead of writing a program with all the rules of syntax, programmers may use machine learning. It works like this:

▶ The computer reads lots of example sentences.

▶ The computer learns which words are more likely to appear together.

▶ The computer generates new sentences based on what it has learned.

The computer will make sentences that match the examples it has seen. Sentences with good syntax are much more likely to appear, so the computer learns to write good sentences. For example, the sentence 'I am happy' is much more likely than the sentence 'I are happy'.

A computer that has learned from looking at billions of sentences is called a **large language model (LLM)**. An LLM can make very realistic sentences on a wide range of topics.

A LLM uses a lot of computer resources. It needs access to lots of real-life language. It uses very powerful computers and a lot of energy.

9:3.6 Make Sentences Program: Digital Activity File

3.6 Generate natural language

Real-life examples

Many computer apps generate text based on previous examples.

▶ A search engine suggests search terms based on what you have already typed.

▶ Predictive texting on a phone suggests the next word, based on probability.

▶ Some websites and apps use LLM to generate long and complex text.

Simple predictive texting can work on your phone. More complex examples may need more computer power.

> **B**
>
> Open a smartphone with predictive texting. Type a single word to get started. Select the next word suggested by the phone, then the next. Soon you will have a whole sentence written by a computer. Does the sentence make sense?

Think maths

Probability is the study of what is more or less likely. Probabilities can be expressed as percentages. For example, 100% probability means something is certain to happen. 10% probability means it only has a one in ten chance of happening.

Summary of learning points

AI is a complex and expanding field in computing. In this unit, we have only had a chance to look at some basic concepts.

▶ AI describes a kind of software that makes decisions or creates content almost as if it can think for itself.

▶ We can create AI using rules or heuristics, or by using machine learning. Machine learning produces the best results.

▶ Machine learning means the computer looks at lots of real-life examples and learns from them – for example, how to make text or images.

Using AI to understand or generate speech and text is called natural language processing (NLP). A computer system that has learned to create realistic text by reviewing billions of examples is called a large language model (LLM).

Benefits and limitations

AI has many benefits.

▶ It can perform useful tasks when there is no human available to make the decision.

▶ It can learn to do useful work quickly and reliably.

AI also has some risks and limitations.

▶ It requires access to large amounts of data.

▶ If the data has mistakes in it, the computer will learn those mistakes.

▶ It uses a lot of electrical and computing power.

▶ It can be easy to confuse real-life pictures and text with fakes made by a computer.

Stop, think

Understanding AI can help to protect us from its risks, while we gain all its benefits. Some governments have made laws to regulate the use of AI. Find out if there are laws like that in your country.

Be creative

Take a random sentence generated by your program. Use it as the first sentence of a short story. Or draw a cartoon to illustrate the sentence.

My cat sings a song

Did you know?

In 1942, a writer called Isaac Asimov wrote a short story about robots. He decided his imaginary robots should be controlled by laws to stop them causing harm. Here is a simplified version of his three laws:

1. No robot shall harm a human.
2. A robot must do what humans tell it to do.
3. A robot must protect itself from harm.

Can you think of a better set of laws?

Stretch zone

Another form of English sentence has this structure:

subject – the word 'is' – adjective

An adjective is a describing word such as 'green' or 'happy'. Write a program to generate random sentences with this structure. You will have to make a list of adjectives.

Test

1. What does 'NLP' stand for?
2. What is the name for a computer system that learns how to make sentences from reading billions of examples?
3. Describe at least one benefit and one limitation of using AI.
4. Predictive texting can suggest the next word in a sentence. Explain how it chooses the word.

3 What have you learned?

Review test

1 Which of these sentences describes AI?
  a Human beings can think like computers.
  b Computers can make complex, autonomous judgements.
  c Computers are made of artificial components.
  d Logical tests are True or False.

2 Which of these phrases describes NLP?
  a A computer that can make realistic photos.
  b A mathematical model of a process.
  c Calculating the probability of an event.
  d Computers generate natural-seeming language.

3 A computer system reviews billions of examples and learns to recognize patterns in the data. What is the name for this?
  a Machine learning
  b A decision tree
  c Heuristic analysis
  d Probability theory

4 Which of these could be done using NLP?
  a Drive a car
  b Produce realistic sentences
  c Autonomous motion
  d Complex mathematical calculations

5 Machine learning has benefits. Which of the following are benefits of machine learning? (There are two right answers – find them both.)
  a The computer does not need any data to find a solution.
  b The computer works out how to solve the problem.
  c The computer never makes any mistakes.
  d The computer develops solutions based on the data.
  e The computer does not need any training.

6 In your own words, describe some of the benefits and limitations of NLP.

Review activity

This program spots if a text message is a question. Use the file for this lesson, or write the code yourself if you have time.

```
message = input("enter your message: ")

if "?" in message:
    print("your message is a question")
```

1. Open the program and look at the code. Run the program to see what it does. Type an example message. What heuristic does the program use to check if the message is a question?

2. The heuristic will miss some questions. Here is a new heuristic.

    `a message that includes the word 'why' is a question`

    Extend the program to use this heuristic.

3. Add a loop to the program so you can check lots of messages. Make a list of all the messages that are questions.

4. If you have time, extend the program to check for other question words as well as 'why'.

Self-evaluation

How did you do?	What is your level?	What your level means
• I answered test questions 1 and 2. • I identified a heuristic in a program.	Developing	You have learned something new in this unit.
• I answered test questions 1 to 4. • I added a new heuristic.	Secure	You have reached the expected standard in this unit.
• I answered all the test questions • I extended and improved the program to make it more useful.	Extending	You are an expert.

What next? To improve your level you can go back and repeat some of this unit.

4 Programming: The fish pond plan

You will learn:

- to build a model of a real-world system
- to use a model to find the answers to real-world problems
- to use logic in your programs.

In this unit, you will make a program to model a real-life system. You will input number values. The computer will work out results from these numbers. Your program will model a fish pond on a farm. It will check the water level in the pond, to make sure there is enough water for the fish that live there.

Making a mathematical model is a fast way to discover if there are problems ahead. The farmer can use a computer model before doing the hard work of building a real-life fish pond.

Activity

The pond in this model is a rectangle shape. You will write a program to calculate the surface area and volume of the pond.

- **Area:** The surface area of a pond is the width of the pond multiplied by its length.
- **Volume:** The volume of the pond is the surface area multiplied by the depth.

The measurements are taken in metres. The area is given in square metres (m^2) and the volume in cubic metres (m^3).

Measure the size of your classroom. Then calculate the floor area and volume of the room.

If you have extra time, try these activities:

- measure the main hall in your school
- measure the size of your teacher's desk
- measure a box or a piece of furniture in your room.

Learning outcomes: Make and use an abstract model of a real-world system; Use Boolean operators in a program

Can a computer model help us understand the real world?

A model based on number values can help us to understand the real world more quickly and safely than trying things out in real life. But a model is a simplification, so treat it with caution. It will lack detail.

abstraction   assumption
Boolean expression
Boolean operator
mathematical model   round
unit of measurement

Talk about …

Computer models are used for many purposes. For example, a model might be used to plan the growth of a city. The planners would make sure they planned all the features the city would need, such as roads and water supply. Only then would they start to build houses.

Imagine you had to make a model of your community. How would you do it? What numbers would you use? How hard would it be to make an accurate model?

4.1 A model pond

You will learn:
- how to use abstraction
- how to make a model of a real-world system.

Key words

abstraction

mathematical model

Case study

The villagers of Redstone Valley have a problem. There used to be a gold mine in the valley. The villagers earned money by working at the mine. But the mine has closed. The villagers need to find another way to bring job opportunities to their valley.

Their solution is to raise a type of fish called tilapia. This is a fish that people like to eat. The villagers will dig fish ponds. They will put water and baby tilapia into the ponds. When the tilapia are full size, the villagers can catch them and sell them at the market.

There is not much water in Redstone Valley. The villagers need to plan how much water they need. In this unit, you will make a program to help the villagers find out the facts for their fish pond plan.

Spiral back

In Books 7 and 8, you learned to plan Python programs. In this lesson, you will plan a program. You will plan the inputs, outputs and processes of the program.

What do we need to know?

The villagers must decide on the size of each pond. They will decide the width, length and depth. They need to know:

- how much water there will be in the pond
- how many fish can live in the pond.

That will help them to plan the ponds for the whole village.

Why use a model?

The farmer could dig a real-life pond and fill it with water. They could find out whether fish can stay alive in the pond. But there are problems.

▶ It takes a lot of time and work to make one pond.

▶ It is even more work to try out ponds of different sizes.

▶ If the pond is not big enough the fish will die, and the plan will fail.

It is better to make a **mathematical model** to test the pond ideas first. A mathematical model uses numbers to stand for all the parts of the system. It uses calculations to predict what will happen in different situations.

If you write a program based on the model, you can try out lots of different numbers quickly and easily. The farmer can use the results to decide the best size to make the ponds. Then they can make the ponds in real life.

Abstraction

To make a model of a real-life system, you must use **abstraction**. Abstraction means making a problem simpler by leaving out details. Which details should you leave out? Which details should you keep? That depends on the purpose of the model.

▶ **Leave out details** that are not needed.

▶ **Keep details** that are needed.

Abstraction turns a complex system into a few key facts. Those facts create a model that meets your needs.

4.1 A model pond

A

A farmer plans to make a pond on his land. He asks you to find out how much water the pond can hold. He also wants to know how many fish can live in the pond. Here are some facts that the farmer can tell you. Which facts do you need to make the mathematical model?

- **A** The farmer's name.
- **B** How many children the farmer has.
- **C** How wide and long the pond will be.
- **D** How deep the pond will be.
- **E** How much water one fish needs to live in.
- **F** The colour of the fish.
- **G** How many miles to market.
- **H** Whether or not the farmer has a truck.
- **I** The other crops the farmer grows on their land.

Values used in the model

The villagers will dig a pond in the shape of a rectangle. You will input the depth, width and length of the pond. Your model will output the surface area and volume of the pond.

▶ The surface area of the pond is width multiplied by length.
▶ The volume of water is surface area multiplied by depth.

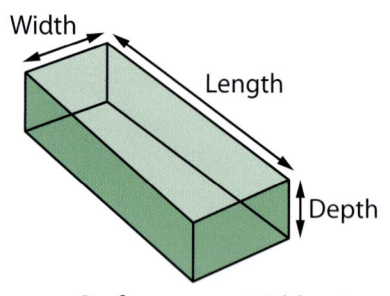

Surface area = Width × Length
Volume = Surface area × Depth

B

This table shows the values used in this model. The last two columns have not been completed.

Value	Input	Calculated	Calculation	Units
Pond width	✓			
Pond length	✓			
Pond depth	✓			
Surface area		✓		
Volume of water		✓		

1. Copy this table into your book or make it using word-processing software. For every calculated field, say what the calculation is
2. State the units used for each measurement. Pick metres, square metres (m^2) or cubic metres (m^3).

Think maths

Find out more about mathematical models of real-life systems.

102

Stretch zone

Each cubic metre of water is enough room for two tilapia fish. Add a new row at the bottom of the table. The value is 'How many fish'. How is this value calculated? (Leave the units column empty.)

Test

Another farmer plans to make a pond. He wants to know how much water he will need to fill the pond.

1. Why is it a good idea to use a model before the farmer digs a real pond?
2. Say one fact about the pond that you need to know to calculate its volume.
3. A model does not include all the facts about a real-life system. Why not?
4. How can you decide which facts to include in the model?

4.2 Make the model

You will learn:
- how to make a program out of an abstract model
- the limitations of abstraction.

Spiral back

In Books 7 and 8, you made Python programs that took user input. You learned to convert inputs to a numerical data type (integer or float).

Case study

The villagers have learned that a pond can hold two fish for every cubic metre of water. Now you have all the facts you need to make a mathematical model.

The inputs are the measurements of the pond:

- width
- length
- depth.

Fish = Volume × 2

The outputs are useful facts about the pond:

- the surface area
- the volume of water
- the number of fish that can live in the pond.

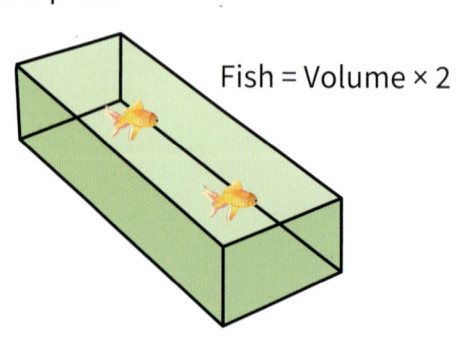

A

1. Open the program for this lesson or make your own version.

2. Run the program. Enter these test values.
   - ▶ Width: 10
   - ▶ Length: 15
   - ▶ Depth: 1.5

The output of your program will look like this. All the answers are zero.

```
width: 10
length: 15
depth: 1.5
area 0
volume 0
fish 0
```

```
### The fish pond model
# inputs
width = input("width: ")
width = float(width)
length = input("length: ")
length = float(length)
depth = input("depth: ")
depth = float(depth)

# processing
area = 0
volume = 0
fish = 0

# outputs
print("area", area)
print("volume", volume)
print("fish",fish)
```

Add calculations

Now you will add calculations to the program to produce the outputs that the villagers need. You must add calculations for:

- ▶ the surface area of the pond (width × length)
- ▶ the volume of the pond (area × depth)
- ▶ the number of fish that can live in the pond (volume × 2).

You will add Python commands to calculate each value. For example, you will change the line

```
area = 0
```

to

```
area = width * length
```

B

1. Open your program. Add formulas to calculate the surface area, volume and number of fish.

2. Run the program. Enter the test values 10, 15 and 1.5.

   The output of your program should look like this.

   If you see these results, your program works correctly.

```
# processing
area = width * length
volume = area * depth
fish = volume * 2
```

```
width: 10
length: 15
depth: 1.5
area 150.0
volume 225.0
fish 450.0
```

9:4.2 Fish Pond Model Inputs: Digital Activity File

105

4.2 Make the model

Limitations of abstraction

When you make an abstract model, you always leave out some details. A model that included every fact about real life would be too complex. It would take a long time to write the program. To run that program would need a very powerful computer.

An abstract model may make facts simpler and more regular. The model will not match reality exactly. Here are some ways that a real-life fish pond might be different from an abstract model.

- The pond might not be an exact rectangle.
- Measurements might not be precise.
- The pond might be deeper at one end than the other.
- Some of the fish might be very big, and need more room.

When we use an abstract model, always remember that it is a simplification.

Key words

integer
round
user-friendly
user interface

Rounding

The villagers entered these values:

- width: 7.55
- length: 9.99
- depth: 2.1

```
width: 7.55
length: 9.99
depth: 2.1
area 75.4245
volume 158.39145
fish 316.7829
```

Here are the results they got.

The results look complicated. There are too many decimal places, and the number of fish should be a whole number – you cannot have part of a fish! There are functions that will fix this problem.

The `round()` function will **round** a number to 2 decimal places before printing:

```
volume = round(volume, 2)
```

The `int()` function will turn a number value into an **integer** (whole number):

```
fish = int(fish)
```

Think maths

Numbers can be rounded up or down. Rounding in either direction introduces some error.

C

Use the `round()` and `int()` functions to make the program more useful. Remember to put this code before the output commands.

```
# rounding
area = round(area,2)
volume = round(volume, 2)
fish = int(fish)
```

Here is the new output.

```
width: 7.55
length: 9.99
depth: 2.1
area 75.42
volume 158.39
fish 316
```

Is the program user-friendly?

The **user interface** is the part of a program that handles user input and displays output. Adding more messages to the user interface could make the program easier for the villagers to understand. When a program is easy to understand, we say it is **user-friendly**.

Here is an example of a more user-friendly user interface.

```
Fish Pond Model
===============
Enter pond width(metres): 10
Enter pond length(metres): 15
Enter pond depth(metres): 1.5


Results
=======
Surface area of the pond is 150.0 square metres
Pond contains 225.0 cubic metres of water
Number of fish: 450
```

Stretch zone

Improve the user interface of the program to make it more user-friendly. You will need to change the input and print commands.

Test

1. An algorithm must include inputs and outputs. What else is included in an algorithm?

2. You need to work out how many fish can live in the pond. What is the calculation to find the number of fish?

3. This program includes a variable 'volume'. It tells you how many cubic metres of water there are in the pond. 1 cubic metre of water is the same as 1,000 litres. Write an extra Python command to calculate how many litres of water there are in the pond.

4. Write a Python command to output the number of litres in a user-friendly way.

Think science

Find out more about the conditions fish need to stay healthy.

4.3 Fill the pond

You will learn:
- ▶ to convert between measurement units
- ▶ to use assumptions to simplify a problem.

Key words

convert

unit of measurement

Case study

The villagers have decided to dig a pond. They will fill it with water using a pipe. As soon as the pond is full of water, they will buy baby fish to put in the pond. They want to know how many days it will take to fill the pond with water.

The time to fill the pond depends on two values:

- ▶ how much water the pond needs (the volume)
- ▶ the speed of water going into the pond (the flow).

The flow into the pond means 'how many litres of water go through the pipe in one second'. The user will input this value.

Convert litres to cubic metres

These input commands will get a figure that tells us the flow of water into the pond. It is a float value (a number with a decimal point in it).

```
flow = input("flow in litres per second: ")
flow = float(flow)
```

The volume of the pond is shown in cubic metres. The flow into the pond is shown in litres. These are measured in different **units of measurement**. It is straightforward to **convert** between litres and cubic metres. Converting means turning a measurement in one unit into a measurement that uses a different unit.

There are 1,000 litres in 1 cubic metre. So, we will divide by 1,000 to turn litres into cubic metres.

```
flow = flow/1000
```

How much time?

To find out how many seconds it will take to fill the pond, we need to divide the volume of the pond by the flow of water per second.

```
time = volume / flow
print("number of seconds:", time)
```

A

1. Open your Python program from 4.2, which calculates the volume of a pond.

2. Add new commands to input the flow of water and calculate how many seconds it would take to fill the pond.

```
# filling the pond

flow = input("flow in litres per second: ")
flow = float(flow)
flow = flow/1000
time = volume / flow
print("to fill the pond (in seconds):", time)
```

3. This image shows this program in use. It shows the inputs and the output of this program. Try entering these inputs. You should get the same result.

```
width: 10
length: 15
depth: 1.5
area 150.0
volume 225.0
fish 450
flow in litres per second: 0.5
to fill the pond (in seconds): 450000.0
```

9:4.3 Fish Pond Calculations: Digital Activity File

4.3 Fill the pond

Convert seconds to days

The program you made tells you how long it will take to fill the pond. This number is shown in seconds. But this number is not very useful. The villagers want to know how many days it will take to fill the pond. How many seconds make one day?

> There are 60 seconds in a minute.
> There are 60 minutes in an hour.
> There are 24 hours in a day.

This Python command will work out the number of seconds in a day:

```
seconds = 60 * 60 * 24
```

This command will divide the total time by seconds to give the result in days:

```
days = time / seconds
```

This command will print the result:

```
print("number of days:", days)
```

Key word

assumption

B

1. Extend the program to show the number of days it will take to fill the pond.

   This image shows this program in use. It shows the inputs and the output of the program.

   ```
   width: 10
   length: 15
   depth: 1.5
   area 150.0
   volume 225.0
   fish 450
   flow in litres per second: 0.5
   to fill the pond (days): 5.208333333333333
   ```

2. Try the program with different input values. Check your results to make sure the program works properly.

Assumptions

In this lesson, you made an abstract model of a pond filling up with water. Here are some facts you left out of the abstract model:

> evaporation might take some water out of the pond
> rainfall might add some extra water to the pond
> there might be leaks out of the pond or the pipe.

To make an abstract model you need to leave out details. Those details could be important. For example, rainfall could help to fill the pond more quickly. In this program, you assume rainfall, evaporation and leakage are zero.

These are **assumptions**. Assumptions are decisions you make to simplify values or to leave them out of the model completely. Assumptions mean your model might be less accurate. But the model is simpler. You should always share your assumptions with the people using the model. That way they know what details you have left out.

In 4.4, you will make a new program to look at evaporation and rainfall.

Stretch zone

Use the `round()` function to show the number of days to two decimal places.

Convert the output so that it shows the number of full days plus extra hours. This is a harder challenge.

Test

In this lesson, you made a program to model how many days it will take to fill a pond with water.

1. If a pond contains 1,000 cubic metres of water, and the flow is 100 cubic metres per day, how many days will it take to fill the pond?
2. Say one reason this answer might not be quite accurate.
3. Describe one assumption used in the fish pond model.
4. Why might you include assumptions when you make a model?

4.4 Evaporation and rainfall

You will learn:
▶ how to make a model more realistic by adding more information.

Case study

In 4.3, you made a program to calculate how long it would take to fill a fish pond. The model included assumptions. You assumed that evaporation and rainfall were zero. In real life, the level of water in a pond is affected by both factors.

▶ **Evaporation** means the sun shines on the pond and some of the water turns into water vapour. The amount of water in the pond goes down.

▶ **Rainfall** into the pond will increase the amount of water.

Both evaporation and rainfall are affected by the surface area of the pond. A wide, shallow pond will collect more rain, but also lose more to evaporation. If the weather is hot and there is not much rain, the water level will go down. If the water level goes down too far, the fish may die.

You will make a program that calculates evaporation and rainfall from the fish pond. That will tell the villagers how much water is left in the pond.

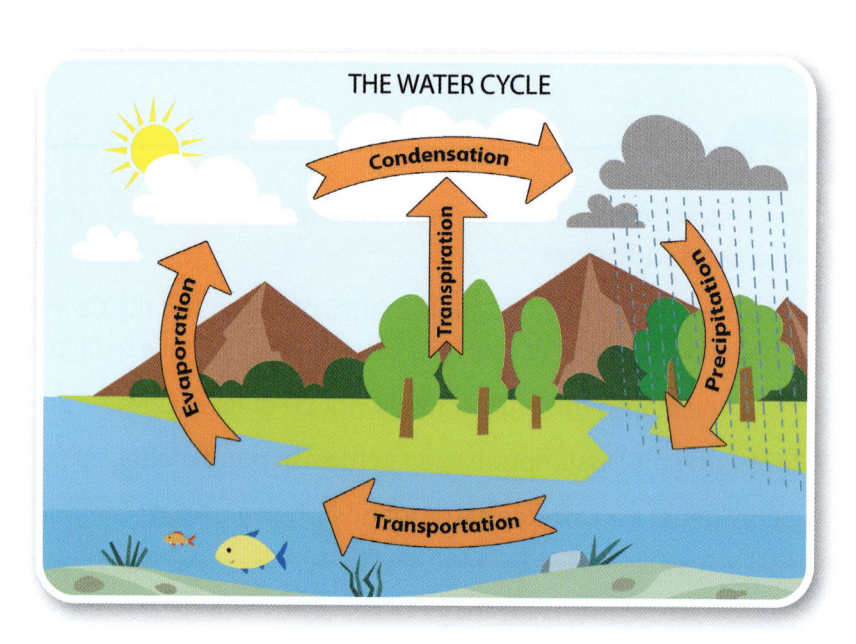

Measurement units

In a mathematical model, all facts are expressed using units of measurement. Using the right units is a key factor in making models of real-world systems. We face the challenge of measurements that use different units.

▶ Rainfall and evaporation are given in millimetres.

▶ The area of the pond is given in square metres.

▶ The volume of the pond is given in cubic metres.

At each stage of the program, we must remember what units we are using and convert our results into the right units.

Evaporation rate

If you hang wet clothes outdoors, they will get dry. If you leave a glass of water in a warm place, the water level will go down. This is caused by evaporation. Liquid water turns into water vapour and rises into the air. Many factors affect evaporation.

To simplify this model, we will use an assumption. We will assume an evaporation rate this month of 75 millimetres of water for every square metre of surface. There are 1,000 millimetres in a metre, so divide by 1,000 to turn millimetres into metres.

```
#evaporation
evaporation = area * 75 / 1000
print("evaporation is ", evaporation)
```

A

1. Open your program from the previous lesson.
2. Add commands at the end of the program to calculate and output the volume of water lost to evaporation.

This image shows this program in use. It shows some example inputs. It shows the outputs. If you enter these inputs, you should get the same output.

```
width: 10
length: 15
depth: 1.5
area 150.0
volume 225.0
evaporation is 11.25
```

Rainfall

This table summarizes the algorithm for calculating the amount of rain that goes into the pond in a month.

	Algorithm	Python command
Input	rainfall that month (in millimetres)	`rainfall = input("rainfall: ")` `rainfall = float(rainfall)`
Processing	rain = rainfall × area divide by 1000 to turn it into cubic metres	`rain = rainfall * area / 1000`
Output	volume added by the	`print("rain is ", rain)`

4.4 Evaporation and rainfall

B

1. Extend the program to show rainfall as well as evaporation. Add the commands from the table on page 113.

```
#rainfall
rainfall = input("rainfall: ")
rainfall = float(rainfall)
rain = rainfall * area
rain = rain/1000
print("rain is",rain)
```

2. This image shows the program in use. In this example, the rainfall was 38 millimetres in the month. Try out your program to make sure it works properly.

```
width: 10
length: 15
depth: 1.5
volume 225.0
evaporation 11.25
rainfall: 38
rain is 5.7
```

How much water is left?

Evaporation takes water away from the pond. Rainfall adds water to the pond. So, we can work out how much water is in the pond at the end of the month.

```
volume = volume − evaporation
volume = volume + rain
print(volume, " cubic metres of water")
```

C

1. Add commands to calculate and display the amount of water left in the pond.

```
# remaining volume
volume = volume - evaporation
volume = volume + rain
print(volume, "cubic meters of water")
```

2. This image shows the program in use. Try out your program to make sure it works properly.

```
width: 10
length: 15
depth: 1.5
volume 225.0
evaporation 11.25
rainfall: 38
rain is 5.7
219.45 cubic meters of water
```

Think science

Find out more about the water cycle and what factors affect evaporation and why.

Stretch zone

Some water will leak from the pond into the soil. In this village, the amount lost by leakage is area multiplied by 20 millimetres. Add this value to the program, alongside evaporation and rainfall. Remember to convert the units of measurement.

Test

1. What unit is used to measure rainfall?
2. The variable 'volume' stores the volume of the pond. What is the data type of this variable?
3. Why do you have to divide rainfall by 1,000?
4. The program in this lesson includes an assumption about evaporation. What is the assumption?

4.5 Use the model to help solve a problem

You will learn:
▶ how to use a model to solve a real-life problem.

Key words

'if' structure

minimum

Case study

If the water in a pond gets too low, the fish cannot get enough oxygen. They rise to the surface of the water and gasp for air. Unless the farmer puts more water in the pond, some of the fish will die.

If there are only a few fish, then it is okay if the volume of water gets quite low. But if there are lots of fish, the pond needs to be full of water. You will use the fish pond model to help the villagers keep their fish alive.

Input the number of fish

First, we need to input how many fish there are in the pond. Remember, the number of fish is a whole number (integer).

```
# input number of fish
fish = input("enter number of fish: ")
fish = int(fish)
```

Next, we need to know the **minimum** amount of water to keep the fish alive. Minimum means the smallest possible value.

Tilapia do not mind some crowding. Two fish can live in 1 cubic metre of water. So, the minimum volume is calculated as the number of fish divided by 2.

```
minimum = fish / 2
print(minimum)
```

A

1. Open the file for this lesson. It is a new version of the program.

2. Add extra commands at the top of the program to input the number of fish and calculate the minimum water needed.

3. Run the program to check it works. For example, if you enter 400 fish, you need 200 cubic metres of water.

```
### The fish pond model

# fish
fish = input("number of fish: ")
fish = int(fish)
minimum = fish/2
print("you need this much water",minimum)
```

```
### The fish pond model

# input size of pond
width = input("width: ")
width = float(width)
length = input("length: ")
length = float(length)
depth = input("depth: ")
depth = float(depth)

# calculate volume, rounded
area = width * length
volume = area * depth
area = round(area, 2)
volume = round(volume, 2)
print("volume is", volume)

# calculate changes to volume
evaporation = area * 75 / 1000
rainfall = input("rainfall: ")
rainfall = float(rainfall)
rain = rainfall * area / 1000
volume = volume - evaporation
volume = volume + rain

# output new volume
print("evaporation is ",evaporation)
print("rain is ",rain)
print("remaining volume is",volume)
```

Show a warning

You will adapt your program to show a warning if the volume of water falls below the minimum safe level. Remember that an **'if' structure** starts with a logical test. If the test is True, then the commands inside the structure will be carried out.

The table shows the algorithm.

	Algorithm	Python command
Logical test	Is the volume of the pond below the minimum level?	`if volume < minimum:`
If test is True	Output a warning message.	`print("Water level`

9:4.5 Evaporation And Rainfall: Digital Activity File

4.5 Use the model to help solve a problem

B

1. Add an 'if' structure at the end of the program, after the commands that calculate the volume of water. It should display a warning message if the volume of water goes below the minimum.

```
# output new volume
print("evaporation is", evaporation)
print("rain is",rain)
print("remaining volume is", volume)
if volume < minimum:
    print("Water level low")
```

2. Try out your program to make sure it works properly.

Model the whole year

The program you have made models the pond for one month. But in real life, the pond must last for the whole year. Now, you will extend the model to repeat for 12 months.

The fish pond model contains several parts:

- input number of fish
- input size of pond
- calculate volume
- calculate changes to volume
- output new volume (and warning).

Some of these parts happen once, and some will repeat every month.

C

Plan and then make your program.

- You want some parts of the program to repeat 12 times. Will you use a 'for' loop or a 'while' loop?
- Which parts of the program will repeat 12 times?
- Add the right type of loop to your program. Put the parts that will repeat inside the loop.
- Run the program and make sure it works.

```
for i in range(12):

    # calculate changes to volume
    evaporation = area * 75 / 1000
    rainfall = input("rainfall: ")
    rainfall = float(rainfall)
    rain = rainfall * area / 1000
    volume = volume - evaporation
    volume = volume + rain

    # output new volume
    print("evaporation is", evaporation)
    print("rain is",rain)
    print("remaining volume is", volume)
    if volume < minimum:
        print("Water level low")
```

Stretch zone

Add commands to make the program more user-friendly.

```
Month 0
---------
enter rainfall (mm): 20
evaporation is 11.25
rain is 3.0
remaining volume 216.75 cubic meters


Month 1
---------
enter rainfall (mm): 0
evaporation is 11.25
rain is 0.0
remaining volume 205.5 cubic meters


Month 2
---------
enter rainfall (mm): 0
evaporation is 11.25
rain is 0.0
remaining volume 194.25 cubic meters
** W A R N I N G **
Water level low - fish in danger
```

✓ Test

1. There is a 'for' loop in this program. How many times will it repeat?
2. Give an example of a measurement that does not change every month.
3. How does this program check if the volume of water is too low?
4. Write a line of code that will output the difference between the volume of water and the minimum safe level.

Digital citizen

Computer systems are used in agriculture of all kinds – not just fish farms. Computers can be used to monitor conditions, make adjustments, or raise alerts if minimum standards are not met. This ensures animal welfare.

Think science

Understanding animal science brings benefits to farmers as well as their livestock. When animals are healthy and happy, farms are more successful.

4.6 Boolean operators

You will learn:
- how to make a model using logic.

Key words
Boolean expression
Boolean operator
NOT operator

Case study

You have made a model of the fish pond through the year. It has worked well and the fish have survived. Now the villagers must decide what to do with each pond:

- add more fish to the pond
- add more water to the pond
- reduce the stock of fish
- clean the pond.

To help the villagers, you will make a new program. This program will use logic.

Boolean values and Boolean operators

The word 'Boolean' is used in computer science to mean logical values and operators. The word comes from the name 'George Boole'. He was a mathematician who invented modern logic. **Boolean expressions** can have only two different values: they can be True or False. Logical tests that compare two values are examples of Boolean expressions.

Boolean operators join Boolean expressions together. They create new True/False values. In this lesson, you will use three important Boolean operators:

- NOT
- AND
- OR

A statue of George Boole

Check the pond

At the end of the year, the villagers check every pond they have made. They ask four questions about each pond.

1. Is the water level too low for the number of fish? (Y/N)
2. Is there room to add more water? (Y/N)
3. Is the water full of plants? (Y/N)
4. Is the water green and cloudy? (Y/N)

This program stores the answer to each question as a Boolean value.

```python
# start with all the values set to False
low = room = plants = green = False
# answer questions to check the pond
question1 = input("is the water low? (Y/N) ")
if question1 == "Y":
    low = True

question2 = input("is there room to add more water? (Y/N) ")
if question2 == "Y":
    room = True

question3 = input("is the water full of plants? (Y/N) ")
if question3 == "Y":
    plants = True

question4 = input("is the water green and cloudy? (Y/N) ")
if question4 == "Y":
    green = True
```

NOT operator

The model can offer advice to the villagers. The first thing they want to know is, can they add more fish to the pond? The answer depends on this input:

▶ Is the water low?

If the water is low, they cannot add more fish. But if the water is not low, they can add more fish. This table show the logic of the decision.

Water is low?	Add more fish?
No	Yes
Yes	No

The output of the process is the opposite of the input value. The logical operation that makes a value into its opposite is *not*. Like the word 'not' in everyday speech, it reverses the truth of an expression.

Using the **NOT operator** produces the correct output.

```python
if not low:
    print("you can add more fish")
```

A

Open the program for this lesson. Add an 'if' structure using the *not* operator to tell the villagers if they can add more fish to the pond. Run the program and check that it works.

AND operator

The villagers need to know when to add water to the ponds. This depends on two answers.

▶ Is the water low?   ▶ Is there room to add more water?

9:4.6 Boolean Operators: Digital Activity File

4.6 Boolean operators

The logic is summarized in the next table.

Is water low?	Room in the pond?	Add more water?
No	No	No
No	Yes	No
Yes	No	No
Yes	Yes	Yes

Key words

AND operator
OR operator

The output of the process depends on two values. Both of the values must be True for the output to be True. The logical operation to check that both values are True is `and`. Like the word 'and' in everyday speech, it combines two expressions to make a bigger True expression.

Using the **AND operator** produces the correct output.

```
if low and room:
    print("you can add more water")
```

B

Extend the program. Add an 'if' structure using the `and` operator to tell the villagers if they should add more water to the pond. Run the program and check that it works.

OR operator

Sometimes the water is clogged with plants or algae. Two inputs tell us this:

▶ Is the water full of plants?
▶ Is the water green and cloudy?

Water that is full of weeds and algae is not good for the fish. Adding water snails to the pond will solve this problem. The snails eat some of the weeds or algae. This makes the pond better for the fish.

This table shows the logic of the decision.

Is water full of plants?	Is water green and cloudy?	Add snails?
No	No	No
No	Yes	Yes
Yes	No	Yes
Yes	Yes	Yes

It is time to clean the pond if the water is green OR the water is cloudy, OR both. The **OR operator** will produce this result. Like the word 'or' in everyday life, it makes an expression which is True if either half of the expression is True.

Using the `or` operator produces the correct output.

```
if plants or green:
    print("add water snails to the pond")
```

C

Extend the program. Add an 'if' structure using the `or` operator to tell the villagers if they need to add snails. Run and check that the program works.

```
if not low:
    print("you can add more fish")
if low and room:
    print("you can add more water")
if plants or green:
    print("add water snails to the pond")
```

Stretch zone

1. This village has five ponds. Put the program in a loop, to produce answers for each pond.

2. If the water is too low for the number of fish and there is no room to add more water, the villagers must take fish out of the pond. Add a new 'if' structure to the program to show this result.

3. Each cubic metre of water is enough for two fish. Enter commands to input the amount of water and the number of fish. Output how many fish should be added or removed from the pond.

✓ Test

1. What are the two possible values of a Boolean expression?

2. What Boolean operator produces a result which is the opposite of the input value?

3. The Boolean `and` operator is used to join two input values. What input values will produce the output True?

4. The `or` operator joins two values to make a larger Boolean expression. What input values will make the expression False?

Digital citizen

Computer models can help communities to work together to achieve their goals. An important goal is to provide good food for everyone. As populations increase, computers are used to improve agriculture and increase food production. Computer skills bring real-world benefits. Computer models help us to reach our goals.

4) What have you learned?

Review test

The government of Redstone Valley make a reservoir to supply the fish ponds with water during the dry season. They build a model to work out the total amount of water that is needed in one year.

Here is the program they made.

```python
# Redstone Valley Reservoir

needed = 0
ponds = 3
print("Enter water needed by each pond")

for i in range(ponds):

    print("Pond", i + 1)
    water = input("How much water: ")
    water = float(water)
    needed = needed + water

print("The total amount needed is", needed)
```

1 How many ponds are included in this model?

2 One piece of information is input about each pond – what is the input?

3 To be safe, the reservoir must hold 1.7 times the total volume needed, as a minimum. Explain how you could adapt the program to calculate and show the minimum.

4 The program simplifies the model of the reservoir using abstraction. State **one** fact about the reservoir that is left out of the model.

5 You identified a fact that is left out of the model. Does leaving it out make the model less accurate? Or does it have no effect on accuracy? Explain your answer.

Review activity

The villagers have spare fields that are not in use. A simple program will help them decide what to do with each field. The program asks two questions.

```
Q1 = input("Is the soil stony? (Y/N)")
if Q1 == "Y":
    stony = True
else:
    stony = False

Q2 = input("Is there a water supply? (Y/N)")
if Q2 == "Y":
    water = True
else:
    water = False
```

1. Open the program and add an 'if' structure, so that if the field is NOT stony, the message 'plant crops' appears.

2. Add an extra 'if' structure, so that if the field is stony AND there is a water supply, then the message 'make a fish pond' appears.

3. If the field is either windy or sunny, the farmer can use it to generate electricity. Extend the program to get this information and display a suitable message.

Self-evaluation

How did you do?	What is your level?	What your level means
• I answered test questions 1 and 2. • I ran the reservoir model and identified the outputs.	Developing	You have learned something new in this unit.
• I answered test questions 1 to 3. • I improved the reservoir model.	Secure	You have reached the expected standard in this unit.
• I answered all the test questions. • I extended the reservoir model to make it more useful.	Extending	You are an expert.

What next? To improve your level you can go back and repeat some of this unit.

9:4.7 Land Use: Digital Activity File

5 Analysing data: Managing a project

You will learn:

▶ how to work as a team to plan and manage a project

▶ how to use software tools to create mind maps, Gantt charts and kanban boards to plan and manage a project.

In this unit, you will learn how people work together on projects. You will practise using many of the tools and techniques that teams use in different kinds of projects.

Planning and delivering a project creates a lot of data and information. A project manager must manage this information. Project managers can use IT tools to help. This unit will show you a toolbox of methods you can use in your technology and digital projects.

Activity

Your headteacher wants students to create something that will celebrate the community that the school is part of. Work in a pair or small team.

Think of two or three suitable projects that will capture the attention of staff, students and visitors, and provide a positive and inspirational celebration of your community.

▶ How will you decide on a final project to go ahead with?

▶ How will you plan the project?

▶ What skills will the project team need to have?

▶ What resources will the project need other than skilled people?

Learning outcome: Use computers to plan or organize teamwork

Does working with others just make everything harder?

There are challenges when we work with others. But the benefits greatly outweigh the problems. Using project management methods, defining roles and communicating clearly can make it easier for everyone.

---

agile method   defect
Gantt chart   kanban board
project   risks   sprint   test case
user story   waterfall method

Talk about …

All IT projects try to deliver a solution to a problem. IT projects require many different skills to solve the problems. Building an IT solution can be as complicated as building a bridge.

Talk about the different skills that are needed to build a bridge. Compare them to the skills that are needed to build a website.

5.1 What is a project?

You will learn:
- what a project is
- what jobs there are in a project team.

Key words

business as usual (BAU)

project

risk

What is a project?

All kinds of organizations and individuals work on **projects**. A project has a specific goal and a set of tasks to reach that goal. A family might have a project to decorate their living room. Their goal would be to have a beautiful room. The tasks to reach their goal might include reading magazines for inspiration, buying paint and brushes, and painting walls.

Projects and business as usual

Organizations in business, government and public services also do projects. These organizations use projects as a way of changing things they do and the way they work. This makes projects different from normal activities. The normal activities are sometimes called **business as usual (BAU)**.

Projects are different from BAU activities because they are:

- **temporary:** a project has fixed start and end dates
- **cross-functional:** a project involves people from different parts of a business
- **unique:** every project is different and aims to solve a particular problem
- **uncertain:** a project involves more uncertainty and risk than BAU activities.

BAU activities create income, for example, through the sale of products. Projects usually create cost because they develop and change things.

Case study

The Cake Factory is a business that makes and sells cakes. They have BAU activities that are part of the day-to-day running of their business. They also have project activities, which allow them to develop and grow their business.

THE CAKE FACTORY

Business as usual activities	Project activities
▸ Buying ingredients	▸ Developing and testing a new cake recipe
▸ Baking cakes	▸ Designing new packaging
▸ Packaging cakes	▸ Building a new factory
▸ Delivering cakes to supermarkets	

128

A

Draw a table with two columns. Write three examples of the BAU work of your school in one column. Write three ideas for projects that the school could do in the second column.

Project risks

You cannot be certain that the result of a project will help increase income in the future. What if customers do not like the new cake recipe? What if the new packaging is not appropriate in some countries? What if the new factory has technical problems?

These 'what ifs' are called **risks**. Every project has risks. It is important that projects are properly planned and managed, so that the risks can be reduced.

The project life cycle

You can divide a project into stages to help you manage it. The most common way of dividing a project into stages is called the project life cycle. The project life cycle has four stages.

All projects start with a planning stage. Once a plan has been agreed, project teams move on to the 'Do', 'Check' and 'Act' stages. A project can go through all the stages and start again at the beginning. When projects go through the cycle several times like this, it is called a 'continuous improvement cycle'.

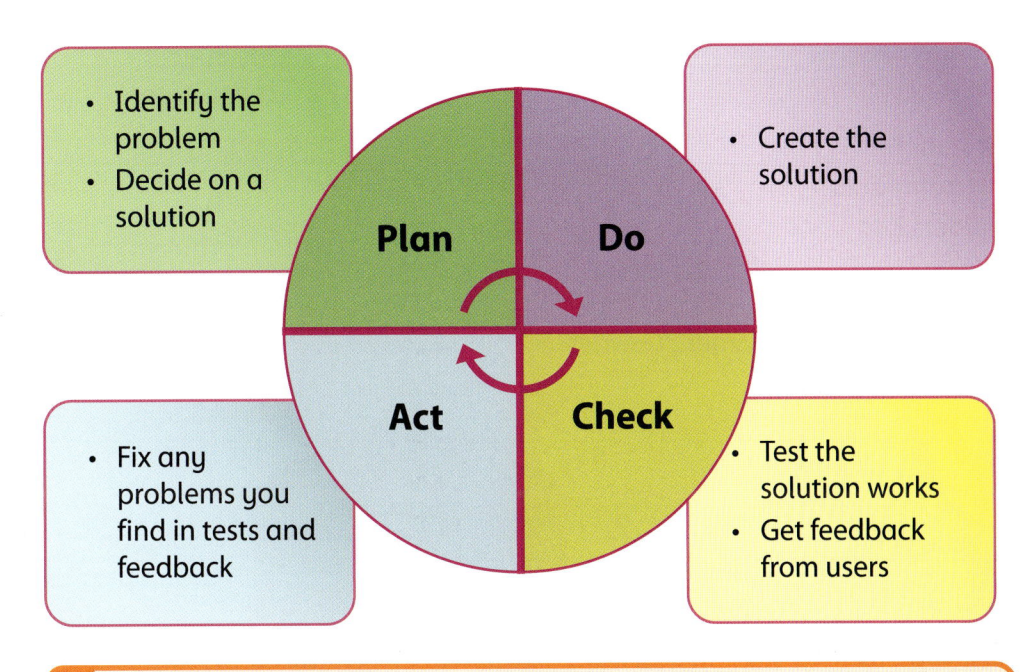

Plan
- Identify the problem
- Decide on a solution

Do
- Create the solution

Check
- Test the solution works
- Get feedback from users

Act
- Fix any problems you find in tests and feedback

B

Open the file for this lesson. Complete Activity 1.

Identify which stage of the project life cycle each task belongs to.

5.1 What is a project?

Project roles

The project manager

The project manager's role is to control the project in each of the project stages. The project manager monitors these issues.

Costs: Project managers have a fixed amount of money to spend on a project. This is called the budget. This money must pay for everything the project needs.

Timescales: Projects should always have a fixed start and end date. Project managers must make sure that the project reaches its goals in the time available.

Quality: Project managers must check that the project team are meeting the quality standards set by the project.

Scope: Project managers must know exactly what the project needs to deliver to achieve its goals. This is called the **scope**. Many projects are delayed or go over budget because project teams add things to the scope. This is often called scope creep.

Risks: All projects have some risks. Project managers must understand the risks and help the project team avoid them.

The project team and stakeholders

There are many ways of organizing a project team. In IT projects, a model like this is often used.

The people who have an interest in the project's outcome are called **stakeholders**. This model divides the stakeholders into two groups.

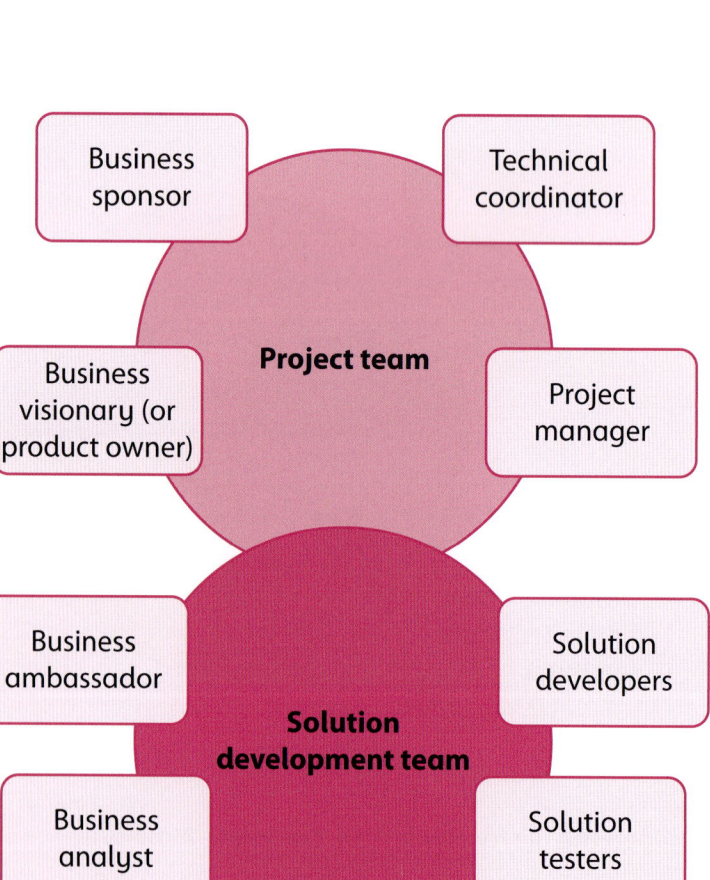

> **Key words**
> scope
> stakeholders

Project team:
- Business sponsor
- Technical coordinator
- Business visionary (or product owner)
- Project manager

Solution development team:
- Business ambassador
- Solution developers
- Business analyst
- Solution testers
- Team leader

The project team

Role	Responsibility
Business sponsor	The person who controls the project budget.
Business visionary	Responsible for making sure that the project delivers benefits to the business.
Technical coordinator	Makes sure the project delivers a product or service that will work with the organization's IT systems.
Project manager	Makes sure the project keeps to its budget and timescale.

The solution development team

Role	Responsibility
Business analyst	Makes sure that the project delivers the right service or product for the organization.
Solution developers and testers	The people who build the product or service.
Business ambassador	Someone who will be a user of the product or service. They can make suggestions on how to improve the solution.
Team leader	Organizes the work of the solution development team.

C

Now complete Activity 2 on your worksheet for this lesson. Match the descriptions of team members to their roles in the team.

Stretch zone

Open the worksheet for this lesson. Complete the 'Stretch zone' activity: Project tasks. List the tasks you expect to be included in an example project.

✓ Test

1. Put these stages of the project life cycle in the correct order:

   (Do)   (Plan)   (Check)

2. What does 'business as usual' mean in an organization?
3. Explain one way in which a project is different from business as usual.
4. Explain the role of a project manager.

5.2 Plan a project

You will learn:
- how to use a mind map to create ideas for a project
- how to use personas to understand what people want from your project
- how to use process diagrams to understand how a project can help a business.

Key words

objective
persona
project goal
requirement

The discovery phase

The planning stage of the project life cycle is often called a 'discovery' phase. This is an important part of a project. Everything else depends on the outcomes of the discovery.

The purpose of the discovery phase is to understand what the project needs to achieve. If anything is overlooked in this stage, it will be harder to achieve the project's goals. The project team do research so that they understand:

- The **project goals** and **objectives**: Project goals need to be divided into objectives. An objective is something that can be measured so you can easily tell when it has been achieved. When you have met your objectives, you will have achieved your goal.

- The **requirements**: These are the instructions for the solution development team.

- The **needs of users**: If you understand your users, you can make sure your product or service works for them.

Create ideas

When you start your project, you might not have a very clear understanding of what you need to deliver. You can use a mind map to create and record ideas of things to research and do.

Case study

The Cake Factory created a mind map to understand everything they would need to do to start up their business.

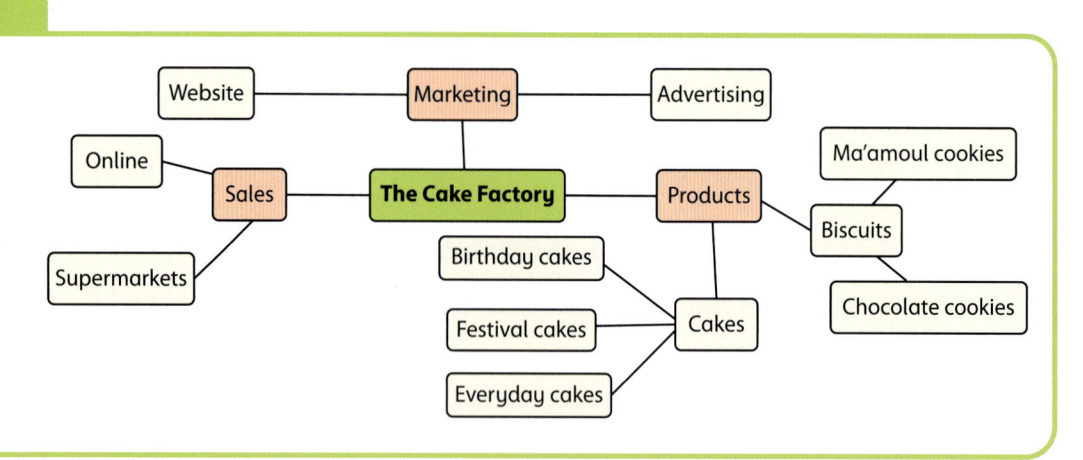

Mind map for The Cake Factory:
- Marketing: Website, Advertising
- Sales: Online, Supermarkets
- Products:
  - Ma'amoul cookies
  - Biscuits
  - Chocolate cookies
  - Cakes: Birthday cakes, Festival cakes, Everyday cakes

132

You can create mind maps on your own or as a team. You can create them using an application or on paper. Start at the centre of your map. Write down an idea or problem. Then add other related ideas as branches. Carry on adding new ideas that relate to the central problem (a new branch) or to an idea in a branch (a twig).

There are many mind-mapping applications available online. You can also use the drawing tools in your word processor or presentation application.

Analyse needs

Most IT projects deliver a product or a service that people will use in business as usual in the future. This could be people inside the organization, who will use a new tool or system you develop. Or it could be customers, who will use the new product or service you develop.

Everyone in your project needs to understand who these people are and what is important to them. They will all have different needs and different expectations. The images below give an example of how the ideas and needs of a user can be different to those of the project team. The project is to design a new model of washing machine.

If the project team had listened only to the solution developer, then the product might have had many features that the customer did not need or want. Money could have been wasted on features no one wants or uses.

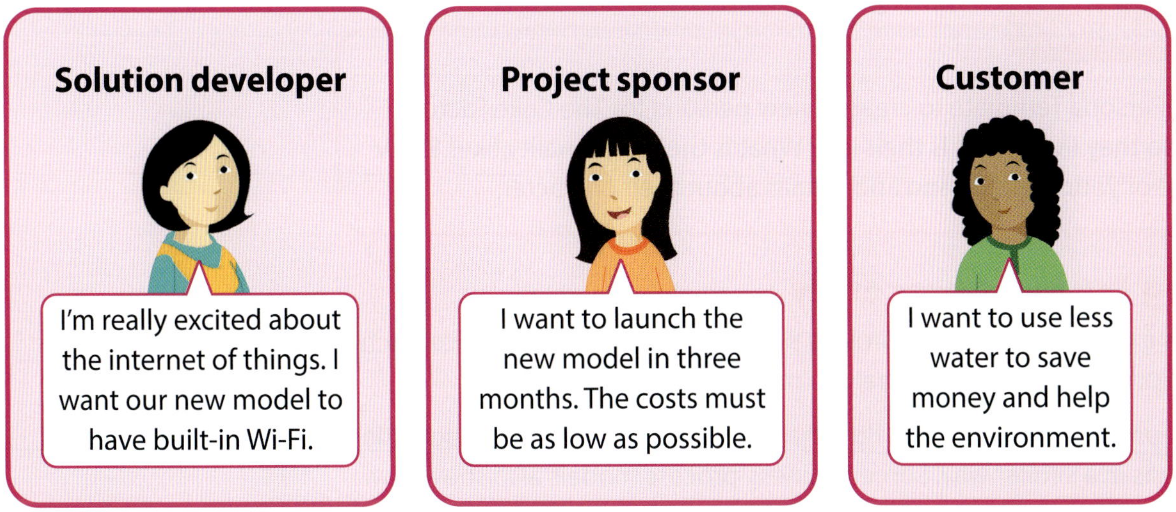

Solution developer: I'm really excited about the internet of things. I want our new model to have built-in Wi-Fi.

Project sponsor: I want to launch the new model in three months. The costs must be as low as possible.

Customer: I want to use less water to save money and help the environment.

Personas

A **persona** is a tool that can help a project team record and share their understanding of their users. A persona is an imaginary person, based on known facts about users and customers. At every stage of the project, the team can use the persona to plan their product or service.

5.2 Plan a project

A

Review this persona created by The Cake Factory's project team.

Name	Mrs Khan
Job	Account manager at The International Bank
Family	Married, with two children
Personality and behaviour	Outgoing, friendly and kind but often rushed because she is very busy
Why would she buy from The Cake Factory?	She loves to treat her children on their birthdays. She does not have enough time to bake a cake herself.
Why would she NOT buy from The Cake Factory?	She is concerned that it might be too expensive. She is concerned that the cake might be delivered too late. She could ask her mother to bake the cake for her children instead.

Write three things that The Cake Factory can do to help Mrs Khan decide to order a custom cake for her children.

Key words

cross-functional diagram

Be creative

Use the Persona Template to create a new persona for The Cake Factory. Where do they live? What is their job? What is their personality like? Draw a picture of your persona and add details about their character.

Mapping business processes

Sometimes a project needs to improve a process that is already in place, such as selling a product online. It can help to model the process.

A business-process model is like a flowchart. It uses symbols to show activities and decisions in a similar way. Some business-process models also show how different people work together. These are called **cross-functional diagrams**.

B

Look at the cross-functional diagram at the top of the next page. What are the four roles identified in the diagram? List the activities carried out by each of the four roles. Which role does the final task?

9:5.2 Persona Template: Digital Activity File

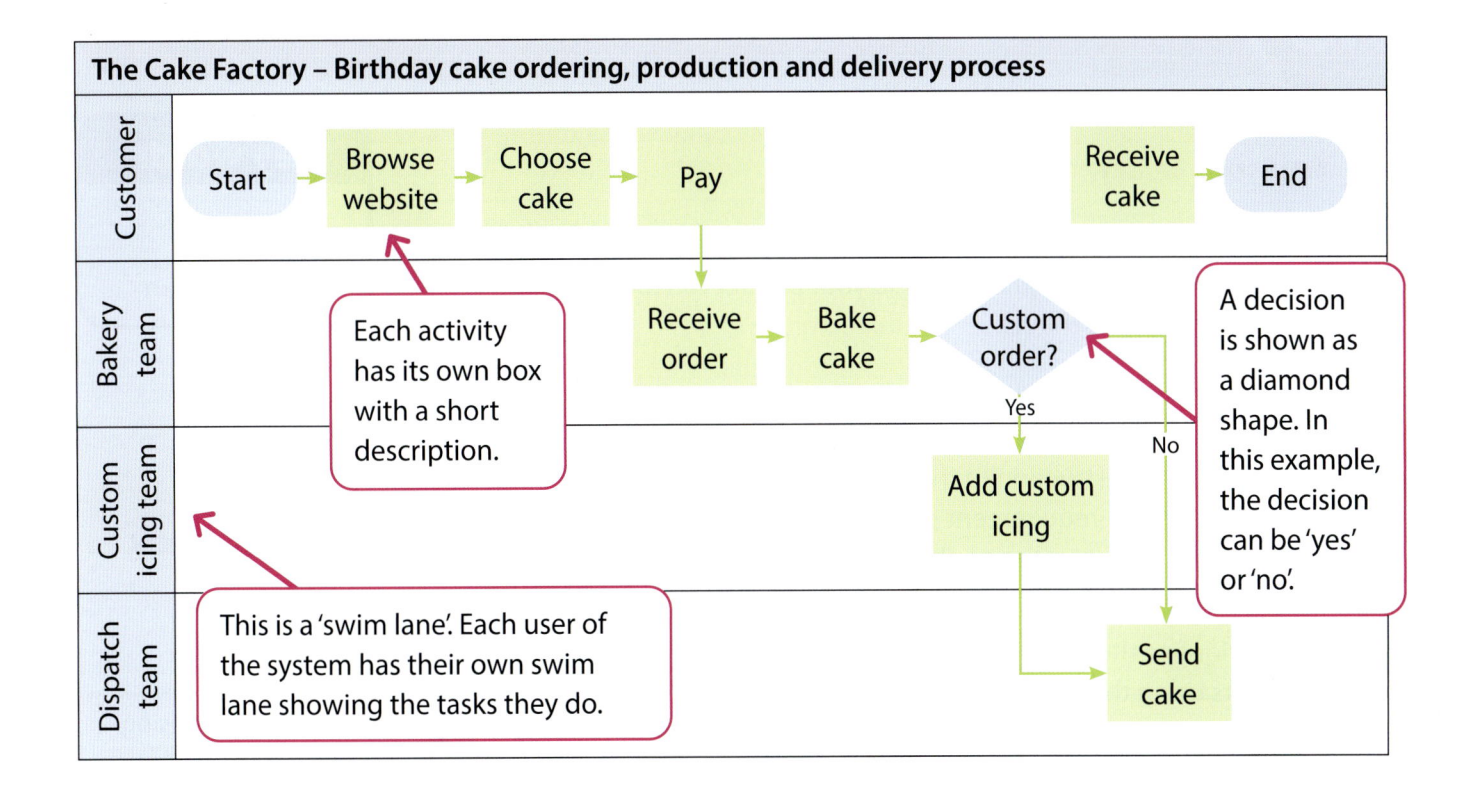

The Cake Factory – Birthday cake ordering, production and delivery process

Customer: Start → Browse website → Choose cake → Pay → ... → Receive cake → End

Bakery team: Receive order → Bake cake → Custom order? (decision)

Custom icing team: Add custom icing (if Yes)

Dispatch team: Send cake

Annotations:
- Each activity has its own box with a short description.
- A decision is shown as a diamond shape. In this example, the decision can be 'yes' or 'no'.
- This is a 'swim lane'. Each user of the system has their own swim lane showing the tasks they do.

Stretch zone

Your teacher will give you the Cross-functional Diagram worksheet. One page shows the roles and tasks involved in buying lunch in the school canteen. The other page shows a blank cross-functional diagram.

1. Label three swim lanes to show the three roles.
2. Put the tasks into the diagram in the right order and join them with arrows.

Test

1. What is a 'persona'?
2. What is a swim lane used for in a cross-functional diagram?
3. Which of these is a valid project objective?
   - 'I want my customers to be happy.'
   - 'I want to improve customer satisfaction by 25% in three months.'
   - 'I think we should be measuring how happy our customers are.'
4. Explain how a mind map can help you write down ideas.

9:5.2 Cross-functional Diagram: Digital Activity File

5 Analysing data: Managing a project

5.3 Understand requirements

You will learn:
- how to use a use case diagram and user stories to design a solution
- how to prioritize requirements so your project can focus on the most important things.

Key words

actor

use case diagram

Requirements

A requirement is an instruction to the project team about a problem they need to solve for the user. A requirement does not tell the project team how to solve the problem. The project relies on the ideas and skills of the team to work out how it should be solved.

The team prioritize the requirements using the 'must have' and 'should have' method. When all the 'must have' requirements have been met, the product or service is ready. The project can still carry on working to deliver the requirements that have a lower priority.

Spiral back

In Book 8, you learned about prioritizing requirements using 'must have' and 'should have'.

Case modelling

In projects that develop an IT system, it can be helpful to start with a **use case diagram**. A use case diagram shows the system, the users and their requirements.

A use case diagram shows four important parts of the requirements.

- **Actors** are the types of people who will use the IT system.
- Use cases are things that an actor wants the system to do. For example, browse the website or place an order. Some use cases are optional. For example, browse a website.
- A system boundary is a box around all the use cases. The system boundary helps show the scope of the system. Anything inside the box is part of the system.
- Associations are lines between the actors and the use cases. They show which actors use each use case in the system.

Drawing a use case diagram is a good way to share information about requirements and check that everyone in the project team understands and agrees the scope of the project. You can create a use case diagram using any software that allows you to draw using shapes.

Case study

The Cake Factory is developing a system to help their customers order a birthday cake.

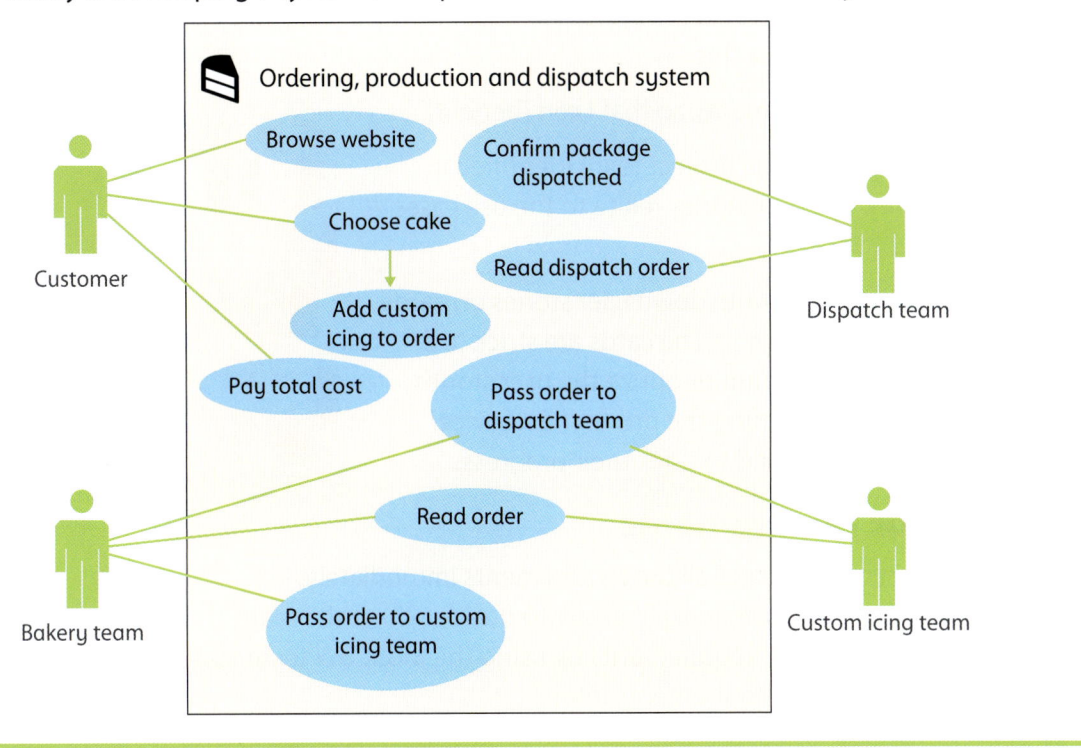

Ordering, production and dispatch system

Actors: Customer, Dispatch team, Bakery team, Custom icing team

Use cases:
- Browse website
- Confirm package dispatched
- Choose cake
- Read dispatch order
- Add custom icing to order
- Pay total cost
- Pass order to dispatch team
- Read order
- Pass order to custom icing team

A

1. Who are the actors in The Cake Factory use case diagram?
2. What use cases do customers want to use?
3. 'Browse website' is one optional use case. What is the other optional use case in the diagram? Why might a customer not use the option?

B

Your school wants to develop an application for students so they can order their lunch in advance.

- Students will use the app to see the lunch menu. They can use the app to order their lunch for that day.
- Parents will use the app to see their child's account, showing how much money they have spent on lunches that week. They can use the app to pay the bill.
- The school chef will use the app to publish the lunch menu. The app will tell them how many students have ordered each lunch choice.

Open the worksheet for this lesson. Use the template to draw a use case diagram to show these actors and how they will use the app.

5 Analysing data: Managing a project

9:5.3 Use Case Diagram: Digital Activity File

5.3 Understand requirements

User stories

There are many ways of writing down the requirements for a project. In software development, designers and developers often use **user stories**. A user story says what an actor wants the system to do, and why. A user story is written down in a sentence like this:

As a [actor], I want to [requirement], so that I can [benefit].

The actors are the ones that the project team identified in the use case diagram. The user stories relate to the use cases in the diagram.

Sometimes the project team write down user stories on cards or sticky notes during a workshop. The cards are stuck to a board or the wall. When the team prioritize the user stories and begin working on developing the product or service, they can move the cards around to track their progress.

> **Key word**
>
> user story

Prioritize your requirements

Sometimes a project cannot meet all the requirements immediately. Prioritizing the requirements can make it easier to decide where the team should start. You can prioritize requirements by using the MoSCoW technique. You can use it to divide your requirements into:

- **M**ust haves: things your technology or service must be able to do. If you do not have these things, your project will fail.

- **S**hould haves: things you should have but do not absolutely need. For example, there might be another way to meet the requirement.

- **C**ould haves: things that would be nice to have, but you can do without.

- **W**on't haves: things that you know you cannot have this time. They might become possible later, so it is useful to make a note of them now.

When they have decided on the priorities, the project team can add the letter M, S, C or W to each user story card. Then they order the cards by priority, with the Ms at the top, then the Ss, Cs and Ws.

> **C**
>
> Look at the case study user stories from The Cake Factory on page 139.
>
> Discuss them with a partner and prioritize them using the MoSCoW technique.

Case study

These are some of the user stories for The Cake Factory's online ordering system.

> As a customer, it would be so exciting if my cake could be delivered to my party by drone.

> As a bakery team member, I need to know if the customer has any allergies before I bake the cake. If I don't, the customer may get ill.

> As a dispatch team member, I think customers might be more likely to buy a cake if they can pay for it in weekly installments.

> As an icing team member, I would like to send a picture of my design for the customer to approve before icing the cake.

Stretch zone

Create one or more user stories from the use cases in the diagram you created in Activity B. Remember to use the format 'As a [actor], I want to [requirement], so that I can [benefit]'.

✓ Test

1. What does each drawing of a person represent in a use case diagram?
2. Put these three levels of priority in the correct order, from most important to least.

    (Could have)   (Should have)   (Must have)

3. Which of these examples uses the correct format for a user story?
    a 'As a customer, I want to add items to my shopping basket so that I can buy the things I want.'
    b 'I must be able to put things in my basket.'
    c 'BasketTotal = (BasketTotal + ItemNumber)'
4. Describe the purpose of a user story.

5 Analysing data: Managing a project

139

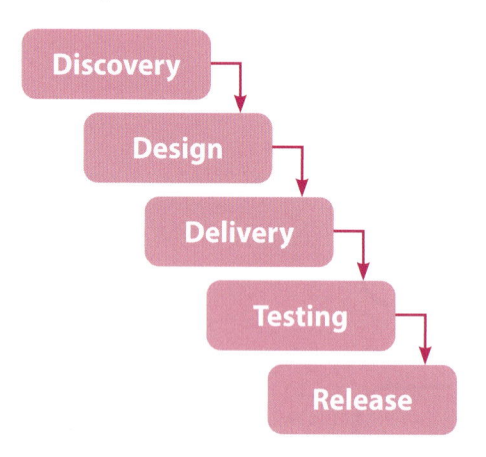

5.4 Plan a project timetable

You will learn:
- how to choose a method to deliver your project
- how to create a project timetable using a Gantt chart.

Key words

agile method
beta
feedback
kanban board
sprint
stand-up
waterfall method

Methods to deliver a project

The **waterfall** and **agile methods** are the two most common ways to deliver IT development projects. The choice that a project team makes affects how they will plan the delivery of their work.

The waterfall method

The waterfall method divides the project into phases that follow after each other. Project teams use this method when they have a clear understanding of the requirements before the work starts.

Phase	Description
Discovery	The team works with the users to create a list of requirements.
Design	The team designs the solution and plans the delivery phase.
Delivery	The team creates the solution.
Testing	The team and the users test the solution.
Release	The team gives the solution to the users to use.

The method is not very flexible. Each phase must be complete before the next starts. If a requirement changes during the delivery phase, it is difficult to return to the discovery phase to change it.

The agile method

The agile method is a more flexible way for teams to plan and manage their projects. This method helps project teams divide their work into smaller parts, called **sprints**. Sprints usually last about two weeks. A sprint includes the discovery and testing for all the work that the team is doing at the time.

Agile teams work together closely during sprints. They have a **stand-up** meeting every day, where they tell each other about their progress and their plans for the day. A project team will often use cards and sticky notes on whiteboards or walls to record their tasks and their progress. This is called a **kanban board**.

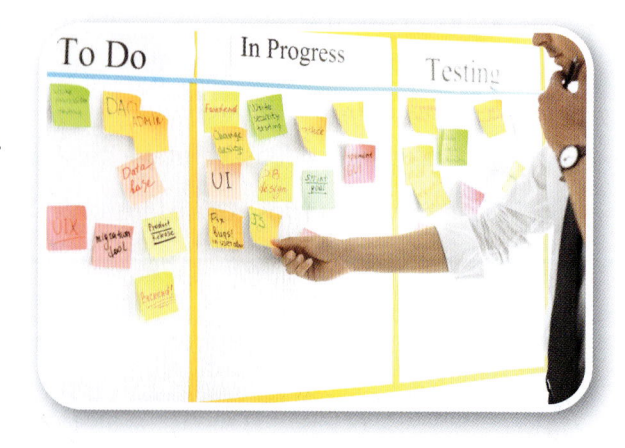

At the end of each sprint, the team can show their work to the users. This is called a show and tell. Sometimes they can release what they have delivered in the sprint to the public. When a project releases their work early like this, it is called a **beta** version. Beta versions of a product or service might not yet have all the functions. But users can expect that an improved version will soon arrive.

Project teams using the agile method can get regular **feedback** from their users. This helps the team to respond to feedback and changes in the requirements more easily and quickly.

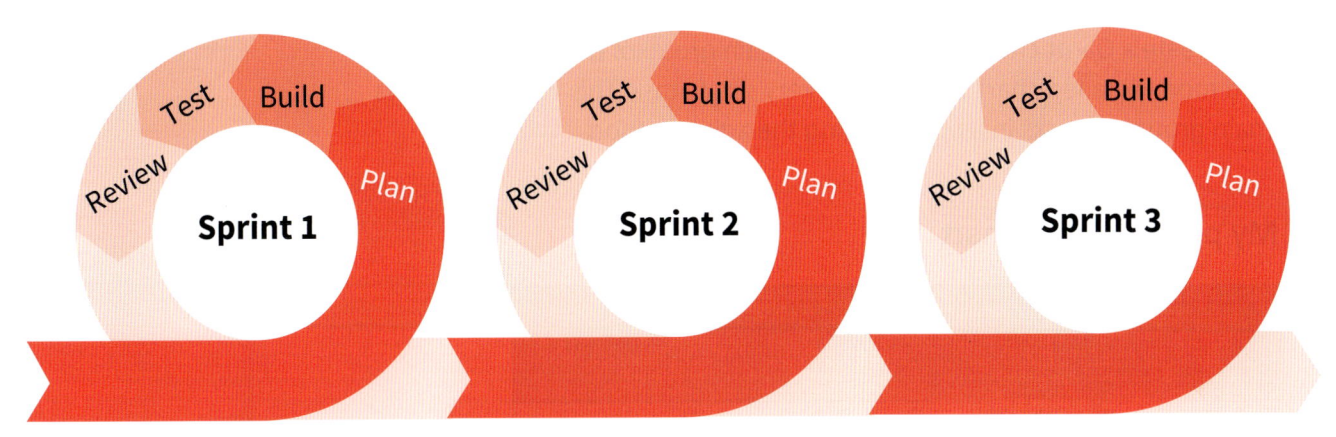

Choosing a method

Teams can choose the method they want to work with. There is no right or wrong choice. The team must choose the method they think fits best with their project and their team.

Here are some guidelines that teams can use to choose a method.

Choose waterfall if …	Choose agile if …
You are certain the requirements will not change.	You think that requirements could change.
Your project can be delivered in a short time.	Your project is likely to take a long time.
Your project team is not in one place or available at the same time.	You can bring the project team together in one place, at the same time, when needed.

A

Look back at the school lunch order application in 5.3. You will be planning the work involved in this project. Work in a small group. Discuss the agile and waterfall methods. Which would you use for this project?

5.4 Plan a project timetable

Create a Gantt chart

When your team has decided what method it will use to deliver the project, you can make a project timetable. Your project timetable shows each task that needs to be completed. It also shows when the tasks should start and end. You can use the timetable to track the project's progress.

One common way of making a project timetable is called a **Gantt chart**. A Gantt chart shows the project plan as a series of tasks on a timeline. Each task is shown as a bar on a graph.

You can create a Gantt chart that shows the main group of tasks, or you can create a more detailed chart that shows every single task. This example shows the main groups of tasks in a project using the agile method.

Key word
Gantt chart

My project Gantt chart

Project Name	Project duration (days)	Project start date	Project end date
The Cake Factory custom cake order system	33	03 June 2019	05 July 2019

Task ID	Task description	Task duration	Task start date	Task end date
1	Project start meeting	1	03 June 2019	03 June 2019
2	Planning workshop 1	1	04 June 2019	04 June 2019
3	Planning workshop 2	1	05 June 2019	05 June 2019
4	Sprint 1	14	06 June 2019	19 June 2019
5	Demo Sprint 1	1	20 June 2019	20 June 2019
6	Sprint 2	14	21 June 2019	04 July 2019
7	Demo & Release 'beta'	1	05 July 2019	05 July 2019

There are many specialist applications that help you plan projects. They can make Gantt charts from the data you enter. You can also create Gantt charts in a drawing program. The example in this lesson was created using a spreadsheet.

You can use the charts functions of a spreadsheet application to create Gantt charts from the data you enter.

A Gantt chart can be useful for different purposes.

▶ It helps you plan the order and the duration (length) of tasks by modelling the impact of changes in your project plan data.

▶ It helps you share the project plan with the project team in a way that is easy to understand.

▶ It helps you react to changes and delays. You can change the dates and durations and see how it affects your project timeline.

B

Your school has decided to develop the lunch order application. All the project tasks are listed in a Gantt chart.

Open the file for this lesson. It is a spreadsheet file containing a Gantt chart. Read the Gantt chart and answer these questions.

1. How many days will it take to develop the app?
2. What is the project end date?
3. What is the first task? How many days will it take?
4. How many days are allocated for testing?
5. Give all the dates when there will be user training.
6. The Gantt chart is incomplete. Use green shading to show the dates of Sprint 1 and Sprint 3.

Stretch zone

The business sponsor is concerned about the project costs. She wants you to reduce the number of days spent on the project by 10 per cent. Use the Lunch Gantt Chart to create a new timeline. Explain what changes you made and how you decided on them.

✓ Test

1. Put these three stages of the waterfall method in the right order.

   (Delivery)   (Release)   (Testing)

2. A Gantt chart lists the tasks in a project. What information does it show about each task?
3. What is a beta release of a product or service?
4. Write down three advantages of using a Gantt chart to plan a project timetable.

9:5.4 Lunch Gantt Chart: Digital Activity File

5 Analysing data: Managing a project

143

5.5 Work on an agile project

You will learn:
▶ how to plan an agile sprint
▶ how to use a kanban board to manage a project.

Key words

backlog
story point
story size
velocity

The backlog

In an agile project, the **backlog** is a to-do list. The list contains all the user stories that describe your project requirements.

Each agile sprint runs for a fixed period, usually two weeks. Before a sprint starts, the project team must decide which user stories to take from the backlog and put into the sprint. This decision is made in a sprint planning meeting.

Plan a sprint

In the sprint planning meeting, the project team looks at all the user stories. The team use three things to help them decide which stories to include in their sprint.

▶ The priority of the user story. Is it a must-have?

▶ The logical order of the user stories. Sometimes one story needs to be delivered before another. For example, the code to put an item in a basket cannot be written until the code for the basket has been developed.

▶ The amount of work that the user story will take to be developed. The team will estimate the amount of effort needed to deliver each story.

Size user stories

At a sprint planning meeting, the project team reviews each story that could go into the next sprint. They give each user story a **story size**. They use this size to decide if they can fit the story into the sprint. Story sizes are usually given in numbers, called **story points**. Story point numbers are used to estimate the difficulty of the story in comparison to other stories.

The project team discusses the story and the possible solutions they could deliver for it. Then they play a story sizing game to help them agree on a size number.

1. After discussing the story and the solutions, each member of the team picks a size number that they think best matches the difficulty of the story.

2. Every team member holds up their number. If all the numbers are the same, then that number becomes the story size. It is added to the user story card on the backlog.

3. If the numbers are different, then the team members each explain why they chose their number. After that, everyone picks a number again. The team repeats this step until everyone agrees on a final story point number.

Use velocity to fit stories into sprints

When the team agrees on all the story sizes, they can add stories from the backlog into the sprint. They add stories until they reach the total number of story points they can deliver in one sprint. This number is the team's **velocity**.

In the first sprint of a project, the team have to estimate their velocity. After this, they can add up the story points they completed in the previous sprint to find their velocity.

5.5 Work on an agile project

A

Open the worksheet for this lesson. It contains six user stories for the school lunch app project. Each story has been given a size in story points.

Working in small groups, play the story planning game. Choose the tasks for your first sprint. The total story points for all the tasks you choose must add up to no more than 12. Choose the tasks with the highest priority.

Work in sprints

A kanban board can be used to manage an agile project during a sprint. It shows what stage the user stories are in.

- Backlog: shows the user stories that are not yet started.
- In progress: shows the user stories that the team has started to work on in the sprint.
- In test: shows completed user stories that are being tested.
- Done (or complete): shows the user stories that are tested and ready to show to users.

You can use an online service or application to create a kanban board. You can also use a wall or any surface that has enough space to stick up your user story cards.

As each stage is completed, the card is moved to the next stage. This means that the project team can use the board to see how they are progressing. They can also use the board to plan their daily work.

Case study

The Cake Factory has made a kanban board to plan their online sales service. They used an online service called Trello.

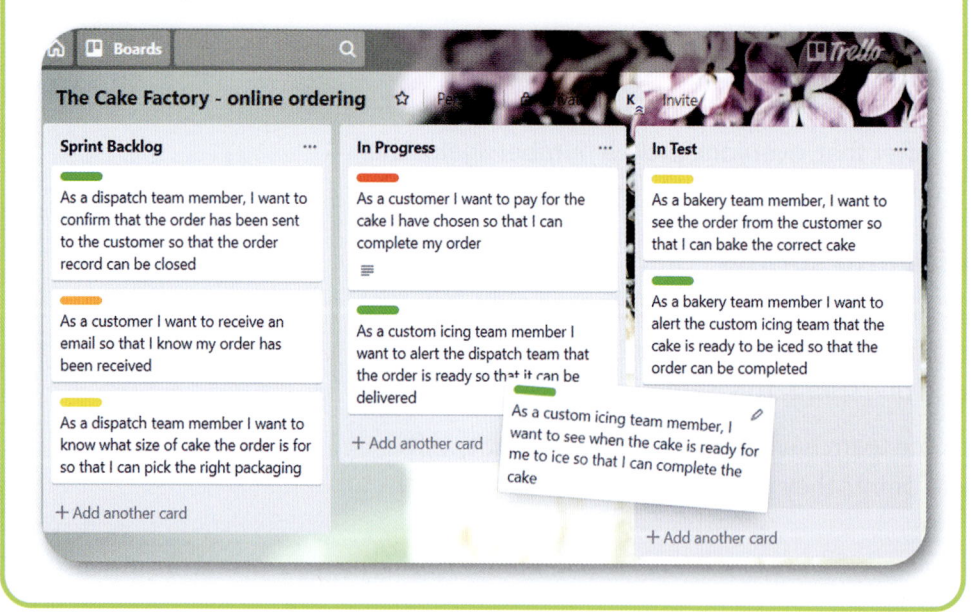

9:5.5 Story Planning Game: Digital Activity File

B

Make a kanban board using a computer application like Trello, or on paper. Take the activities that your team chose in the planning game. Choose two of the activities, one to be 'in progress' and the other to be 'in test'. Place the activities in the correct section of your kanban board.

Daily stand-ups

The daily stand-up is a short, daily meeting. It is called a 'stand-up' because it is so short that people do not need to sit down. It helps the team stay informed about the project and allows them to respond to changes in the plan if things go wrong or get delayed.

The team meets around the kanban board. Each team member says three things:

▶ what they achieved yesterday

▶ what they are planning to do today

▶ what problems, or 'blockers', might stop them from achieving their goals today.

Stretch zone

Carry out online research into how kanban boards are used in business. Software is available to help teams to make and use kanban boards. Do you prefer to use software or to make a real-life board with cards pinned to it?

✓ Test

1. What is the purpose of a daily stand-up meeting in an agile project?

2. Which of these columns would you find on a project's kanban board?

   (Recycle bin)   (Delay)   (In test)

3. Why do agile project teams play the story sizing game at the start of every sprint?

4. Explain how a project team can calculate its velocity at the end of a sprint.

5.6 Test and feedback

You will learn:
- how different types and levels of tests can be done at each stage of the project
- how a test scenario can help find problems and defects
- how positive and negative tests check how the system behaves.

Key words

scenario

test

test case

All digital projects must thoroughly **test** the products and services they create. The project team needs to know that its product or service works. It also needs to know that the users are happy with it. Different kinds of tests help to find this out.

Levels and types of testing

On larger projects, software testing is usually done by a specialist team. On smaller projects, members of the solution development team can do the tests. When the project team are happy with the quality of the product or service, they will invite a group of users to test it. The product or service cannot be released until it passes all these tests.

Levels of testing

Tests are carried out at different levels.

Unit testing

The team tests small parts of the product. In an agile project, a team can do unit tests during sprints.

↓

Integration testing

The team tests that two or more parts of the system, such as a website and a database of products, work together.

↓

System testing

The team tests the finished solution. For example, browsing a website, selecting a product, making a payment, receiving an email confirmation.

↓

Acceptance testing

The users test the product or service from end to end. They check that the product meets their requirements and that they agree it is ready to be released.

Types of test

At each level, the project team might decide to use different testing methods. This table shows the main types of test.

Test type	Purpose	Used in levels
Smoke testing (or build verification testing)	Tests for signs that the product is not working. Called smoke testing because smoke coming from a machine is a sign that something is wrong.	Unit, Integration
Functional testing	Tests that the product or service meets the functional requirements and specifications.	Unit, Integration, System, Acceptance
Usability testing	Tests if the system is easily usable.	Unit, Acceptance
Security testing	Tests to check the system is safe and data cannot be stolen.	Integration, System
Performance testing	Tests that measure how quickly the system responds to users. Does it crash or fail when busy?	Integration, System
Regression testing	Tests that any changes to the system work and do not cause new problems.	Unit, Integration, System
Compliance testing	Tests that the system meets any legal requirements.	System

Use scenarios to test

A **scenario** is a simulation of how a user would use the product or service. The test designer creates scenarios from the requirements and uses them to create a document called a **test case**.

A test case tells the testers what to do and how the system should respond. The testers follow the instructions and record if the system does something wrong or unexpected.

5.6 Test and feedback

> **Case study**
>
> The testing team at The Cake Factory have written a test case for their new online ordering service.
>
> **Test case:** Customer adds a customized birthday cake to their order
>
> | Test steps | Expected result | Actual result | Pass/Fail |
> |---|---|---|---|
> | 1 Select cake type from drop-down list | System displays three cake options. Cake options can be selected. Order price is updated. | As expected | P |
> | 2 Select 'Custom Icing' to add personal icing message | User can select 'Custom Icing' option only if 'Icing' option is NOT 'Chocolate'. System displays text entry box. | As expected | P |
> | 3 Enter message text | User can enter text up to 25 characters including spaces. User can NOT enter any special characters. | I was able to add characters # and % | F |

Key word

defect

Positive and negative tests

There are two types of test: positive and negative. A positive test checks how the system behaves when it is used correctly. For example, the test for entering the number of cakes could be to enter the numbers 1, 2 and 100 in the amount box. All of these values are valid.

A negative test checks how the system behaves when it is used incorrectly. The test case will ask the tester to deliberately add invalid data, such as 0, −10 or 'abcdefg' in the amount box.

The test designer will use a combination of positive and negative tests.

A

A tester is running a test on this 'Subscribe' box. Why have they entered the data for 'Name' and 'Email' shown in the image? Write some positive test data for each of the two fields.

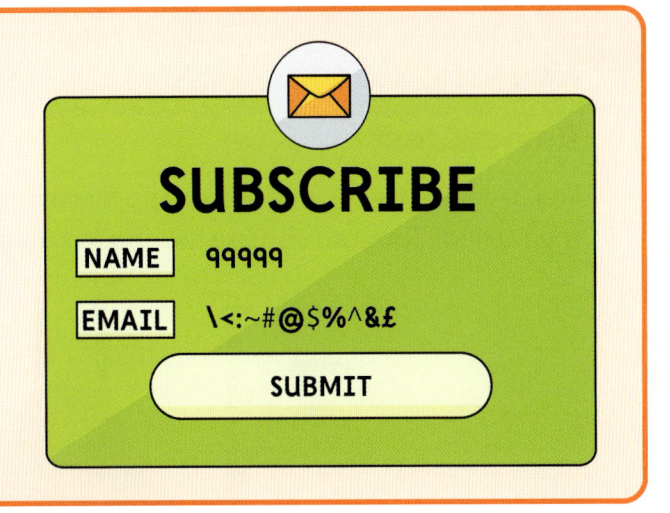

SUBSCRIBE
NAME 99999
EMAIL \<:~#@$%^&£
SUBMIT

Record defects

When a tester finds that the system behaves in a wrong or unexpected way, they record the behaviour as a **defect**. A defect is any behaviour that does not meet the requirements. At the end of the test, the list of defects is passed back to the solution developer to fix. When the defect is fixed, the tester repeats the test case to check that it now passes the test.

B

Open the worksheet for this lesson. Use the test cases table on the second sheet of the spreadsheet to perform the tests on the birthday calculator on the first sheet. Record any defects you find.

Stretch zone

Review the birthday calculator and its test cases. What other tests do you think could help the project team find errors in the app? Add one or more new test cases to the second sheet of the spreadsheet.

✓ Test

1. Explain why project teams must test their products or services.
2. What is a defect?
3. Which of these is not a type of software test?

   Positive test   Negative test   Indifferent test

4. Describe how a scenario can help a user test a system.

9:5.6 Software Testing: Digital Activity File

5 What have you learned?

Review test

You have been asked to make an app for students so they can see a list of after-school activities at their school. They can also use the app to sign up to an activity.

1 Is the work of developing the app business as usual or is it a project?

2 You will make the app. It will take five days to find out the information you need, three days to plan, and ten days to make the app. Think about today's date. If you start tomorrow and work every day, what day will you finish the work?

3 Give **three** items of information you need to find out before you can start making the app.

4 Write **two** software applications that you can use to help plan and manage the project.

5 In question 4, you identified two software apps to help manage the project. Give **one** example of how you would use each application.

6 Write **two** advantages of using software applications to create project documents compared to making the documents by hand.

Review activity

Open the worksheet for this lesson. It contains a half-completed Gantt chart called Tropical Beach Gantt Chart. In this activity, you will complete the chart.

Hana is the new IT project manager at the Tropical Beach Dive Shop. The dive shop wants to increase sales by offering a new online booking service. The service will allow customers to book a dive trip before travelling to Tropical Beach.

9:5.7 Tropical Beach Gantt Chart: Digital Activity File

Hana wants to start the project on 1 November. The team will need three sprints. Each sprint will be ten days. There will be a five-day acceptance test after the last sprint.

1. Open the Gantt chart. Use the chart to find answers to the following questions:
   - What is the start date of the project?
   - What is the end date of the project?
   - How many days does the project last?
   - How many tasks are there in the project?

2. The Gantt chart shows four tasks. Add the start and end dates for tasks 2, 3 and 4. Shade the cells to show the tasks in the Gantt chart.

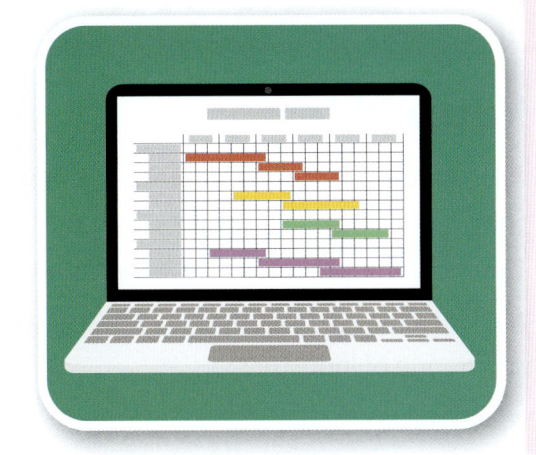

3. There will be a demo on the last day of every sprint. Write down the dates of the demos.

4. Hana needs to bring forward the project end date by five days. Change the Gantt chart to suggest a way of doing this that still leaves at least three days of acceptance testing.

Self-evaluation

How did you do?	What is your level?	What your level means
• I answered test questions 1 and 2. • I understand that people work in teams to complete projects that provide solutions to problems.	Developing	You have learned something new in this unit.
• I answered test questions 1 to 4. • I understand how IT applications help me work as a member of a team.	Secure	You have reached the expected standard in this unit.
• I answered all the test questions. • I can say how IT applications can improve the work of project teams.	Extending	You are an expert.

What next? To improve your level you can go back and repeat some of this unit.

6 Understanding technology: Inside the CPU

You will learn:

- about the three important parts of the central processing unit (CPU) and how they work together
- how computers can solve logic problems
- how the components of a robot combine to perform useful tasks in a range of industries.

A computer's processor (sometimes called the 'microprocessor') is at the centre of every computer system. The processor is responsible for all the work your computer does. It controls everything you see on screen. The processor is made up of millions of microscopic electronic switches.

In this unit, you are going to discover how the microscopic switches work. You will learn how improvements in processor technology have led to the development of robots across a range of industries.

Activity

Work in small groups to play a 'True' or 'False' game. Team A think of a secret object. Team B must work out what the object is by making statements that can be answered with either 'True' or 'False'.

For example:

Team A choose a lion as their secret object. They tell Team B the object is an animal.

Team B try to guess the object:

- Is a type of bird: False
- Has a mane: True
- Is a lion: True

The winner of each round is the team that discovers the secret object in the fewest guesses.

Learning outcomes: Use or describe simple electronic logic (for example, AND, OR and NOT gates); Outline the structure of the processor and the fetch-execute cycle; Discuss the hardware that enables robotics

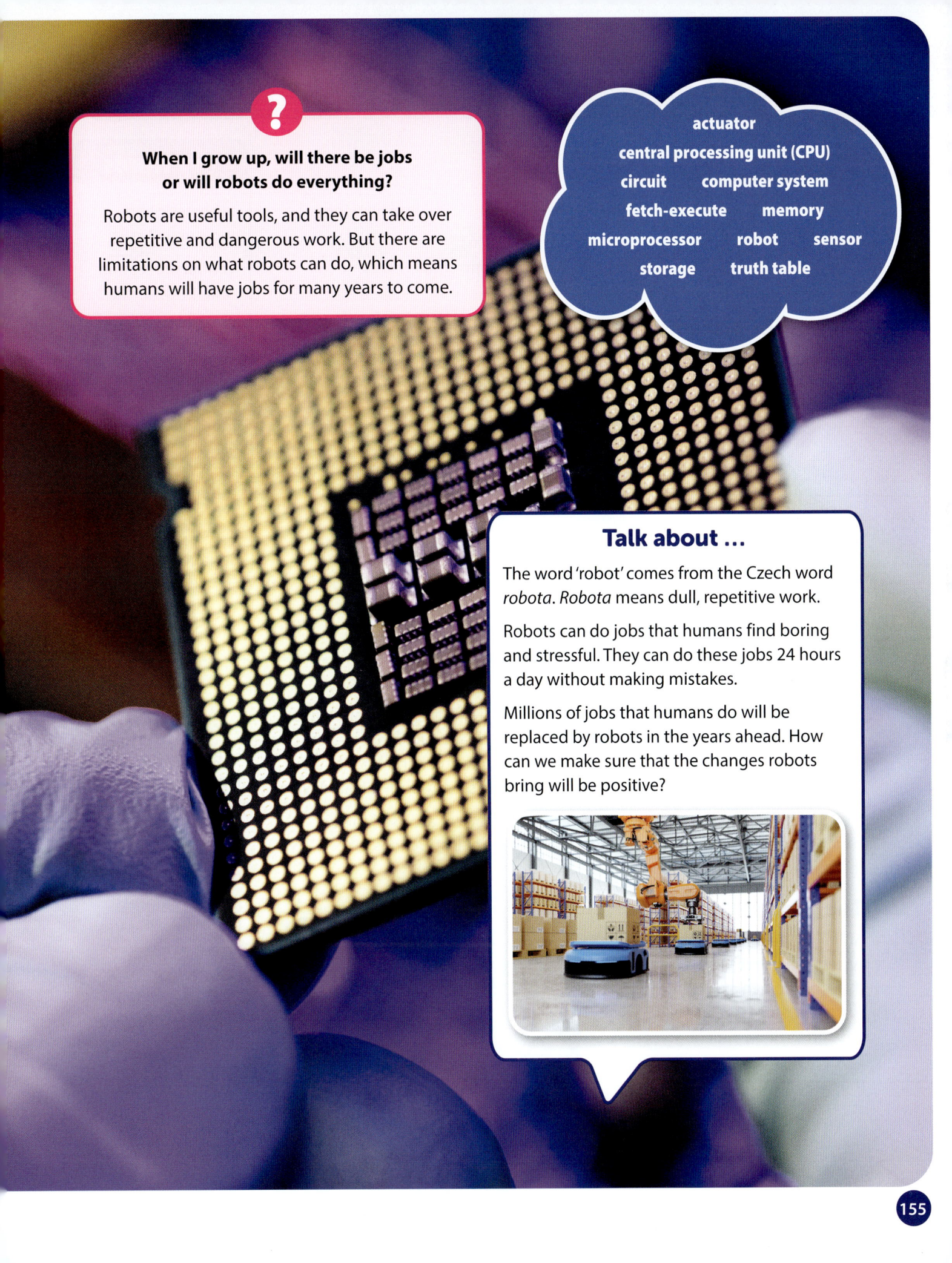

When I grow up, will there be jobs or will robots do everything?

Robots are useful tools, and they can take over repetitive and dangerous work. But there are limitations on what robots can do, which means humans will have jobs for many years to come.

> actuator
> central processing unit (CPU)
> circuit   computer system
> fetch-execute   memory
> microprocessor   robot   sensor
> storage   truth table

Talk about …

The word 'robot' comes from the Czech word *robota*. *Robota* means dull, repetitive work.

Robots can do jobs that humans find boring and stressful. They can do these jobs 24 hours a day without making mistakes.

Millions of jobs that humans do will be replaced by robots in the years ahead. How can we make sure that the changes robots bring will be positive?

6.1 The computer system

You will learn:
- about the parts of the central processing unit (CPU) and how they work together
- how computers can solve logic and arithmetic problems.

Computer systems

A **computer system** is a set of equipment that works together to help you do useful work. The system can be drawn as a simple diagram.

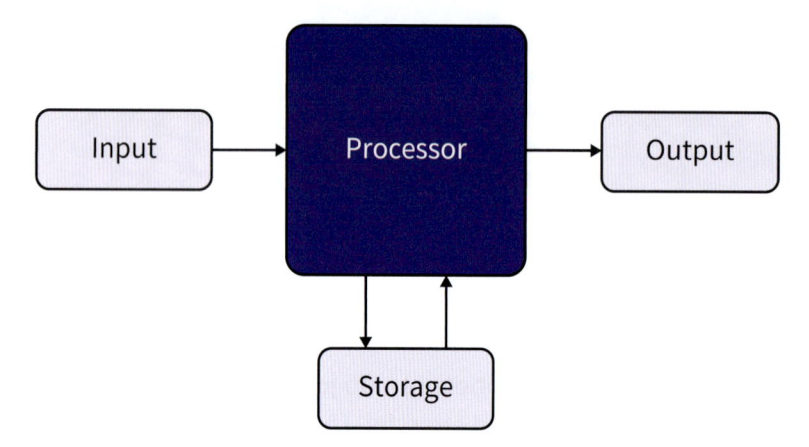

```
Input → Processor → Output
            ↕
         Storage
```

A computer system has **input devices** and **output devices**. Input devices allow data to be put into your computer. They convert information into digital data that can be processed by a computer. A keyboard is an input device. Output devices take digital data processed by the computer and turn it into a form humans can read and understand. A computer screen is an output device.

A computer system has **storage devices**. Storage devices are used to save your work and to store programs. Programs are lists of instructions for the computer.

The processor

At the centre of your computer system is a **processor**. A processor does the work in a computer system. A processor is small enough to fit on your fingertip. Modern processors are so small they are called **microprocessors**.

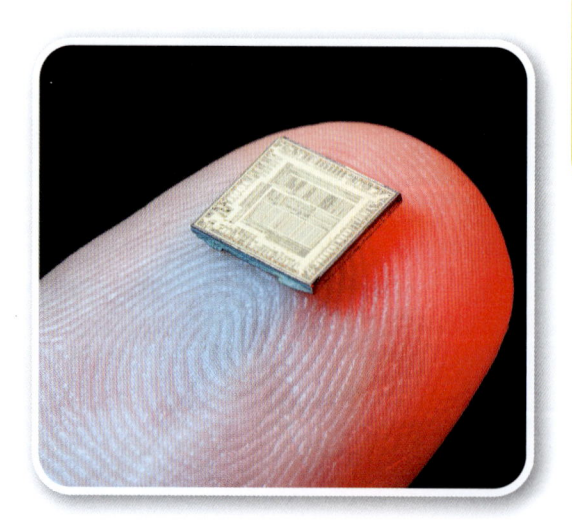

Key words

arithmetic and logic unit (ALU)
central processing unit (CPU)
clock
computer system
control unit
input device
microprocessor
output device
processor
storage device

Spiral back

In Book 7, you learned that every file a computer uses is made up of digital data. The brain of a computer is a microprocessor. Now you will learn how the processor does its work.

A

Draw a diagram of a computer system like the one on page 156. Write as many devices you can think of under the input, output and storage boxes in your diagram.

The central processing unit (CPU)

The **central processing unit (CPU)** is another name for the microprocessor at the centre of your computer system. It is the name to use when you study the computer processor in detail. The CPU has three important parts: the **control unit**, the **arithmetic and logic unit (ALU)**, and the **clock**.

The control unit

The control unit manages the work done by the CPU.

- ▶ When an instruction arrives at the CPU, it goes to the control unit.
- ▶ The control unit works out what the instruction means.
- ▶ The control unit makes sure that the other parts of the CPU do the work needed to carry out the instruction.

The arithmetic and logic unit (ALU)

The ALU does all the calculations in the CPU. If you are working on a maths problem, you might use a spreadsheet to do your calculation. The control unit uses the ALU in the same way. The control unit sends instructions to the ALU. The ALU carries out the instructions.

The clock

The CPU's clock sends out regular electrical pulses just like the tick of a clock. A clock in your home ticks once every second. The clock in the CPU of your computer ticks around 3 billion times every second. Every time the CPU clock ticks, the control unit sends an instruction to the ALU.

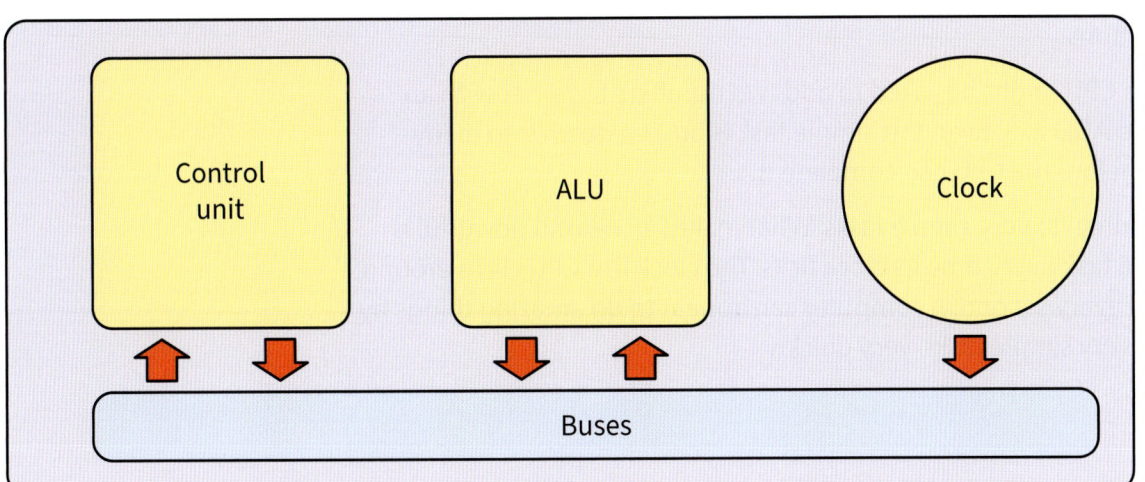

The CPU

Control unit | ALU | Clock

Buses

6.1 The computer system

Buses

The three parts of a CPU are joined together by connections called **buses**. Buses are high-speed connections that carry data around inside the CPU. They are like the buses you see travelling around towns and cities. Instead of carrying passengers, the buses in a CPU carry data at very high speed.

How the CPU works

Think about the last time you played a game on a computer. The screen is full of colour. The images you see are lifelike. Objects move just like they do in the real world.

On-screen movement is smooth and fast. If you are playing a game, you can give instructions through a joystick or game controller. The action on-screen responds immediately to your command. High-quality audio is being played while you play.

> **Key word**
> bus

When you play a game on a computer, it is easy to think that the CPU must be doing very complicated things. In fact, the CPU can perform only very simple instructions.

For example, a CPU might be asked to add two numbers together with an instruction like 'ADD 2, 3'. Even this simple task is broken down into many smaller tasks before the CPU can complete it.

So, a CPU can only do very simple tasks. What makes it seem so powerful is that it can do a task every time its clock ticks. The clock in a CPU clicks around 3 billion times every second. A computer can appear to do amazing things by doing a lot of very simple tasks, very quickly.

B

This activity will give you an idea of how fast a computer CPU does its work. You need two team members for this game, and somebody to time them. Read the instructions and make sure you understand them. Have a practice run.

Start the timer.

1. Team member A: Say an action: 'Add', 'Multiply' or 'Subtract'.
2. Team member B: Write down the action.
3. Team member A: Say a single-digit number (1 to 9).
4. Team member B: Write down the number.
5. Team member A: Say a single-digit number (1 to 9).
6. Team member B: Write down the number.
7. Team member A: Tell team member B to work out the answer to the sum.
8. Team member B: Work out the answer.
9. Team member B: Write down the answer.
10. Team member A: Read the answer out loud.

Stop the timer and note how many seconds the task took.

A CPU can carry out the same task 300 million times every second. Multiply the number of seconds it took you to complete the task by 300. That is the number of times (in millions) that a CPU would have done the task in the time it took your team to do it once.

Stretch zone

Three students worked together on Activity B. Explain which part of the CPU each team member represents in the activity.

Test

1. What are the three main parts of a CPU?
2. How does data move between the parts of a CPU?
3. Explain why a computer can seem to do very complicated tasks when its processor can only carry out simple operations.
4. Write two places that instructions for the CPU come from.

6.2 The fetch-execute cycle

You will learn:
- what computer memory is
- what happens when a computer carries out an instruction.

Key words
cloud storage
fetch-execute cycle
flash memory
hard disk drive (HDD)
memory
random access memory (RAM)
secondary memory
solid state drive (SDD)

Memory and the CPU

The CPU is the part of the computer that carries out instructions. The CPU contains a control unit, the ALU and a clock, all connected by fast links called buses.

Another component a computer needs is **memory**. Part of a computer's memory is called **random access memory (RAM)**. RAM is used to store the instructions and data the CPU needs to do its work. RAM is located close to the CPU. It is joined to the CPU by buses.

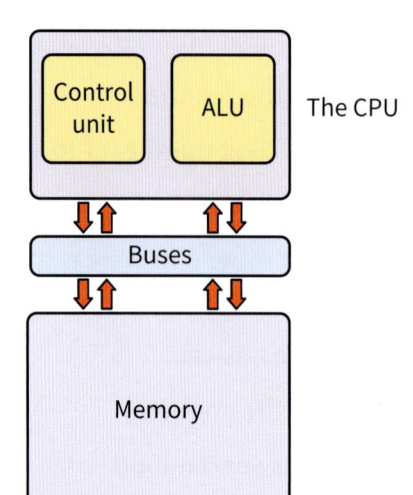

The CPU — Control unit, ALU, Buses, Memory

What is RAM for?

RAM holds:
- instructions that tell the computer what to do
- data that the computer uses in its work
- the result of each instruction, which the CPU sends back to memory when it has completed the instruction.

Memory and storage

RAM is made of microscopic electrical switches. The switches can be on or off. Everything inside the memory is stored using these on/off signals.

If the electricity to your computer is turned off, all the data in RAM will be lost. This is why you must always save your work before you turn the computer off. When you save your work, it is copied from memory to storage. Some examples of storage devices are:

- **hard disk drive (HDD)** or **solid state drive (SSD)**
- a **flash memory** drive
- the storage on your school network
- **cloud storage** on the internet.

A storage device keeps data even when the computer is turned off. That means that your work is not lost. Storage is also called **secondary memory**.

Advantages and disadvantages

Both RAM (electronic memory) and storage have advantages and disadvantages.

RAM is very close to the CPU. The CPU can get data and instructions from RAM quickly. But any data stored in RAM is lost when the computer is switched off. Also, RAM is quite small compared to secondary memory. It only stores what it needs to for the computer to do its work.

Secondary memory is further away from the CPU. It takes longer for the CPU to get data and instructions from secondary memory. But secondary memory can keep data and instructions safe when they are not needed, or when the computer is turned off.

> **A**
>
> Copy and complete this table to show the advantages and disadvantages of RAM and secondary memory. The first section is done for you.
>
> | | RAM | Secondary memory |
> |---|---|---|
> | **Advantages** | It is close to the CPU. The CPU can get data and instructions from RAM easily and quickly. | |
> | **Disadvantages** | | |

The fetch-execute cycle

The CPU carries out instructions millions or even billions of times a second. Every time it carries out an instruction, it follows these steps.

▶ **Fetch:** The control unit 'fetches' an instruction from RAM. The instruction travels down the bus from RAM to the control unit. The computer might also need to fetch some data from RAM.

▶ **Decode:** The instruction is in the form of a binary number code. The control unit knows all the binary number codes. The control unit 'decodes' the instruction, so it knows what to do.

▶ **Execute:** The control unit sends a signal to the ALU to tell it what to do. The ALU carries out the instruction. 'Execute' means carry out an instruction.

▶ **Save:** If the instruction produces a result, then the ALU sends the result back to RAM.

These steps are called the **fetch-execute cycle**.

6.2 The fetch-execute cycle

You have created programs in Python. Here is a single command written in Python.

```
answer = 2 + 3
```

To carry out this instruction, the computer must complete at least one fetch-execute cycle.

> **Key word**
> cache

- **Fetch:** The control unit fetches the instruction (add) and the data values (2, 3) from RAM.
- **Decode:** The control unit decodes the instruction and sends a signal to the ALU, telling it to add the numbers together.
- **Execute:** The ALU carries out the instruction, and adds the two numbers together.
- **Save:** The ALU sends the result of the addition back to RAM. The result is saved in a memory location with the label 'answer'.

Fetch-execute diagram

You can draw the fetch-execute cycle using a simple diagram like this.

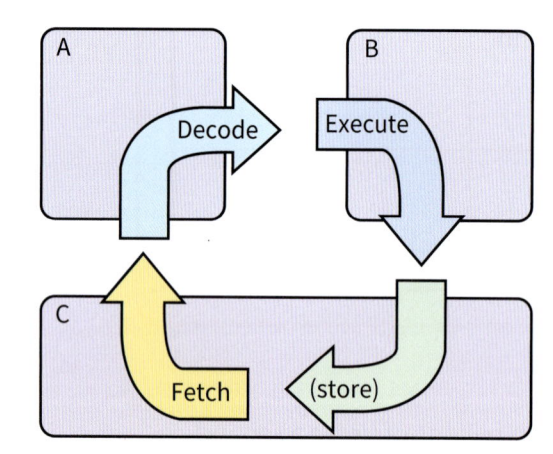

A — Decode → B — Execute ↓
C ← Fetch — (store) ←

> **B**
>
> The parts of the fetch-execute cycle happen in different places:
> - in memory
> - in the control unit
> - in the ALU.
>
> Draw the diagram of the fetch-execute cycle. Instead of letters A, B and C, put the name of the place where each part of the cycle happens.

Memory and computer speed

In the last lesson, you learned that the speed of the clock affects the speed of the computer. But the size of memory is also important.

RAM

If a computer has lots of RAM, then more data and instructions can fit into the memory. The CPU can get the data and instructions very quickly. If a computer does not have very much memory, then the data and instructions will not all fit into memory. Some will have to wait in storage. The computer will run more slowly.

Cache size

The CPU has a small amount of memory that is even closer than RAM. This is called **cache**. It is very quick for the CPU to get data and instructions from cache. If a computer has a big cache, then it will be able to get more data and instructions quickly. It will run faster.

Stretch zone

A friend wants to buy a fast computer. Write an email telling them what to look out for when they choose a computer. One factor is clock speed, but there are others. Tell your friend about some other factors that affect the speed of a computer. Explain why each one is important.

✓ Test

1. What is the difference between memory and storage?
2. List the four stages of the fetch-execute cycle.
3. Describe what happens during the 'execute' stage of the fetch-execute cycle, and where it happens.
4. Explain why a computer with lots of RAM will run faster than a similar computer with less RAM.

6.3 The computer and logic

You will learn:
- how a computer processes logical problems
- how to write a logical argument
- how to draw a truth table.

Key word

logical statement (argument)

Arithmetic and logic

When you play a computer game, you see the result of the ALU performing arithmetic. For example, the strength of your character increases when you pick up energy. A value is added to your existing strength total.

A game would not be interesting if it only used arithmetic. A game must also include challenges. For example:

- Does the treasure chest contain gold coins?
- Does the key open the treasure chest?

Challenges like these cannot be solved using arithmetic. They need logic.

What is logic?

Think about the statement 'the treasure chest contains gold'. There are two possible situations. The statement can be true or false. 'The key opens the treasure chest' is a logical statement. A **logical statement (argument)** is used to say if something is True or False. (In this course, 'True' and 'False' start with a capital letter when we refer to Boolean logic. See page 120 of this book for more about Boolean logic.).

> **A**
>
> 'It is raining' is a logical statement. It could be True or False. Write two more logical statements about the weather.

Logic and the ALU

The computer is a digital device. A computer processor is made up of electrical switches. The electrical switches in a computer can be on or off. A computer is called a two-state device.

Logic also has two states. The two states are True and False. A logical statement can be True or it can be False. A computer's ALU can process logical statements. It can do so because both logic and the computer use two states.

OFF	ON	ON	OFF	ON	OFF
0	1	1	0	1	0

In a computer, we use binary to show the state of a switch. A '1' is used to say a switch is 'on'. A '0' says a switch is 'off'. We can also use binary to show the state of a logical statement. A '1' can be used to show a statement is True. A '0' can be used to show it is False.

Linking logical statements

Logical statements can also be used to draw conclusions from data and make decisions. To use logic to draw conclusions, you must be able to combine logical statements.

Here are two logical statements about a computer game:

▶ Player has no lives.

▶ Game is over.

Each of the two statements can either be True or False. You can link the two logical statements using the words IF and THEN:

▶ IF Player has no lives THEN Game is over.

When two statements are linked, they can be used to draw conclusions. We can say:

▶ IF 'Player has no lives' is True THEN 'Game is over' is also True.

▶ IF 'Player has no lives' is False THEN 'Game is over' is also False.

> **B**
>
> When have you used logical statements while learning computing skills? Write down any occasions you can think of. For each, give an example of the logical statements you have used.

Parts of a logical statement

To make it easier to talk about logic, the two parts of a linked statement have names. In a logical statement, everything between the IF and the THEN is called the proposition. Everything after the THEN is called the conclusion. The whole statement is called a logical argument.

	Proposition		Conclusion
IF	Player has no lives	THEN	Game is over

165

6.3 The computer and logic

C

Activity A used 'It is raining' as an example of a logical statement. This statement is used as a proposition in the table below. The conclusion 'Umbrella is opened' has been linked to the statement. Now we can say that if 'It is raining' is True, then 'Umbrella is opened' is also True.

	Proposition		Conclusion
IF	It is raining	THEN	Umbrella is opened

In Activity A, you wrote two more logical statements about the weather. Copy the table. Write a conclusion to match each of the propositions you wrote.

Key word
truth table

Truth tables

A **truth table** is a way of laying out a logical statement in table form. It makes it easier to understand the logic. A written description can be confusing, especially for complex logical statements.

There are four steps in creating a truth table.

1   **Write out the argument.** Write IF and THEN in upper-case letters to show how the statements are linked: IF Player has no lives THEN Game is over

2   **Create the column headings.** Your table needs a column for each statement in your argument. There are only two statements in this example but there can be more. Write the conclusion in the last column on the right. There is no need to use IF or THEN in your table.

3   **Add a row for every possible response to the proposition.** In this example, the proposition is 'Player has no lives'. There can only be two responses: False or True.

Player has no lives	Game is over
False	
True	

4 **Complete the conclusion column.** Fill in the correct value for each possible response to the proposition.

Player has no lives	Game is over
False	False
True	True

In this example, we have used logic to show that when a player has no lives in a game, then the game is over. Logic also shows that when the statement 'Player has no lives' is False, then 'Game is over' is also False. While you have lives, you can keep playing.

D

1. Create a logical statement in the same form as the example. You might use an example based on a computer game you play. You might choose a sport or hobby you enjoy.
2. Now draw the truth table for your statement.

Stretch zone

The logic described in this lesson is sometimes called Boolean logic. You saw in Unit 4 that the name 'Boolean' comes from the inventor of modern logic, George Boole. Use the internet to find two facts about George Boole and his life.

✓ Test

1. Put these terms in the order they appear in a logic argument:

   THEN   conclusion   proposition

2. What are the two states used in logic?
3. What two types of operation can an ALU do? Give an example of each.
4. Say why a computer's ALU can process logic problems.

6.4 Complex logical statements

You will learn:
- ▶ how to link logical statements using AND/OR
- ▶ to write logical arguments with more than two statements.

Increasing complexity

In the last lesson, you learned that computers can perform logic operations as well as arithmetic. You saw how a simple problem can be written as a logical statement like this one:

IF Player has no lives THEN Game is over.

All the examples in the previous lesson had just two parts linked by a THEN statement.

In this lesson, you will learn how to use logic to describe situations where there are more parts to the logical argument. Here is an example. Your local football club want to sign a new star player. The manager has asked the team owner to sign a player who scored 30 goals last season. The manager also wants the player to be left-footed. Here are the key points:

- ▶ Club signs player.
- ▶ Player is left-footed.
- ▶ Player scored 30 goals.

Using AND to link logical statements

The team manager writes the problem as a logical statement. He will hand the team owner a truth table to make sure the right player is found. He will use the four stages described in 6.3.

1. **Write out the argument.** The first step is to identify the conclusion. There is only ever one conclusion to a logical argument. The conclusion is a desired outcome. In this case, the conclusion is 'Club signs player'.

   Once you have identified the conclusion, any other statements are part of the proposition. In this case, there are two statements: 'Player is left-footed', 'Player scored 30 goals'.

   The two statements must be joined together. Statements in the proposition can be joined using AND or OR. In this case, the manager wants both statements to be True. If both statements must be True, join them with AND.

   IF Player is left-footed AND Player scored 30 goals THEN Club signs player.

2. **Create the column headings.** In this example, the table must have three columns. The conclusion must always go in the column on the far right of the table.

Player is left-footed	Player scored 30 goals	Club signs player

3. **Add a row for every possible response to the proposition.** A two-part statement always needs the four responses in the table below. Read them carefully. Make sure you understand that no combination of True/False is missed out.

Player is left-footed	Player scored 30 goals	Club signs player
False	False	
False	True	
True	False	
True	True	

4. **Complete the conclusion column.** The two parts of the proposition are joined by AND. This means that the conclusion will be True only if both parts of the proposition are True.

Player is left-footed	Player scored 30 goals	Club signs player
False	False	False
False	True	False
True	False	False
True	True	True

The final table tells us that 'Club signs player' is True only when both 'Player is left-footed' AND 'Player scored 30 goals' are True. If either of the statements is False, then 'Club signs player' is also False.

6.4 Complex logical statements

A

Sonia wants to buy her mother a present. She wants to buy a blue vase. She has $5 saved for the present. She sees a vase in a shop window.

Write a logical argument and truth table to determine if she can buy the vase.

Using OR to link logical statements

Here is a different kind of problem. An extra life is awarded in a computer game if the player reaches 10,000 points or collects five stars during a game. In this example, use the word OR to join the statements together. It will look like this:

IF 10,000 points reached OR five stars collected THEN extra life awarded.

A truth table will help to make sense of this statement. 'Player gets extra life' is True if either '10,000 points reached' OR 'Five stars collected' is True. The completed table looks like this:

10,000 points reached	Five stars collected	Player gets extra life
False	False	False
False	True	True
True	False	True
True	True	True

Notice that the True and False entries are the same as in the previous example. If you replace False with a 0 and True with a 1, you will have the binary numbers 00, 01, 10, 11. In decimal, that is 0, 1, 2 and 3. That may help you remember how to write the True and False entries into the table.

The table can be used to draw conclusions. The table tells you that if a player reaches 10,000 points or gathers five stars, they get an extra life in the game. Also, the player gets an extra life if both 10,000 points are reached, and five stars are collected.

B

A building is equipped with smoke sensors and heat sensors. If either sensor is triggered, an alarm must sound so that the building can be cleared. Write a logical argument and truth table to describe this system.

Think maths

How are truth tables similar to Venn diagrams? Could you display the information in a truth table in a Venn diagram?

Stretch zone

A bank is equipped with a high-security safe. To open the safe:

- a key must be turned in a lock
- a personal identification number (PIN) must be entered
- the alarm must be turned off.

Draw a truth table for this system. Your table will need eight rows.

Test

Complete the missing word in questions 1 and 2.

1. IF Mark 40% or greater _____ Work handed in on time THEN Student gains pass.
2. IF Sun is shining _____ It is raining THEN Wear a hat.
3. How many combinations of True/False are there for a logical argument with three parts to the proposition? (For example, IF a AND b AND c THEN d.)
4. What is the maximum number of conclusions in a complex logical argument?

6.5 Logic gates

You will learn:
- how to describe the AND, OR and NOT logic gates used in a computer
- how to draw truth tables for logic gates
- how computer logic gates compare to logic in the real world.

Key words
AND gate
gate
NOT gate
OR gate

A computer can carry out complicated tasks such as creating realistic game worlds. It can navigate spacecraft through space. How is this possible when a computer is only made up of switches that can be turned on or off?

The switches can be combined into larger units called **gates**. Gates allow electrical signals to pass through, but only if they meet certain conditions. In this lesson, you will learn about three types of gate:

- the **AND gate**
- the **OR gate**
- the **NOT gate**.

You have learned that logical statements using AND and OR can be used to describe situations we come across in everyday life and in computer games. Now you will learn how the computer's ALU uses logic gates to control programs such as games.

The AND gate

You have learned how using AND in logical statements can describe problems. For example, you drew a truth table for the logical argument:

IF Player is left-footed AND Player scored 30 goals THEN Club signs player.

Imagine you are writing a football manager game. How will the computer running the game make sure the manager signs the right player?

The CPU is made up of millions of on-off switches. Those switches are organized into larger units called gates. One of those gates is the AND gate. Each type of gate that a computer uses has its own symbol. The symbol for the AND gate is shown in the image.

The AND gate has two inputs. They are called A and B. The gate is part of a digital device so it can only understand binary. The value of each input can be either 0 or 1. The output of an AND gate is 1 if both input A and input B are 1. Otherwise it is 0.

You can draw truth tables for gates in the same way that you drew them for logical statements. Use 0 and 1 instead of True and False.

The truth table for an AND gate looks like this:

A	B	Output
0	0	0
0	1	0
1	0	0
1	1	1

Check that you understand why the pattern of zeros and ones is as it appears in the table.

The output of an AND gate is only 1 when both input A **and** input B are 1.

The pattern of zeros and ones in the AND gate truth table is exactly the same as the pattern of True and False in the truth table for the AND logical statement. That is how the CPU is able to use gates to carry out logical operations.

The OR gate

Another type of gate the computer uses is an OR gate. The OR gate has its own symbol too.

The OR gate has two inputs, A and B. It has one output. The value of each input can be either 0 or 1. The output of an OR gate is 1 if either input A or input B or both is 1.

The truth table for the OR gate looks like this. It is exactly the same as the OR truth table you saw in 6.4. Because of this, the CPU is able to use the OR gate to perform logic.

6.5 Logic gates

The truth table for an OR gate looks like this:

A	B	Output
0	0	0
0	1	1
1	0	1
1	1	1

Check that you understand why the pattern of zeros and ones in the output column is as it appears in the table.

Key word

circuit

The NOT gate

Other gates are used in a computer. They help us get the answers we need. A NOT gate has only one input and one output. A NOT gate reverses the input. If the input is 1, the output is 0. If the input is 0, the output is 1.

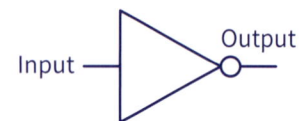

The truth table for a NOT gate looks like this:

A	Output
0	1
1	0

Gates always have only one output. Most gates have two inputs: only the NOT gate has one input.

A

Download and complete the Logic Gate Truth Tables worksheet for this lesson.

Circuits

In this lesson, you have learned about the AND gate and OR gate. You have seen that they can be used by the ALU to solve logic problems. That is because they act in the same way as logic statements in the real world.

Gates become more powerful and more useful when they are joined together. When gates are joined together, they form a **circuit**. Here is a simple circuit.

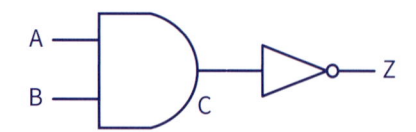

9:6.5 Logic Gate Truth Tables: Digital Activity File

To create a truth table for a circuit, you must create a column for every input and output. You must include any connections that link two gates. In this example, there are two inputs to the left of the circuit (A and B) and an output on the right (Z). You also need a column for C, which is both the output of the AND gate and the input to the NOT gate.

First, enter all the possible values for the inputs, A and B. Then enter the values for column C. This is the output of the AND gate. Finally, enter the values for column Z, using the values in column C as the input.

A	B	C	Z
0	0	0	1
0	1	0	1
1	0	0	1
1	1	1	0

B

Draw the truth table for this simple circuit.

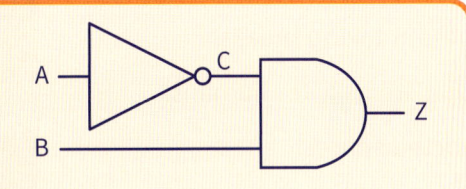

Stretch zone

Other logic gates used in computers include the NOR gate and the NAND gate. Research the web to find out about these two gates. Draw the symbol and a truth table for each of them.

Test

1. How many outputs does a logic gate have?
2. Describe what a NOT gate does.
3. When does an OR gate give an output of 1? Explain your answer using a truth table.
4. The shapes of the AND, OR and NOT gate symbols have something in common. What is it? Why do you think they share that shape?

6.6 Robots in the real world

You will learn:
- what robots are used for
- about the technology used in robots.

Key word

robot

What is a robot?

A **robot** is a machine that is designed and programmed to carry out tasks quickly and accurately. A robot is autonomous. This means it can work independently without human intervention. A robot senses and responds to its environment.

Features of robots

- Robots carry out repetitive work without getting bored or making mistakes.
- Robots work quickly, without taking breaks.
- Robots work in places that are risky for humans.
- Robots can work in restricted spaces.
- Robots work with dangerous chemicals and materials.

How are robots used?

Robots are vital tools in many industries. The car and electronics industries already depend on robots. The range of jobs that robots are used for is growing as robot design improves.

Robots in manufacturing

In manufacturing, robots do repetitive jobs such as soldering electrical components or making microprocessors. Accuracy is very important in the production of microprocessors. A tiny mistake can mean the processor does not work properly. A human might make a mistake when they get tired. Robots do not get tired.

Robots in agriculture

Agriculture is one of the fastest growing areas for robots. Robots can be used in glasshouses and out in the fields. Crop spraying by plane is one of the most dangerous jobs humans do. Robots are now used to spray crops. Robots are being developed to harvest crops including soft fruits like berries.

Some farmers drive tractors guided by satellites to plough fields. Fully autonomous machinery will soon be a feature on farms to plough, harvest and care for crops.

Robots in medicine

Surgeons work with robotic surgical instruments to perform surgery they could not do with their own hands. This means that surgery can take less time and patients recover faster.

Robotic equipment is used to scan patients to create a detailed 3D image of internal organs. This helps doctors to make an early and accurate diagnosis of illness. A robot has been developed that lifts a patient in and out of bed. It is more comfortable for the patient and saves nurses from injury.

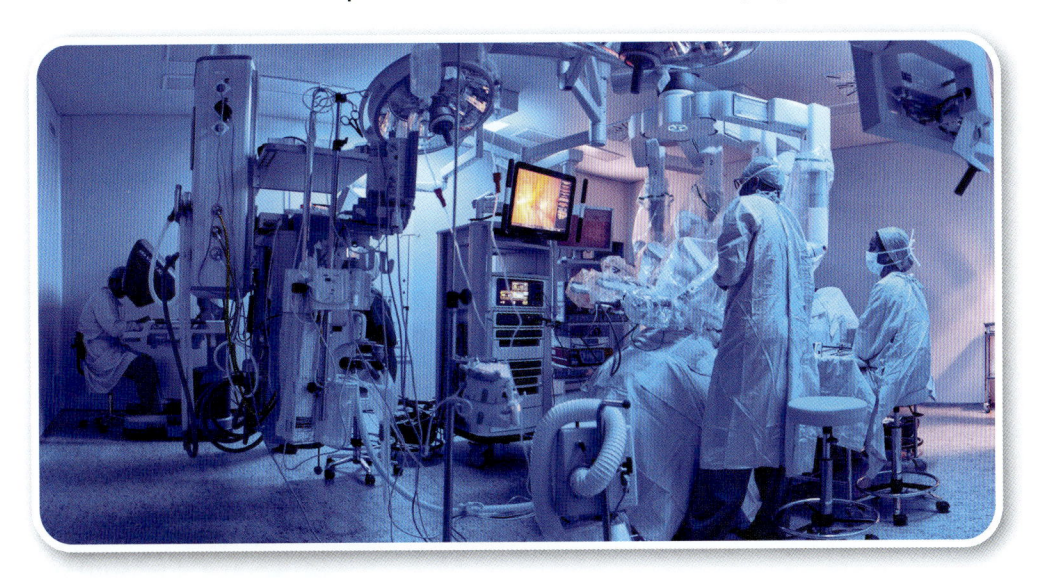

Robots in distribution

Distribution centres store goods that are sent out to shops or to customers who have purchased them online. Robots are used to collect the goods that are to be sent to shops and customers. Distribution centres use drones and autonomous robot vehicles to deliver goods like medicines to remote areas quickly.

Disaster recovery

Natural and man-made disasters create dangerous environments for humans to work in. Buildings might be damaged and unstable. Areas might be polluted with chemicals or radioactive material. Fires might break out. Robots are ideal for this situation. They have sensors to help assess dangers. Infrared sensors can help detect people that need to be rescued.

A

Choose one of the industries described above where robots are used. Do research on the web to find out more about the jobs robots do in this industry.

6.6 Robots in the real world

The parts of a robot

There are three main parts in a robot.

- ▶ **Sensors** are used to get information from the world that the robot operates in.
- ▶ **Actuators** are the motors that make the parts of the robot move.
- ▶ The **controller** is the microprocessor that controls the robot. It receives signals from the sensors, just like our brain gets messages from our eyes and ears. It sends messages to the actuators telling the robot how to respond to the situation detected by the sensors

The technology of robots

The growth of robots has depended on the advances in technology. Some key technologies robots depend on are:

Sensors

To be autonomous and act independently, robots must be able to sense the world around them.

- ▶ Proximity sensors use infrared light beams to detect the position of nearby objects.
- ▶ Bumper switches tell a robot that it has hit something.
- ▶ Pressure pads are used to control robot hands as they pick objects up. They stop the robot hand crushing objects.

There have been important new developments in recent years.

Vision-guided robotics (VGR) allows robots to use video cameras to see in 2D and 3D. Sophisticated software allows a robot to identify objects and interact with them. In older robot systems, items had to be in the right position for the robot to pick up and use.

Voice recognition and **natural language processing (NLP)** are giving robots a sense of hearing. In time, we might be able to speak and give complex instructions to a robot and it will be able to understand and carry them out immediately.

Microprocessor development

Microprocessors have become smaller and more powerful. This has allowed powerful processors to be embedded into robots.

Key words

actuator

controller

natural language processing (NLP)

sensor

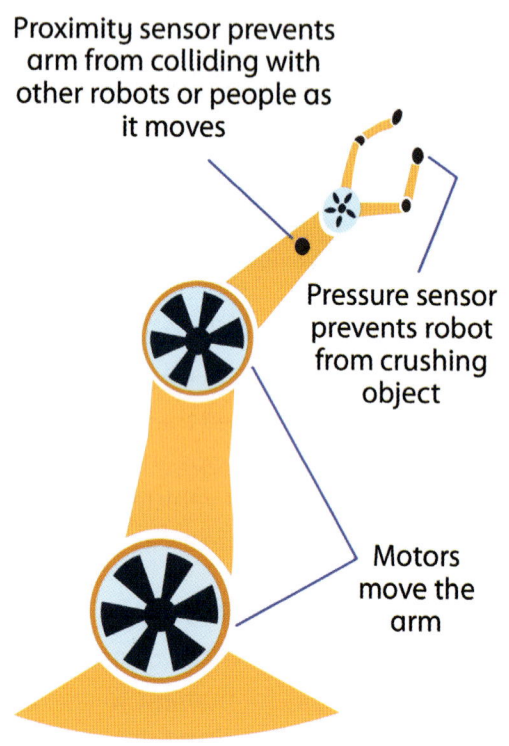

vision-guided robotics (VGR)

voice recognition

Proximity sensor prevents arm from colliding with other robots or people as it moves

Pressure sensor prevents robot from crushing object

Motors move the arm

Embedded processors are important. They allow the robot to carry the processing power they need with them.

Parallel processing uses several CPUs working together to create faster, more powerful processors. Two, four or even eight CPUs work together to control sophisticated robots.

Artificial intelligence

Artificial intelligence (AI) means using computers to make decisions almost as if they are able to think for themselves. Robotics is a major area of research in AI. AI allows robots to learn and improve the way they do jobs without human input.

Real-time operating systems (RTOS)

RTOS have been developed to allow robots to work safely in the real world. RTOS run many jobs at the same time. If an important job starts, it is given all the processing power it needs. For example, if the RTOS detects a possible collision, the process that avoids collision is given all the processing it needs. Other jobs stop until it is safe for them to restart.

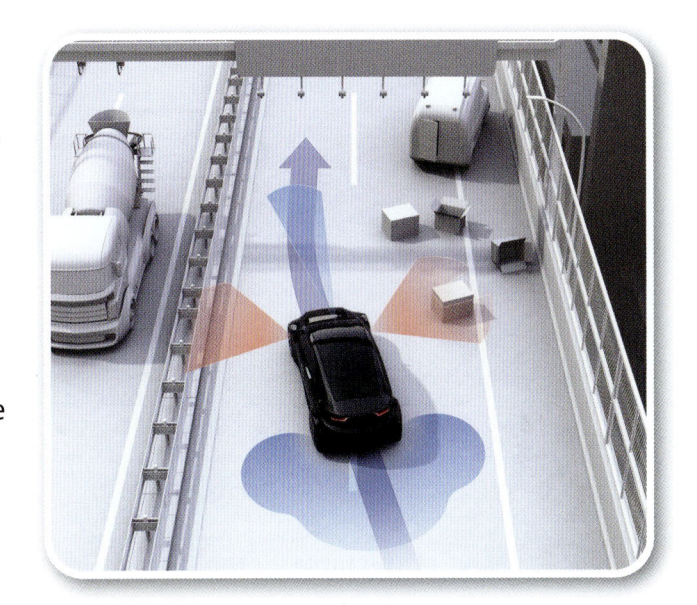

B

Design a robotic assistant to work alongside your school technician. What jobs will the robot be used for? What sensors and technology will it use? What are some of the risks and challenges (for example, busy corridors, stairs and doors)? If you have time, sketch your robot.

Stretch zone

An autonomous car drives itself with no human control. Would you feel comfortable being driven around town in an autonomous car? Write down the arguments for and against.

✓ Test

1 Describe how robots can help doctors.
2 What are the advantages of using robots in manufacturing?
3 Say two ways that sensors allow computers to sense the world around them.
4 Say how artificial intelligence can improve the way robots operate.

6 What have you learned?

Review test

1 This is a diagram of a computer system. Draw this diagram and add the following labels in the right place.

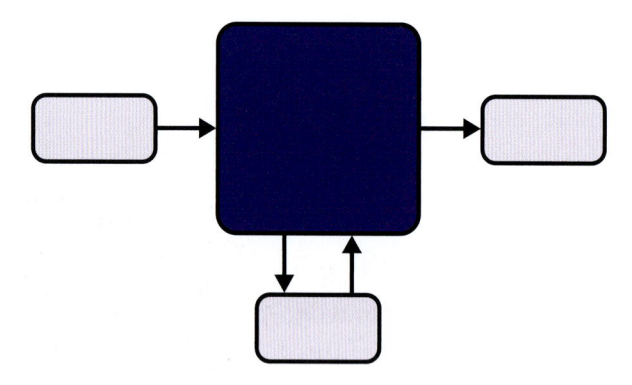

- Processor
- Input
- Output
- Storage

2 Draw a diagram of an OR gate.

3 Draw a truth table for the OR gate you drew in question 2.

4 This diagram shows the parts of a processor, plus the memory. Copy the diagram and add the following labels.

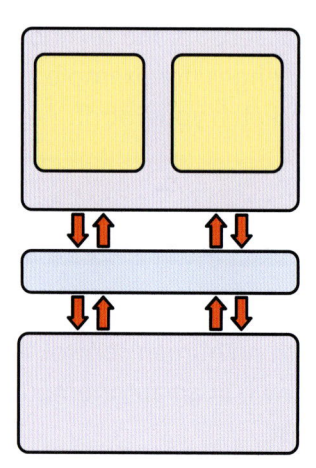

- CPU
- Memory
- ALU
- Control unit
- Buses

5 Describe **one** way you can improve the performance (speed) of a computer.

6 Draw a simple circuit made of an AND gate followed by a NOT gate. Draw the truth table for the circuit.

Review activity

Write a report about the use of robots in an industry or profession. For example, manufacturing, agriculture or medicine.

1. Describe some of the ways that robots are used in the industry you have chosen.
2. Say what developments in technology have led to greater use of robots in the industry.
3. Choose one of the technologies you described in activity 2. Give examples of how that technology has made robots more useful.

Self-evaluation

How did you do?	What is your level?	What your level means
• I answered test questions 1 and 2. • I described how robots are used in industry.	Developing	You have learned something new in this unit.
• I answered test questions 1 to 4. • I described developments in robot technology.	Secure	You have reached the expected standard in this unit.
• I answered all the test questions. • I gave examples of how a new technology has made robots more useful.	Extending	You are an expert.

What next? To improve your level you can go back and repeat some of this unit.

7 Creating web content: Use JavaScript

You will learn:

▶ to make a website that includes interactive buttons and a drop-down menu

▶ to make a web page that responds to user input by changing text and images

▶ to write JavaScript commands and functions for your web page.

In this unit, you will create web pages that respond to user input. Most modern web pages allow you to click buttons and use menus that change what you see on the site. These are called interactive or responsive websites. The JavaScript language is used to add these features to websites. In this unit, you will learn to write simple functions in the JavaScript language.

Activity

In the first three lessons of this unit, you will make a web page that shows flash cards. Flash cards have a question or challenge on one side, and the answer on the other side. Use paper or card to create a set of flash cards. Here are some ideas:

▶ Maths quiz, with maths questions on one side, and the answers to the questions on the other.

▶ Language quiz, with the language you are learning on one side, and your first language on the back.

▶ Chemistry quiz, with the formula of an element on one side, and its common name on the back.

▶ A picture quiz for any school subject, with diagrams on one side, and names or other details on the back.

Learning outcome: Create an interactive web page, for example, using JavaScript

? Why might you want to make a web page interactive?

Web pages that are written using only HTML are 'static'. You can make an HMTL web page interactive by adding small programs and functions using the programming language JavaScript.

There are lots of reasons why you may want to make your page interactive. For example, so a user can click on a button to change the colours or fonts used in the web page, making it easier to read for those with dyslexia. By giving the user choices, you increase their interest and engagement with the content of the page.

> drop-down menu   e-commerce
> function   HTML ID   identifier
> JavaScript   trigger   variable

Talk about …

In 7.4–7.6, you will create a web page with a pretend online shop. Nowadays, people do a lot of shopping online. This has many advantages, but it can also cause problems for communities. Discuss the good and bad sides of online shopping for you, your family and your community.

7.1 User control over text size

You will learn:
▶ to add a JavaScript command to a web page.

Key words

accessibility

JavaScript

A programming language for the internet

You have learned to write programs using Python. In this unit, you will learn to write programs in another programming language – **JavaScript**.

JavaScript is the most commonly used programming language in the world. It is used to write very short programs – called scripts. These 'scripts' are sometimes downloaded automatically when you open a web page. Sometimes the JavaScript commands are added to the HTML file, and sometimes they are saved as external script files. Usually, your computer will get the HTML and other files through an internet connection. The browser will use the files to display the website for you to look at and use.

Spiral back

In Books 7 and 8, you learned to use HTML and CSS to create and format a web page. You will need those skills in this unit.

A flash card example

You will make a web page with interactive revision 'flash cards' using JavaScript. You may have used paper flash cards in the past to help you study. One side of a flash card has a fact you want to remember. The other side has an answer or answer prompt. You say the answer and then turn over the card to see if you were right. The example topic we use here is logic gates (see Unit 6), but you can choose a topic that interests you.

The HTML file

This HTML file creates a website for flash cards. It has one flash card so far.

When the HTML file is opened in a text-editor app, it looks like this.

```
<!DOCTYPE html>
<html>

<head>
<title>Lesson 9.7.1</title>
<style>
body {background-color: lightyellow; color: black; font-family: Arial }
</style>
</head>

<body>
<h1>Flash cards</h1>
<p>Answer the question and then flip the card to see the answer</p>
<h2>TOPIC 1: Logic gates</h2>
<p>Guess the name of this gate</p>
<img id="flash1" src="not_gate_image.jpg" width="200"></img>
</body>
</html>
```

A

1. Save the HTML file to your own storage area. Save the image file 'not_gate_image.jpg' into the same folder. If you are using your own theme, create your question image and save it in this folder.

2. Open the web page in your browser. It should look like the page shown here.

Flash cards

Answer the question and then flip the card to see the answer

TOPIC 1: Logic gates

Guess the name of this gate

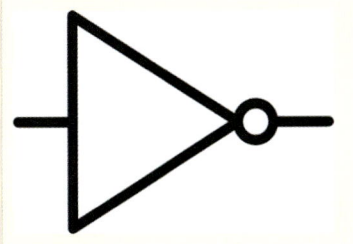

3. If you have time, make changes to the background and font colours and the font family.

Add a button

The purpose of JavaScript programs is to give the user some control over the web page. For example, some users might want the text to be larger. Now you will add a button to the web page. When the user clicks the button, the web page will use a larger font size to make it more **accessible**.

You can add a button to a web page using these HTML tags.

```
<button>Larger text</button>
```

The words between the two tags will appear on the button. You can add the button anywhere you like, but perhaps somewhere near the top of the page.

Flash cards

Larger text

Answer the question and then flip the card to see the answer

7.1 User control over text size

When the user clicks the button

Now you can add a short JavaScript command inside the start tag of the button. The JavaScript command begins with the word `onclick`. That means the command will happen when the user clicks the button. We say that clicking the button **triggers** the command.

```
<button onclick="">Larger text</button>
```

The command that follows the button click is entered between the quote marks. We want the computer to change a **style attribute** of the document. For example, to increase the font size to 35 pixels. You can pick any number.

```
document.body.style.fontSize='35px'
```

Putting this all together, this code creates a button that increases the size of text in the web page.

```
<button onclick="document.body.style.fon-
tSize='35px'">Larger text</button>
```

Here is the completed HTML file with all these changes.

```
<!DOCTYPE html>
<html>

<head>
<title>Lesson 9.7.1</title>
<style>
body {background-color: lightyellow; color: black; font-family: Arial }
</style>
</head>

<body>
<h1>Flash cards</h1>
<button onclick="document.body.style.fontSize='35px'">Larger text
</button>
<p>Answer the question and then flip the card to see the answer</p>
<h2>TOPIC 1: Logic gates</h2>
<p>Guess the name of this gate</p>
<img id="flash1" src="not_gate_image.jpg" width="200"></img>
</body>
</html>
```

> **Key words**
> function
> trigger
> style attribute

Flash cards

[Larger text] ← This is the new 'Larger text' button.

Answer the question and then flip the card to see the answer

TOPIC 1: Logic gates

Guess the name of this gate

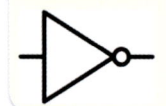

Flash

[Larger text]

This is what the web page looks like once the new button has been clicked.

Answer the question and th

TOPIC 1: Logic g

B

1. Open the HTML file and add a button. Add an `onclick` command as shown on this page.
2. Open the page in your browser, and check that the button works. You should see the text on the page get a lot bigger.
3. To return text to its original size, refresh the web page.
4. Make sure your HTML file and the image file are both saved ready to use again next lesson.

Digital citizen

It is important to design web pages to be accessible to all kinds of user, including those with disabilities. Adding JavaScript **functions** to a web page can give users control over the way the page is displayed. They can pick fonts, text colours and sizes that make the page easy to read. See if you can find any examples of accessibility options on a website for a large company or healthcare provider.

Test

1. What language is used to write short scripts that are linked to a web page?
2. What software can open a web page and read the short scripts made in this language?
3. What HTML tags are used to create a button on a web page with the text 'Click Here' on it?
4. The following command was added to the start tag of a button. What happens if the user clicks the button?

   ```
   onclick = "document.body.style.color='red'"
   ```

Stretch zone

Add a second button to your flash card web page. This button will make the text smaller. You can choose a suitable font size.

7 Creating web content: Use JavaScript

187

7.2 Add night mode

You will learn:
▶ to add a JavaScript function to a web page.

Key words

night mode
identifier

Night mode

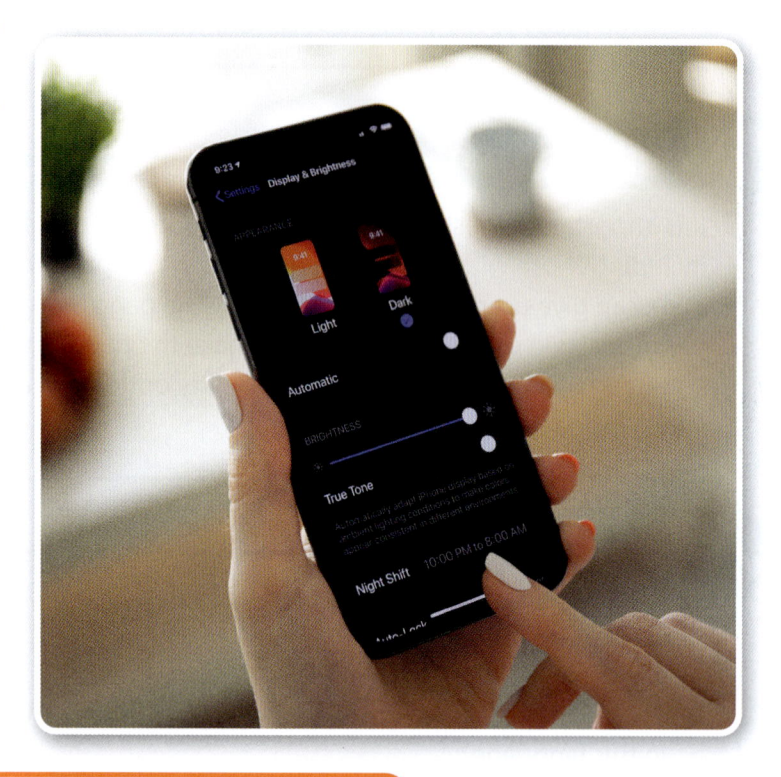

Some people prefer to look at web content in 'dark mode' or '**night mode**'. This means the content is displayed using light text on a dark background. Some people switch to night mode when using a phone or computer in a darker room.

Many web pages include a JavaScript function that lets users switch to night mode. In this lesson, you will make a button that turns on night mode.

You already know how to make a button using HTML tags. The text to appear on the button comes in between the tags.

`<button>Night Mode</button>`

A

1. Open the HTML file you saved at the end of the previous lesson. If you do not have this available, use the HTML and jpg files provided.
2. Add a button at the top of the page with the words 'Night Mode'.
3. Save the file and try it out in your browser.

A JavaScript function

Last lesson you created a button that made text size larger. This is a single command. You put the command into the start tag of the button. But to turn the website into night mode, you need to make more than one change:

▶ make the background black
▶ make the font colour light grey

9:7.2 Add Night Mode: Digital Activity Files

This is too much to fit into the button tag. Instead, you will store these commands as a JavaScript function. A function in JavaScript, just like a function or procedure in Python, is a group of commands. The function is given a name called an **identifier**. If you put the function name into any part of the program, the computer will carry out all the stored commands.

In this example, we will make a function called 'nightmode' that changes the background and text colours.

Make the script

If you want to put JavaScript into a web page, you must put it in between HTML 'script' tags.

```
<script> </script>
```

You can put these tags anywhere in a web page – including in the head or body of the page. And you can put more than one set of tags in a page. So it is quite flexible.

As you learned when Python programming, you should choose a suitable name for the function that reminds you of what the function does. A function is defined like this.

```
function nightmode() {}
```

Finally, you have to enter the commands that belong inside the function. In JavaScript, the commands go inside curly brackets. The commands are separated by semicolons. You can put them on the same line or on different lines.

Here are the two commands to set the style of the body of the web page.

Javascript command	Effect it has
`document.body.style.background = 'black';`	Makes the background black
`document.body.style.color = 'lightgrey';`	Makes the font light grey

Putting all of that together, the next image shows the completed JavaScript `nightmode()` function.

```
<script>
function nightmode() {
document.body.style.background ='black';
document.body.style.color = 'lightgrey';
}
</script>
```

This function can be added to the HTML file anywhere inside the head or body of the web page.

7.2 Add night mode

Link the function to the button

You used the `onclick` command last lesson. The `onclick` command triggers another command. In this case, we will trigger the nightmode function.

```
onclick = "nightmode()"
```

Putting this trigger into the button tag gives this complete line of HTML.

```
<button onclick = "nightmode()">Night Mode</button>
```

Here is the completed HTML file with all these changes.

```
<!DOCTYPE html>
<html>

<head>
<title>Lesson 9.7.2</title>
<style>
body {background-color: lightyellow; color: black; font-family: Arial }
</style>
</head>

<body>
<h1>Flash cards</h1>
<button onclick="document.body.style.fontSize='35px'">Larger text</button>
<button onclick = "nightmode()">Night Mode</button>
<p>Answer the question and then flip the card to see the answer</p>
<h2>TOPIC 1: Logic gates</h2>
<p>Guess the name of this gate</p>
<img id = "flash1" src= "not_gate_image.jpg" width = "200"></img>

<script>
function nightmode() {
document.body.style.background="black";
document.body.style.color="lightgrey";
}
</script>
</body>
</html>
```

B

1. Add the `nightmode()` function to your HTML file.
2. Adapt the new button so that it 'triggers' the function.
3. Save the file and try it out in your browser. If you click the button, the web page will go into 'night mode'.
4. Refresh the page to return to normal mode.

Flash cards

Larger text Night Mode

Answer the question and then flip the card to see the answer

TOPIC 1: Logic gates

Guess the name of this gate

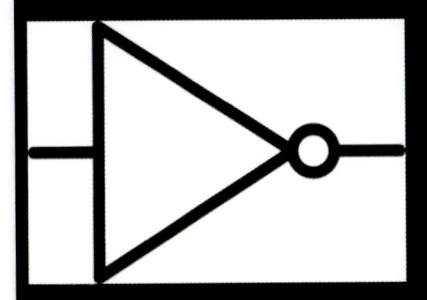

✓ Test

1. What is the name for a group of JavaScript commands saved with a name called an identifier?
2. What tags are used to mark JavaScript in an HTML file?
3. What type of brackets are used to group together the commands of a JavaScript function?
4. What symbol is used to separate the comands of a JavaScript function?

◉ Stretch zone

You can put the `onclick` command inside an image tag instead of a button.

▶ Add a small image of the moon to your web page. Use the `onclick` command to link it to the `nightmode()` function.

▶ If you have extra time, create a `daymode()` function and link it to an image of the sun.

NIGHTMODE

DAYMODE

7.3 Flip a card

You will learn:
- to give an HTML element an ID
- to link a JavaScript function to an image.

Key words

HTML element

HTML ID

NOT Gate

Flip the card

You have created a web page with a flash card. Now you will add functionality so that the user can 'flip' the card. The user can click on the image, and it will change to show the other side of the flash card with the answer. Here is the new image. It is called 'answer_image.jpg'.

A

You will need a new image that shows the other side of the flash card. You can use our image (called answer_image.jpg) or make one of your own. Make sure the chosen image is saved in your folder.

If you want your answer card to look colourful, you could use an online 'quote maker' app.

Note: You will need the answer image in this lesson, but you have not linked it to the web page yet.

9:7.3 Flip A Card: Digital Activity Files

Change one element

The JavaScript commands you used in 7.1 and 7.2 affected the whole body of the web page. JavaScript commands that affect the whole body of the page begin like this.

```
document.body
```

In this lesson, you will make a JavaScript function that affects just one **HTML element** (the flash card). A JavaScript command that affects a single element starts like this.

```
document.getElementById().
```

The command says 'get element by ID'. ID is short for 'identifier'. An **HTML ID** can be used to identify a single element on the page.

Give your image an ID

The JavaScript command 'gets' an element using its ID. So, the element we want to change has to have its own 'ID' (identifier).

Remember that an image element is defined by these HTML tags.

```
<img> </img>
```

Attributes inside the start tag define the source of the image and the size of the image. The image on this page uses a source file called 'not_gate_image.jpg'.

```
<img src= "not_gate_image.jpg" width = "200"></img>
```

Now a new ID attribute must be put inside the start tag of the image.

```
<img id = "flash1" src= "not_gate_image.jpg" width = "200"></img>
```

In this example, the image has the ID 'flash1'.

> **B**
> Edit the HTML file and give your answer image element the ID 'flash1'.

Write a new function

The next step is to write a function that will change a single element. Remember that all JavaScript functions must go inside the `<style> </style>` tags.

The name of a function should remind you of what the function does. For example, 'flipcard'.

```
function flipcard() {}
```

The JavaScript commands go inside the curly brackets. First, get the element we want to change.

```
{document.getElementById("flash1").}
```

7.3 Flip a card

Then change its source to the new image file.

```
{document.getElementById("flash1").src="answer_image.jpg"}
```

Putting all of this together, here is the complete JavaScript code for the new function.

```
function flipcard() {
    document.getElementById("flash1").src="answer_image.jpg"
}
```

This image shows the script part of the HTML file. It includes the `nightmode()` function from 7.2, and the new function `flipcard()`.

```
<script>

function nightmode() {
document.body.style.background ='black';
document.body.style.color = 'lightgrey';
}

function flipcard() {
document.getElementByID('flash1').src="answer_image.jpg"
}

</script>
```

C

Create a JavaScript function called 'flipcard', as shown here. Save the HTML file.

Trigger the function

Finally, the new function must be linked to the image so that if the user clicks the image, it will trigger the function. That uses the `onclick` command as before.

```
<img id = "flash1" onclick = "flipcard ()"
src= "not_gate_image.jpg" width = "200"></img>
```

← This is the `onclick` command.

The next image shows the body of the HTML file, with the image edited to include the `onclick` command.

```
<body>
<h1>Flash cards</h1>
<button onclick="document.body.style.fontSize='35px'">Larger text</button>
<button onclick="nightmode()">Night Mode</button>
<p>Answer the question and then flip the card to see the answer</p>
<h2>TOPIC 1: Logic gates</h2>
<p>Guess the name of this gate</p>
<img id="flash1" src="not_gate_image.jpg" width="200"></img>
```

D

1. Add code so that if the user clicks the image, it triggers the function.
2. Save the HTML file and test it in your browser. The card should 'flip' when you click the image. Correct any errors that you find.
3. Refresh the page to return it to its original state.

Summary

This has been quite a complicated task:

- Add an ID to the image element.
- Write a new JavaScript function that changes this element.
- Use the `onclick` command to trigger the new function if the user clicks the image.

If you have completed all these steps, the flash card website now works perfectly.

✓ Test

1. A JavaScript function can be triggered by a click. What does 'triggered' mean in this case?
2. What is the difference between a JavaScript command and a JavaScript function?
3. In this JavaScript command, what element is changed?

   `{document.getElementById('mypic').src='football.jpg'}`

4. The command in question 3 changes an element of a web page. How is the element changed?

◎ Stretch zone

1. Add a second flash card to your web page. You will need to find or make an image for the top side and the answer side of your new flash card.
2. Add functionality so that when the user clicks the flash card, the image changes to show the answer.

7.4 An e-commerce web page

You will learn:
- to use your HTML skills to make a new web page.

Key words

drop-down menu

e-commerce

What is e-commerce?

E-commerce is the general name for buying and selling things online. Most e-commerce sites include JavaScript commands to let the user explore the site and set different preferences. In 7.4, you will make an e-commerce site. This is a practice lesson. It will give you the opportunity to use and explore the HTML commands you have already learned.

First you must decide what you want to sell in your pretend e-commerce site. Here are some suggestions:

- clothing
- stationery
- musical instruments
- sports equipment.

Note: Your web page must include at least one image of the type of product you want to sell.

Example web page

We created an example web page that looks like this. So far, this web page only sells one item – a red T-shirt. Later in the lesson, you will add extra options.

This web page has several HTML elements you have seen before:

- style attributes that set the text colour, font, and background of the page
- headings and paragraphs
- an image
- a button.

It does not have any JavaScript yet.

Remember, you do not have to copy this page, it is just here to suggest contents and layout.

Spiral back

In Unit 7 of Books 7 and 8, you created a web page using HTML. You learned to use style attributes to format the appearance of individual items on a web page. You will use these commands again in this lesson.

One-stop shop

For every pretend purchase.

Buy a T-shirt

Choose your preferred colour.

Click to buy

A

1. Decide on what you want to sell in your pretend online shop.
2. Find an image to use in your web page and save it in a suitable folder.
3. Make an HTML file in the same folder to define the web page.
4. Open your file in the browser and check that it looks the way you want. Make changes until you are happy with your web page.

HTML example

This is the HTML file for the example web page we have provided. You can use this for reference or for ideas about the contents and style of an e-commerce site.

```html
<!DOCTYPE html>
<html>

<head>
<title>Lesson 9.7.4</title>
<style>
body {background-color: lightgreen; color: black; font-family: Georgia }
</style>
</head>

<body>
<h1>One-stop shop</h1>
<p>For every pretend purchase.</p>
<h2>Buy a T-shirt</h2>
<p>Choose your preferred colour.</p>
<img id="Tshirt" src="red_tshirt_image.jpg" width="300px"></img>
<br>
<button>Click to buy</button>
</body>
</html>
```

What are the options?

Now you will give the user of your web page some choices. You must decide what the choices are. For example, if your web page sells stationery, your choices might be pen, pencil or notebook.

Add a drop-down menu

A **drop-down menu** is a good way to present options to the user. In HTML, a drop-down menu is defined using these tags.

```html
<select> </select>
```

9:7.4: An E-Commerce Web Page: Digital Activity Files

7.4 An e-commerce web page

In between the two tags, you can define a list of options to choose from. Each option is enclosed in these tags.

`<option> </option>`

The next image shows a drop-down menu that gives the user a choice of colour. The menu also has an ID ('choosecolour') so it can be used later in a JavaScript function.

This is what the web page now looks like. The drop-down menu is in place. The student has changed the title of the shop.

```
<h2>Buy a T-shirt</h2>
<p>Choose a colour.</p>
<select id = "choosecolour">
   <option>Red</option>
   <option>Blue</option>
   <option>Black</option>
   <option>Orange</option>
</select>
<br>
```

B

1. Decide on what choices you want to offer the user.
2. Add a suitable drop-down menu to your web page.
3. Open your file in the browser and check that it looks the way you want. Make changes until you are happy with your web page.

✓ Test

1. What is e-commerce?
2. What HTML tags mark the start and end of a drop-down menu?
3. Write the HTML to define a drop-down menu with the options 'pen', 'pencil' and 'notebook'.
4. Write the head section of a web page that defines the style as green text on a purple background.

⊙ Stretch zone

You can add style tags to almost any part of a web page. For example, this code adds style attributes to the button at the bottom of the web page.

```
<button style="color:red; background:yellow; font-size:35px; width:300px; height:50px">Click to buy</button>
```

These attributes make the button look like this.

One-stop shop

For every pretend purchase.

Buy a T-shirt

Choose a colour.

[Red ▼]

[Image: red t-shirt]

[Click to buy]

This is just an example. Use style attributes to set the appearance of the button on your web page.

7 Creating web content: Use JavaScript

199

7.5 Improve the colour menu

You will learn:
▶ to give the user control over the display in your web page.

Key word

asset

Find a new image

In 7.4, you created an e-commerce web page with a drop-down menu. The menu gave the user a choice of items. The choices will depend on the topic of your web page. Now you have to find a selection of images that match the choices in the menu.

These images will form the **assets** of your web page. Assets are the items needed to complete a project. Web page assets are the files you need to make the web page work properly.

How to get the assets

Because this is an educational activity about a pretend shop, you can make sensible use of some images found on the internet. Look for images that are copyright-free, for example, Creative Commons. Another fun way to get images is to take photos of items with a mobile phone or digital camera, and email them to your school email address, or save them to the school network. All the assets should be stored in the same folder as the HTML file that defines your web page.

Check the file types

Images can be saved as different file types. Images used on web pages are often these file types

File extension	How to say it
.jpg	jay-peg
.svg	ess vee jee
.gif	giff or jiff

If you are worried that an image you want to use is not a good file type, it is easy to change it.

1. Open the image in a suitable image-editing application, such as Paint.
2. Choose 'Save as'.
3. Pick a suitable file type from the drop-down menu.

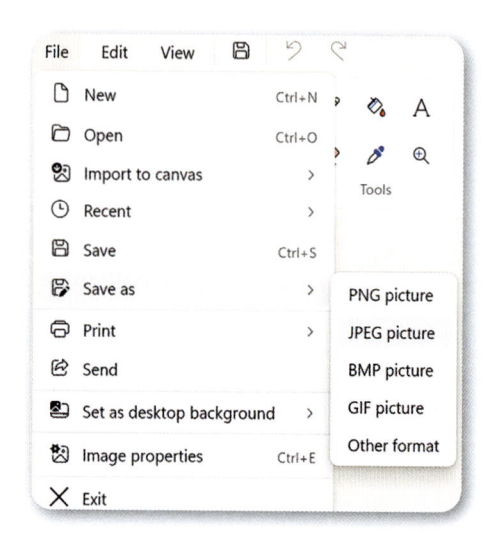

A

1. Find images to match all the options in your drop-down menu. Make sure each image is a suitable file type, such as jpg.
2. If you cannot find suitable images, you can use the image files we have provided, showing different coloured T-shirts.
3. Save the image files in the same folder as your HTML file.

Drop-down menu

You are going to create a new JavaScript function to change the image in your web page. First, you must change the drop-down menu so that it triggers the function. Look at the start tag of your drop-down menu.

```
<select>
```

It should already include an ID that you added last lesson. But you can add it now. In this example, it is called 'choosecolour' because the menu chooses between different colours. But use an ID that makes sense for your page.

```
<select id = "choosecolour">
```

Next, you must add a trigger. In 7.1–7.3, you used the trigger `onclick`. But this time you will use the trigger `onchange`. That means the new function will be triggered every time the user makes a choice from the drop-down menu. In this example, we have called the new function `setpic()` because it will change the picture on the web page. You can use a different name if you prefer.

```
<select id = "choosecolour"; onchange = "setpic()">
```

Here is the completed drop-down menu code with all these changes.

```
<select id="choosecolour"; onchange="setpic()";>
  <option>Red</option>
  <option>Blue</option>
  <option>Black</option>
  <option>Orange</option>
</select>
```

B

Open the HTML file you made last lesson or use the one we have provided. Look at the drop-down menu. Make sure it has a suitable ID and that it triggers a function called `setpic()`.

7.5 Improve the colour menu

Make the setpic() function

Now you will write the `setpic()` function. Remember some features of JavaScript functions.

▶ JavaScript functions go inside `<script>` tags.

▶ All the commands of the function are enclosed in curly brackets { }.

So, the function starts like this.

```
<script>
function setpic() {
}
</script>
```

Change the image on your web page

The `setpic()` function will change the image on the web page. You learned how to do this in 7.3. Here is our example.

```
<script>
function setpic() {
document.getElementbyID("TShirt").src="blue_tshirt_image.jpg"}
</script>
```

This function includes only one image. In our example, it loads the blue T-shirt picture. In 7.6, you will extend the function to include more images.

> **C**
>
> 1 Write the `setpic()` function. You can use these commands in your program but you might need to make changes:
>
> | In our code | How you should change it |
> | --- | --- |
> | `getElementbyID("TShirt")` | Change 'TShirt' to the ID of the image element on your web page |
> | `src = "blue_tshirt_image.jpg"` | Change 'blue_tshirt_image.jpg' to the name of one of your image assets |
>
> 2 Open your file in the browser and check that it looks the way you want. Your `setpic()` function should change the image on your web page when you use the drop-down menu.
>
> 3 Try out the drop-down menu. It should let you change the image. To change it back to the original, refresh the web page.

✓ Test

1 Name an image file type that is suitable to use on a web page.

2 How are curly brackets used in a JavaScript function?

3 Here is the start tag of a drop-down menu. What function is triggered when this menu is changed?

```
<select onchange = "background()">
```

4 What action by the user will trigger the function in question 3?

Stretch zone

Extend the `setpic()` function. Change the background colour of your web page as well as the image.

7.6 Complete your web page

You will learn:
▶ to choose between many different images using a drop-down menu.

Key words

'if' structure

index number

variable

Give the user greater choice

In 7.5, you made a function called `setpic()`. This function changes the image on your web page to a new picture. But it only lets the user choose one new image. In this lesson, you will adapt the function to select any image from the list of choices on the drop-down menu.

You will use new JavaScript commands. These are similar to commands you have learned in Python, but not identical. You will learn commands to:

▶ create a **variable** and give it a value

▶ get the **index number** of an item in a list

▶ make a selection using 'if'.

All of these commands will go inside the function.

Create a variable

In Python, we can create a variable and give it a value with a line of code like this.

```
variable = value
```

JavaScript is similar, but it is best practice to use the keyword 'let'.

```
let variable = value
```

In this example, we will store the number of the user's menu choice. A short name is suitable. In our example, we are using the short name 'x' for the variable.

```
let x =
```

Get the user's menu choice

The value that we need is the number of the user's choice from the drop-down menu list.

Look at the start tag of the menu to remind yourself of the ID of the drop-down menu. In our example, it is 'choosecolour'.

```
<select id="choosecolour"; onchange="setpic()";>
  <option>Red</option>
  <option>Blue</option>
  <option>Black</option>
  <option>Orange</option>
</select>
```

Is it the same in your web page, or have you chosen a different ID for the drop-down menu?

The JavaScript command to get index number is called `selectedIndex`. Putting it all together, the command looks like this.

```
let x = document.getElementById("choosecolour").selectedIndex;
```

You will have to adapt this command to use the ID of your menu.

> **A**
> 1. Open the HTML file you made last lesson. Find the `setpic()` function.
> 2. Add a command to the function to create a variable and store the index number of the user's choice from the menu list.
> 3. Save the file.

How menu items are numbered

In our example, the drop-down menu has these choices. Each item has an index number, although the number is not shown on the page.

0. Red
1. Blue
2. Black
3. Orange

Notice that the numbering starts at 0, just like in a Python list. You have to remember that when you use the number to make the image selection.

Selection using 'if'

You have used **'if' structures** in Python programs. A Python 'if' structure begins with the word 'if' followed by a logical test. If the test is True, the commands that follow are carried out.

JavaScript is very similar. It uses the word 'if', a logical test and a set of commands. There are some differences:

▶ The logical test is put into round brackets.

▶ The commands that follow are put into curly brackets.

▶ There is no need for indentation or line breaks, but you can use them if you want.

Like Python, JavaScript has other selection structures using commands like 'else' and 'elseif'. But we will only use 'if' for now.

9:7.6: Complete Your Web Page: Digital Activity Files

7.6 Complete your web page

Complete the function

In our example, if the user choice from the drop-down menu is 0, then the image should be the red T-shirt.

```
if (x==0) {document.getelementbyid("Tshirt").src="red.jpg"}
```

This command uses the values from our web page example.

▶ The ID of the image element is Tshirt

▶ The source file is red.jpg

The names you use might be different. You will have to adapt this command to use the ID of your image element, and the name of the source file you want to use.

The next image shows the completed function. The only option not shown is the orange T-shirt picture. If you choose to use our example, you will have to fill that part in for yourself.

```
<script>
function setpic() {
    let x=document.getElementById("choosecolour").selectedIndex;
    if (x==0) {document.getElementById('Tshirt').src="red_tshirt_image.jpg"}
    if (x==1) {document.getElementById('Tshirt').src="blue_tshirt_image.jpg"}
    if (x==2) {document.getElementById('Tshirt').src="black_tshirt_image.jpg"}
}
</script>
```

B

1 Extend the `setpic()` function using 'if' commands. Make sure all the choices on the drop-down menu are matched to a suitable source file.

2 Save the file. Open it in your web browser. Test the drop-down menu. It should now work.

Javascript

In this unit, you have experienced just some of the things that JavaScript can do. JavaScript can:

▶ change the appearance of a web page

▶ let the user choose different images

▶ add functionality to the buttons and menus of a web page.

JavaScript is used to make web pages responsive to user input. You have seen that JavaScript is part of the web page. Java Script is downloaded onto your computer as part of the web page. The JavaScript functions run on your computer.

More complex processes, such as paying money to an online shop, or joining a social media site, are not usually handled by JavaScript. In these cases, you need to exchange data with a distant website, using an internet connection. Different and more complex languages are used for this type of work. When personal data like this is shared, security measures are needed to protect your details and to prevent cybercrime.

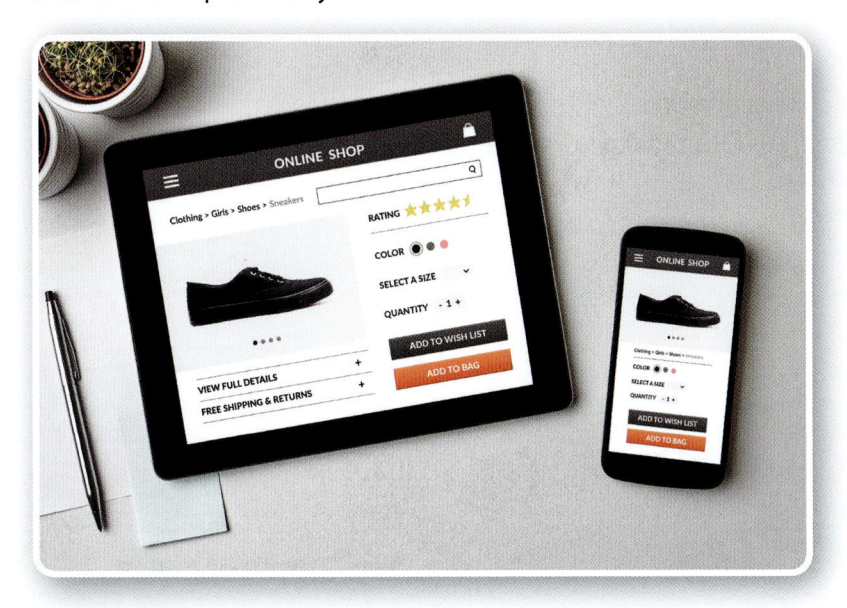

✓ Test

1. When would a JavaScript programmer use the keyword 'let'?
2. What is the index number of the first item in a drop-down menu?
3. Say what is the same or different about using 'if' in JavaScript and in Python.
4. JavaScript is not the only language that can be used to add functionality to a web page. Explain the type of task that JavaScript is most suitable for.

Stretch zone

In 7.1 and 7.2, you added buttons to your flash cards website to let users select larger text and night mode. Add buttons to your e-commerce page to allow the user to change style features, such as colour and text size.

If you have time, extend your web page by adding new items to buy.

7 What have you learned?

Review test

Here is part of an HTML file. It includes a button that calls a JavaScript function.

```
<!DOCTYPE html>
<html>
<body>
<h1>Before and after</h1>

<p>Change your face into a cartoon. </p>
<button onclick="newface()">Click to change</button>
<br>
<img id = "Face" src= "photo.jpg"></img>
<br>

<script>

function newface() {
   document.getElementById('Face').src = "cartoon.jpg"
}

</script>

</body>
</html>
```

Answer these questions about the commands you see.

1. What words will appear on the button?
2. What is the name of the JavaScript function?
3. How does the user trigger the JavaScript function?
4. The image has the ID 'Face'. What is the name of the image source file?
5. In your own words, explain what happens when the function is triggered.

Review activity

We have provided an HTML file that includes some JavaScript.

Open and edit this file:

1 Add a button to the page with the words 'Try it out' on it.

9:7.7: Before And After Web Page: Digital Activity File

2. Add a command to the button so that when the user clicks the button, it triggers the JavaScript function `colourchange()`.

3. The JavaScript function changes the colours of this web page to red text on a yellow background. Now change the function to use two different colours of your own choice.

4. If you have time, create a second button that triggers a new function, for example, changing the web page to night mode.

```html
<!DOCTYPE html>
<html>
<head>
<style>
body {background-color: lightyellow; color: black}
</style>
</head>

<body>
<h1>Before and after</h1>

<p>Change the colours used in this web page. </p>

<script>
function colourchange() {
   document.body.style.background = "yellow";
   document.body.style.color = "red";
}
</script>

</body>
</html>
```

Self-evaluation

How did you do?	What is your level?	What your level means
• I answered test questions 1 and 2. • I edited a web page to get user input.	Developing	You have learned something new in this unit.
• I answered test questions 1 to 4. • I edited a web page to link user input to a JavaScript function.	Secure	You have reached the expected standard in this unit.
• I answered all the test questions. • I adapted how the web page responds to user input.	Extending	You are an expert.

What next? If you want to improve your level you can go back and repeat some of the learning in this unit.

Glossary

abstraction Making a problem simpler by leaving out details that you do not need.

accessibility Making something as easy to use for someone with a disability as it is to use for someone without a disability.

actor One of the types of people who will use your product or service.

actuator A machine controlled by a processor, for example, a motor that makes things move. It is controlled by software.

addictive design Features used in technology design to encourage users to spend more time using an app. Examples include notifications, infinite scrolling and the 'like' button.

agile method A method of delivering projects in short cycles of work, called sprints.

AI (artificial intelligence) The use of computers to make decisions and create content almost as if they are able to think for themselves.

AI hallucination A mistake or inaccuracy made by AI. For example, an error made in generated content or data processing.

AND gate A gate where the output is True only if both inputs are True.

AND operator A Boolean operator that joins two Boolean values. The result is True if both the original values are True.

AR (augmented reality) A technology that enhances the real world by overlaying digital information onto it, usually through the screen of a device like a smartphone or through a wearable technology like smart glasses.

arithmetic and logic unit (ALU) The part of a computer's central processing unit that compares numbers and performs arithmetic.

asset An item that is used in a digital project, such as an image in a web page.

assumption A value that is left out of a mathematical model, or set to a fixed level. We use assumptions to simplify the model.

auto-caption Text subtitles on a video that are generated by AI using natural language processing (NLP).

backlog A list showing all the work that needs to be done in a project. Backlog items can be moved across a kanban board as they are worked on.

beta A version of a product or service that is being tested by a few users before it is offered for sale.

bias Treating a person or thing favourably or unfavourably based on a general idea about them that may not be true.

Boolean expression An expression that can have the value True or False.

Boolean operator An operator that joins Boolean values to make larger Boolean expressions (see AND, OR and NOT operators).

brief A set of instructions that tells you what you should do for a particular job or task.

bus A fast connection that transfers data between the control unit and other parts of the processor.

business as usual (BAU) This phrase describes all the usual actions and events that occur in the running of a business.

cache Very small amount of memory that is very close to the CPU, allowing fast loading of instructions and data.

caption Text that will be shown while a video clip or still image is being played.

central processing unit (CPU) The key component of a processor. The CPU controls all arithmetic and logic operations in a computer.

circuit A number of gates joined together to form a larger, more complex structure.

clock Part of the CPU. The clock controls the timing of each operation inside the computer.

cloud storage Remote storage that you access through an internet connection.

cluster (data) A group of data that shares similar characteristics and is significantly different to other clusters in a database.

compression (file) A method of reducing the size of digital files, such as images or sounds. Some compression methods lead to a loss of quality in the digital file.

computer system A processor linked to input, output and storage devices, which acts as a system to solve a problem.

control unit Part of the CPU. The controller manages each computer instruction to create solutions.

controller Central part of a robot that receives signals from sensors and instructs actuators to move.

convert (units) If a model uses a range of different measurement units, you must convert the measurements to use the same units before you can combine them in the model.

cross-functional diagram A flowchart to show how different people work together.

cryptocurrency A digital currency created using encryption algorithms.

curate Select what content to show, how to group it and what order to show it in.

cutaway (film) A short shot that shows something different from the main subject that is being filmed.

deep learning A form of machine learning that combines many methods into a highly complex learning process. Deep learning typically uses a type of computer structure called a neural network.

defect Any behaviour of a system that does not meet the requirements. Sometimes called a bug.

digital audio workstation (DAW) An audio production app or platform designed for recording, editing and mixing digital audio files.

drop-down menu A menu that opens up when you click on it, showing the choices.

e-commerce Buying and selling through the internet.

embed To display content from another source or service in an application or web page. For example, you can embed video and audio from streaming services in other web pages.

empathy Imagining how others are feeling.

ethics of care Being kind to ourselves and others online.

expert system An algorithm that represents the knowledge and decision making of a subject expert.

feedback Information about the effect of something, which we can use to regulate or improve it. Examples include feedback from an audience for digital content, or feedback from a physical system in robotics.

fetch-execute cycle The sequence of events that takes place every time an instruction is carried out in a computer. The full sequence is fetch-decode-execute-store.

file format The structure of a file that tells a program how to use its contents. Different applications save files as different file formats (types). File formats can be identified by the letters after the dot in the filename. For example, the file 'mysong.mp3' is an MP3 file that contains audio content and is compressed.

final proof Your final check of spelling and formatting of your text for a project or product.

flash memory Small, portable solid-state drive used to transfer data from one computer to another.

follower A person who has chosen to see the content that a company or individual makes online, by having it appear in their social media.

function A modular program structure that carries out commands and makes a new value.

Gantt chart A visual form of timetable using a bar chart format.

gate (logical) An electronic device that is the basic building block of a computer processor.

generative AI A type of AI that creates content, such as images text and video, by learning from a wide range of sample content made by humans.

global (edit) When a change to a project, product or service needs to be made throughout the whole thing.

hard disk drive (HDD) A storage drive that contains lots of moving parts and a metal disk. They can store large amounts of digital data.

heuristic A rule that helps you make a quick decision. A heuristic is like a guess, or a rough estimate. But it is a guess based on careful thinking about the problem.

hosting service A service that stores software, multimedia content, files and other digital assets online so that they can be accessed and used by people over the world wide web. File-sharing applications, media streaming services and websites rely on hosting services to store their content and make it accessible to users.

HTML (Hypertext Markup Language) The programming language used to set the content and format of websites.

HTML element An item on a web page defined by HTML tags.

HTML ID A name given to an HTML element so it can be referred to in a JavaScript program.

humane design Technology design that aims to make life better for everyone.

identifier A name given to any element or item that we need to refer to in a program.

'if' structure A conditional or selection program structure that starts with the key word 'if' and a logical test. If the test is True, then the commands inside the structure are carried out.

index number (programming) A number that represents the position of an item in a list.

infographic A visual way of representing data and information.

input device A computer device that converts signals from the real world into digital data.

integer A whole number without a decimal point.

JavaScript A programming language that is mainly used to add short programs, or scripts, to web pages.

kanban board A board, wall or software application that shows work in progress during a project.

large language model (LLM) A computer system that learns to produce language by looking at billions of examples.

logical statement Also called an assertion. A logical statement makes a claim about the world. The claim can be either True or False.

machine learning When AI systems are programmed to learn new and better ways to do tasks.

mathematical model A model of a real-life system that uses numbers to stand for all the parts of the system.

meme An image format that is adapted by different people to show different messages. Memes are shared very quickly across the internet.

memory Small storage areas close to the CPU that hold instructions and data needed for immediate operations.

metadata Data that describes other data, such as the content of a digital file. For example, information about the format of a file.

metaverse A virtual reality space in which people can interact with each other, with digital objects or devices.

microprocessor A circuit that contains all the functions of a central processing unit of a computer.

minimum The smallest possible value something can have.

MR (mixed reality) A technology that places digital objects in a real-world environment and allows you to interact with them.

multimedia platform An application or online service that allows users to make, share or view multimedia content. Multimedia platforms allow users to combine media like text, images, audio and video.

natural language processing (NLP) A computer system that can understand and produce natural-seeming human speech.

night mode A display setting that uses a dark background with lighter text to reduce eye strain and improve visibility in low-light conditions.

non-fungible token (NFT) A unique, digital item (an exclusive online collectible) with a special code that shows it is the only authentic copy.

NOT gate A gate that flips the input from True to False or vice versa.

NOT operator A Boolean operator that changes a Boolean value. The result is True if the original value is False. The result is False if the original value is True.

objective Something you plan to achieve. You can measure objectives so you know if they have been achieved. Sometimes called a goal or target.

obligation Something you have to do, either because you feel it is morally right or because someone in authority tells you to do it. A responsibility or duty.

OR gate A gate where the output is True if either or both of the two inputs are True.

OR operator A Boolean operator that joins two Boolean values. The result is True if either or both of the original values are True.

orientation Which way something faces. For example, whether a document or screen is in portrait or landscape mode.

outline plan A general description of the main features of something, but not the detail.

output device A computer device that converts digital data into a form humans can read or understand.

page (blogs, websites) Part of a website with content that you want to keep separate. Readers use the site menu or links to navigate to pages.

persona An imaginary person with an assumed identity.

post (online) Any content shared by a user on a social media or blog site. On most platforms, the most recent post is the first one that users see on the page or feed.

prejudice 'Pre-judging' or making a judgement in advance. A prejudice is a judgement you make about a person without knowing anything about them as an individual. For example, based on the group they belong to.

preview To view something before it is published.

processor A device that processes digital data to solve a problem.

project A piece of work that has a start and end date, and a specific set of goals. Projects often bring people together in teams to work to deliver the goals.

project goal A project outcome that can be measured.

publish To make content available to other people, for example, making information available via an online platform or printing a magazine.

random access memory (RAM) Part of the computer memory. Data in RAM is lost when power is turned off.

reinforcement learning Reinforcement is anything that makes something stronger. During reinforcement learning, feedback tells the computer when it has moved towards the right goal. The feedback strengthens its learning.

requirement A feature or function that is needed in a project. The requirements guide the direction of a project. In programming, it is an instruction telling the programmer what the program should do.

resolution A measure of the quality of a digital image based on the number of pixels used in the image.

risk Anything that could cause a problem or cause harm, for example, factors that could cause a project to fail.

robot A machine designed and programmed to carry out tasks without human intervention (autonomously).

rough cut An early version of a film that the director and editor create. Usually, a rough cut has some mistakes – it is 'rough'. There are no special effects, titles or music.

round To shorten a number by reducing it to a set number of decimal places. For example, 2.777 rounded to 1 decimal place is 2.8

scenario A simulation of how a system might be used. Testers use scenarios to create test cases.

scope The bounds of something, setting out everything that is included. For example, all the goals and deliverables of a project.

screen format The shape and orientation of a screen. Also called the aspect ratio.

script The written text for what people will say for a play, video or audio broadcast.

secondary memory Alternative name for storage devices that contain extra storage.

segment Part of a TV programme, webcast video or podcast.

self-regulation Being able to stop when you might be doing something risky.

sensor Part of a robot that senses the environment the robot is working in.

shot type The framing of a video image created by the position of a camera relative to the subject. Typical shot types (sometimes also called 'camera angles') include: wide (or long), medium and close-up. These shots differ by how much of the subject and background/foreground is seen in the frame.

social media Online platforms and technologies that connect people, and enable them to share content.

solid-state drive (SSD) A storage device with no moving parts. It stores digital data using the electrons in a solid substance. Solid-state drives are lightweight and hold a lot of data.

speech emotion recognition (SER) A computer program that can work out how people are feeling by analysing their speech or writing.

sprint A short cycle of work in a project. A sprint always has a defined start and end date. At the end of a sprint, the project team will show the work they have done in a demo.

stakeholder A person who has a strong interest in a project. For example, an investor who has put their money into the project, or a user who will make use of its results.

stand-up A short meeting of a project team to share updates about the project.

storage device A computer device that stores files and instructions so that they can be retrieved and used again.

story point A number value given to a story to represent its size. Story point numbers are used to estimate the difficulty of the story in comparison to other stories.

story size A way of measuring how difficult and time-consuming a user story is to deliver.

stream Listen to or watch media content, such as audio, video or games, by receiving it in a continuous stream from the internet, instead of downloading a copy of the file to your own device.

style attribute One of the style features of web content, that can be altered in an HTML or CSS file.

supervised training When an AI system is given a lot of data that has already been organized and labelled.

syntax The rules of a programming language.

test A method of checking a product or service to make sure it is a good quality.

test case A script that a tester follows to test the behaviour of a system. A failed test means that there is a defect.

training The first stage of machine learning. The computer is given access to example data and sometimes feedback or labels. The computer must work out how to solve a problem.

trigger To make the computer carry out some commands, such as a JavaScript function.

truth table A way of laying out a logical statement in table form. It makes it easier to understand the logic.

Unicode A number code used to store text characters in digital form. It is based on an older code called ASCII, but extended to cover thousands of different characters and symbols, including emojis.

unit of measurement Every physical measurement, for example, of size or weight, uses units. Units are standards of measurement that are used by scientists all over the world, for example, metres, litres and seconds.

unsupervised training When an AI system is given a lot of data that is not sorted or organized. The computer has to find the patterns for itself.

use case diagram A diagram showing how actors (users) want to use a system that is being developed. Use case diagrams help IT project teams understand the scope and requirement of their projects.

user-friendly Easy for a user to use. A program that is easy to use can help to prevent errors.

user interface The user interface of a program handles user input and shows program output.

user story A way of writing down a user's requirement that a system needs to meet. User stories are written in plain language to help project teams understand exactly what they have to deliver.

variable A named area of memory that stores a value.

velocity The number of story points a team can deliver in one sprint.

VR (virtual reality) A computer-simulated environment, using 3D models. The viewer can move around the environment and interact with it using a special headset and sensors.

vision-guided robotics (VGR) Systems that allow computers to input data and instructions from video signals.

voice recognition A system that enables computers to take data and instructions from spoken input.

waterfall method A method of delivering projects in phases that follow on from each other in order.

wearable technology (wearables) Items of computing equipment that can be worn on the body, like smart watches and smart glasses.

widget An application or a small part of an interface that allows you to perform a function or access a service. Widgets can be embedded in web pages or on the home screen of computers, tablets or smartphones.

XR (extended reality) A term used to describe the group of technologies that include virtual reality, augmented reality and mixed reality.

Jobs for the future

I am an **audio engineer**. I record and edit audio tracks and upload them to streaming platforms.

I am a **store manager**. I use spreadsheet apps to keep track of stock, costs and profits. I can find and check specific order details if a customer has a problem.

I am a **software engineer**. I work with a team to write and test the program code to create new software apps.

I am a **project manager**. I use spreadsheet software to create and update project schedules. I use virtual meeting software to keep in touch with and manage a small team of people.

I am a **content moderator**. I use computer software to check for harmful content on my company's online platform. I can delete harmful content and block users who do not follow the agreed user policy. I report criminal behaviour to the police.